Everyday Opportunities for Extraordinary Parenting

Everyday Opportunities for Extraordinary Parenting

By Bobbi Conner

SOURCEBOOKS, INC.®
NAPERVILLE, ILLINOIS

This publication is designed to provide accurate and authoritative information in regard to the subject matter covered. It is sold with the understanding that the publisher is not engaged in rendering legal, accounting, or other professional service. If legal advice or other expert assistance is required, the services of a competent professional person should be sought.—*From a Declaration of Principles Jointly Adopted by a Committee of the American Bar Association and a Committee of Publishers and Associations*

All brand names and product names used in this book are trademarks, registered trademarks, or trade names of their respective holders. Sourcebooks, Inc., is not associated with any product or vendor in this book.

Published by Sourcebooks, Inc.
P.O. Box 4410, Naperville, Illinois 60567-4410
(630) 961-3900
FAX: (630) 961-2168

Library of Congress Cataloging-in-Publication Data
Conner, Bobbi.
Everyday opportunities for extraordinary parenting: simple ways to make a difference in your child's life / Bobbi Conner.
   p. cm.
ISBN 1-57071-625-0 (alk. paper)
1. Child rearing. 2. Parenting. 3. Parent and child. I. Title.
HQ769 .C643 2000
649'.1—dc21

00-044042

Printed and bound in the United States of America
PX 10 9 8 7 6 5 4 3 2 1

For Billy, Cassidy, Olivia, and Peter

It's called the Silver Rule…every grown-up has
been given the honor and responsibility to make a quiet and
steady difference in the life of a child.

This book is dedicated to the millions of grown-ups who
apply this rule to the living of their lives with their own families
and the other children they encounter.

acknowledgments

• • • • • • • • • • •

I have been blessed with a rich professional and personal life that has led me to the writing of this book.

My sincere thanks to each of the child development, pediatric, parenting, and educational guests who have spoken with me over the past fifteen years on *The Parent's Journal* (*TPJ*) public radio series. The insight and information these expert guests have so generously shared has been tremendously helpful to listening parents, myself included.

A special thanks to the many public radio station managers who recognize "parenting" as an essential topic worthy of airtime and broadcast *The Parent's Journal* each week. Thanks also to Huggies diapers and Pull-Ups training pants for having an appreciation for and belief in this public radio program and consequently for providing the funding that has made this radio series possible for the past fifteen years.

For assistance in producing *TPJ* radio series, thanks to Bruce Roberts and Madeleine Kelly; and for many long hours of typing program transcripts, my thanks go to Ellen Pruitt. Special thanks go to Bruce Joseph and Nina Graybill for their professional support and encouragement.

To Todd Stocke and Katie Funk at Sourcebooks, a heartfelt thanks for their enthusiasm for this book and fine job editing and fine-tuning.

On a personal note, I express the deepest gratitude to my own family. The belief in the wonder and strength of growing children that resides close to my heart comes from my real-life experiences with my own family. My parents, grandparents, sister, husband, and children have provided me with a strong and nurturing place to continue to grow; first as a child, and later as a mother.

contents

● ● ● ● ● ● ● ● ● ● ● ● ●

Chapter One: Everyday Opportunities for Parenting   1

How do we learn to be good parents with no prior experience in parenting? What can we learn from the experts? What is parental intuition? How do feelings help guide us in our role as parents? This chapter provides an overview of the ingredients of good parenting and serves as a guide to finding the daily real-life opportunities to respond to your child's many needs.

Chapter Two: Getting to Know Your Child   19

Parenting requires a tailor-made response based on the temperament, strengths, and differences of each child. This chapter looks at the process of getting to know your child and helps you apply what you know to your ongoing job of parenting.

Chapter Three: Nurturing and Establishing Security and Stability   29

This chapter provides a look at your child's need to be nurtured from birth through the teen years. How do you transmit a sense of security to your child? What makes your family stable despite ever-changing circumstances? Includes a glimpse into the value of predictable daily routines and ordinary family interactions in the life of your growing child.

Chapter Four: Encouragement and Recognition   47

This chapter provides a look at the wonder of encouragement in your child's life. How do your actions and responses help shape your child's self-esteem? What real-life events and activities set the stage for recognition or rejection?

Contents

Chapter Thirteen: Integrity

Honesty comes naturally to very young children. What is the parents' role in encouraging the continuation of honesty throughout childhood? Fairness is a learned behavior.

Chapter Fourteen: Faith

Children possess a natural belief and trust in goodness that is the basis for spiritual development and faith. What is the parents' role in encouraging their child's sense of faith and belonging to a world that recognizes and incorporates decency and goodness?

Part Four: Making Their Way in the World

Chapter Fifteen: Learning to Communicate

How do children learn to communicate? This chapter looks at the communication skills children need to express care for themselves and care for others. How can a shy child learn to communicate his or her desires and needs? How do parents become good listeners so that even older children continue to talk about what's on their minds?

Chapter Sixteen: Independence

The ultimate goal for a parent is to prepare a child for independence. This process begins in baby steps and continues throughout childhood in bits and pieces. What is your role in assisting your child's solo flight? This chapter takes a look at what creates confidence in your child.

Chapter Seventeen: Responsibility

How do small children begin to experience a sense of responsibility? This chapter points out the day-to-day opportunities to learn and be recognized for responsibility. What chores are appropriate?

Chapter Eighteen: Competition

What positive role does competition play in the lives of growing children? What motivates competition within the family, with others? What important life skills do boys and girls gain from involvement in organized sports? This chapter explores the role of parents, coaches, and others.

Chapter Nineteen: Learning to Cope with Stress

In today's fast-paced world, all children need to learn to cope with stress. What can parents do to minimize stress to their child? What self-calming skills work for babies, children, and teens?

Chapter Twenty: Humor

An appreciation and expression of amusement and delight are important ingredients of childhood. Humor provides an important emotional bridge between parents and children and brothers and sisters.

In the fall of 1985, I had an idea that grew into a nationally syndicated radio program for parents.

For years, I had been enthusiastic about using a radio talk show as a way to share information on practical matters of living, rather than as a vehicle for controversy or political debate.

At that time, I had been working for nearly eight years as the producer and host for two informative call-in shows on public radio. One program was locally broadcast, the other was heard throughout the state of Ohio. Both created a lively and efficient vehicle for gathering and sharing information on a broad range of practical, how-to topics.

In 1985, I was also a thirty-two-year-old parent with two small children in diapers. I was enthralled with the wonder and responsibility of raising my own children. I wanted to learn as much as possible about how children grow and what they needed to be happy, healthy, and well-adjusted. I wanted to become a good and effective parent.

I began to search the airwaves to see what public radio had to offer on the topic of parenting. I found nationally syndicated how-to programs on every subject except raising kids. There were national programs on gardening, finance, stereo systems, and auto repair. I was surprised to find that there was not one nationally syndicated radio program that focused exclusively on raising children. Yet, I knew there were millions of parents like me who would turn on their radios to hear intelligent and informative conversations about the many challenges of raising children.

With radio broadcast experience under my belt and a heartfelt enthusiasm for chatting about children and parenting issues, I decided it was time to establish a nationwide radio program about the important subjects involved in raising children.

In February 1986, I traveled to Cleveland to meet with the late Dr. Benjamin Spock to discuss my plans to create a national radio program for parents. Dr. Spock and his wife, Mary Morgan, were very enthusiastic about my plans, and Dr. Spock agreed to be my first guest. Weeks later, he helped me create a high-caliber, lively pilot program that I used to secure funding for the project. (Dr. Spock has since appeared on the program numerous times as a guest.)

On November 1, 1986, I hosted the first edition of *The Children's Journal*, my nationally broadcast radio program. (I later changed the name of the program to *The Parent's Journal* to avoid confusion over whether this was a program for children or about children but for parents.) From its humble beginning, the show has grown tremendously over the years.

It is now fifteen years later. *The Parent's Journal* is heard coast to coast on more than 150 public radio stations. I have conducted over twelve hundred in-depth interviews about child development and parenting topics. I have had the distinct pleasure of interviewing hundreds of lively and wise pediatricians, child-development experts, child psychiatrists and psychologists, educators, and others about the challenges that face parents each and every day—from the mundane to the profound.

Because I have been blessed with two children of my own to raise, I have tried to incorporate what I have learned during my many hours of professional interviews into our everyday family life. I have experienced many of the same ups and downs that all parents face, from sleepless nights to the excitement that the tooth fairy brings, from homework hassles to brilliant works of art on the refrigerator door. I have learned that the recommendations of experts are only meaningful when put into action in our everyday lives. Sometimes it's hard to make this leap from sound parenting theory to real-life experience.

I have learned above all else that the greatest gifts a parent gives his or her child are given through the ordinary actions of caring for a fussy baby or making dinner with a child playing alongside. Simple, everyday activities create opportunities to contribute to a child's life in lasting ways.

Sometimes life's hectic pace interferes with a parent's ability to appreciate the deep meaning found in the ordinary routines of each day. However, if you take an informal survey of people from all walks of life after they reach sixty-five or seventy, when there is more time for reflection, you'll hear this philosophy repeated often: "Some of the greatest significance is in the routine moments of life."

If you ask this specific question to people of retirement age: "When you look back on your long life, what are some of your most significant memories; what has mattered most?" These are the answers you might hear: "It was taking my brother fishing on Lake Marion every Saturday." "Attending my daughter's piano recitals throughout her childhood." "Baking a special birthday cake for each child in our large family." "I took my son bowling every Thursday from the time he was five years old, just the two of us. We had some wonderful times together on Thursday nights." "It was all the ordinary moments with the people I loved best of all." There's a hefty dose of wisdom for parents with young children in these remembrances.

The lives of children are shaped by these ordinary moments with parents and families. In fact, from the child's perspective, the present moment is where life is lived. Children are born with this wisdom; they seem to focus on that which has the greatest potential to help them grow.

It is my hope that parents will embrace this approach to life while their children are still growing and developing, rather than when the children are gone. No matter what your specific circumstances, age, profession, education, or finances, you are given hundreds of thousands of opportunities to turn these ordinary moments with your child into something of extraordinary significance.

With the publication of *Everyday Opportunities for Extraordinary Parenting*, I hope to share some of what I have learned during the past fifteen years of hosting *The Parent's Journal* and raising my own children to help you live your life with your child to its fullest each day.

How This Book Is Set Up

There isn't a magic recipe for raising children that can be printed and distributed for guaranteed success. All children are different, all parents are different, with varying temperaments, values, and family circumstances.

Everyday Opportunities for Extraordinary Parenting is a collection of information and practical ideas about the many important ingredients that go into raising a child. I like to think of it as an "ingredients book" for raising children. Each chapter identifies an ingredient important to a growing child, highlighted by relevant quotes from the many guests who have appeared on *The Parent's Journal* over the years.

The first part of each chapter describes a specific ingredient that your child needs in order to grow and thrive intellectually, emotionally, and socially. The second part of each chapter offers practical suggestions to work that specific ingredient into your daily routine with your child. These are arranged by age: infant, toddler, preschool child, school-age child, preteen, and teen. My hope is that this will inspire you to find ways to put your good intentions as a parent into action to help your child thrive.

the foundation for good growing

• • • • • • • • • • •

chapter one

Everyday Opportunities for Parenting

It was a glorious spring day, made to order. The two parents at the end of the third row sat quietly, like all the others seated in folding chairs, awaiting their child's graduation from college. What wasn't apparent, however, was the tremendous emotion stirring on the inside—in the hearts and minds and memories of these two parents. First, there was a remembrance of their daughter's now humorous first day of kindergarten, when her new dress was drenched by a mud puddle. The mother recalled her daughter's first smile on a clammy August morning. The father remembered the time during a junior high school basketball game when she shot the ball from the three-point line and it went in! Both of their minds danced back to her first spoken words as a baby. These parents have separate minds and hearts and yet share memories of ordinary moments that have now taken on extraordinary significance.

Being a good parent is tough work. You will commonly be pushed to your full capacity. You may experience fatigue the likes of which you've never felt before. You may discover strength you never knew you had. You will learn things that your prior years of education and career never taught you. You undoubtedly will experience great joy, challenge, and change. If you are a parent of a newborn baby, you might scarcely be able to imagine what it will be like to parent a teenager. If you are deeply immersed in your child's busy, active preschool years, you may have little time or inclination to contemplate the years that lie ahead. If you are in the throes of parenting your lively, independent teenager, your remembrance of what used to settle his colic when he was two months old might be vague.

Each age in childhood brings with it a different focus for you as a parent. Much of your energy is put into responding to the moment-to-moment ups and downs of family life. And yet, throughout childhood, the basic ingredients essential for growth and development remain the same. And it is you, the parent, who has the responsibility to work these ingredients into your child's daily routine.

A Starting Point for Good Parenting

The starting point for all the interviews I have conducted during the past fifteen years on *The Parent's Journal* radio series is also the starting point for good parenting. It is expressed in two simple question: What do children need to grow and thrive? and How can we, as parents, provide that?

> "Most people are educated to believe that wealth is money. What I really believe is that wealth is time! And so I encourage people to think about new definitions of wealth that define it as that which you value most highly."
>
> —Dr. Mary Pipher, clinical psychologist, author of *Reviving Ophelia* and *The Shelter of Each Other: Rebuilding Our Families*

I have asked these questions while exploring hundreds of different topics concerned with raising children, from self-esteem to independence, from discipline to creativity. I have phrased them in a thousand different ways. I have asked prominent pediatricians, child psychologists, psychiatrists, educators, and child-development experts.

The answers I have received have created a road map for good parenting that is the basis for this book. The foundation is built on the notion that *good parents must respond to the needs of their children at each stage of their development*. The chapters of this book identify many of the important needs of children and offer practical suggestions for meeting those needs as they grow through all the stages of development: infancy, toddler, preschool, school-age, preteen, and teen years.

Understanding the Stages of Child Development

We are fortunate to live in a time when many studies about how children develop have been undertaken. We now have good, trustworthy information that helps us understand the stages that children pass through during their growing years, from newborn through the teen years. This information is valuable to parents because it helps us grasp how children look at their world and how they learn, behave, and communicate at various ages. An understanding of the toddler stage, for example, may give you a clear idea of why your toddler throws temper tantrums. This understanding may help you figure out a way to respond to your child's temper tantrum that is effective at curbing the behavior and at the same time empathetic to your child's need to become independent. At the end of this chapter, you will see a summary of each of these important stages: infant, toddler, preschool, school-age, preteen, and teen. These summaries identify some of the developmental milestones that typically occur during each of these important stages.

> "Remember that young children expect that adults are all-knowing and all-powerful. They really believe that their parents are godlike creatures. They have all the knowledge and wisdom in the world, they've created everything!"
>
> —Dr. David Elkind, professor of child development at Tufts University and author of *The Hurried Child* and *Parenting Your Teenager in the '90s*

What Do Children Need Most from Parents?

First, of course, children need good, nutritious food and good medical care. These needs are essential to all children. Since I'm not a nutritionist or a doctor, I am leaving these important medical topics to experienced health-care professionals. Your pediatrician will be a valuable adviser in meeting these important medical and nutritional challenges. Also, there are wonderful parenting books that provide good nutritional guidelines and address medical problems and remedies that every parent needs to know. (See the recommended parenting books

The Long-Term Job Description of Parenting

You provide many of the important ingredients for good growing for your child throughout all of childhood.

Your job encompasses the following:

1. Developing your child's individual identity
2. Establishing security and stability
3. Encouraging and recognizing accomplishments
4. Guiding and disciplining
5. Providing opportunities for exploring
6. Encouraging creativity and curiosity
7. Promoting learning at school
8. Developing problem-solving and decision-making skills
9. Helping your child to discover perseverance, courage, optimism, and honesty
10. Encouraging spiritual development
11. Teaching good communication skills
12. Embracing independence and responsibility
13. Helping your child to develop a healthy attitude toward competition
14. Dealing with stress
15. Encouraging a sense of humor
16. Teaching respect
17. Encouraging kindness and compassion in words and actions
18. Creating a healthy family to which your child belongs

listed in Recommended Reading for Parents under Health and Development.)

This is a book of ingredients for the rest of good growing in childhood. Two of the most powerful ingredients—love and commitment—are not mentioned specifically by name, but are the motivation behind every facet of raising children and are woven into every chapter.

Essential Ingredients for Growing

Here are the essential ingredients for good growing in childhood that will be explored in this book: appreciation for your child's individuality, security and stability, encouragement, discipline, exploring, creativity, education, problem-solving and decision-making skills, perseverance, courage, optimism, integrity, faith, communication, independence, responsibility, competition, coping with stress, sense of humor, respect, kindness and compassion, and a healthy family in which to belong.

> "In the old days, people would bring out the switch or bring out the belt as a means of getting kids to do stuff. Today, we don't do that anymore, and there's more skill involved in parenting."
>
> —Dr. Anthony Wolf, clinical psychologist and author of *It's Not Fair, Jeremy Spencer's Parents Let Him Stay Up All Night*

You may find other important ingredients that have not been identified in the chapters of this book. Add those ingredients to your child's life, because it is your style, your values, and your hopes and dreams for your child that make you the expert on raising your own child.

Fine-Tuning Parenting Skills

Parenting is a delicate mix of feelings, thoughts, and actions. In order to be a good parent, you must marshal all of your talents, emotions, intellect, and intuition to develop parenting skills to apply to your role as a parent.

Use Your Best Thinking Skills

Parenting takes an incredible amount of sharp thinking! Some of this thinking falls into the commonsense category. Some falls into the analytical/problem-solving category. Parenting is a role that is worthy of your best efforts to think and figure as you go. A half hour of brainstorming about a specific problem related to your child's behavior, for example (either alone, with your spouse, with a close trusted friend, or with your own parent), can go a long way toward finding solutions to some of your biggest challenges as a parent. You may at times want to jot down information about what you've observed regarding your parenting challenges and some possible solutions.

Factor in Feelings

The assortment of feelings you are likely to have in the course of your child's growing years is rich and expansive. Many of these loving and prideful feelings help you find strength to live up to your responsibilities to be a good parent. These feelings of what is best for your child can be powerful motivators to sustain your efforts even in traumatic situations.

You will also need to develop skills to manage those feelings of anger or disappointment that your child's behavior might precipitate on occasion. Anticipate these feelings ahead of time. Recognize that you will be angry or upset with your child from time to time throughout his or her childhood. Remember that one of the ways children learn how to behave properly is through occasional misbehavior. This is true at each age of childhood. Keep in mind that your objective is to guide your child to proper behavior, not humiliate or stifle your child's spirit. Try planning in advance how you might respond when these angry feelings occur. Above all else, call upon your strong feelings of love and commitment to your child to temper your feelings of anger. Be true to your overall pledge to find positive ways to help your child grow, even when the going gets tough.

If at any time you or your partner has physically violent outbursts of anger directed toward your child, you must recognize that your behavior threatens your child's health and safety. Get help immediately from a trained professional in your community who deals with family violence and abuse prevention, or call your local chapter of Parents Anonymous for support and assistance.

"Whether you have one parent or two, you need somebody who is there consistently that you can count on....you need to have somebody at home who is interested in you and who cares about you and believes in you and will also take the bother to discipline you."

—Dr. Louise Bates Ames, cofounder of the Geselle Institute for Human Development, author of over thirty books on child-development topics

Use Your Intuition

I have spent a considerable amount of time probing the question of what "parental intuition" is with many experts and parents alike. I've heard a wide assortment of answers. I've come to think of intuition as a "knowing feeling" that is created by a combination of information and past experiences mixed with feelings.

Intuition is a powerful tool for parenting your child. Very often your intuitions will be based upon your special knowledge of your unique child: what she is like, how she responded in a similar situation before, what upsets or delights her, what her vulnerabilities are. This essential knowledge feels as if it resides in the pit of your stomach—or is lodged somewhere in your heart. Much of this parental intuition comes from careful observation of your child and listening carefully to your child.

> "Time is the essential element of parenting. We're in the parenting business to raise a child who's adaptable, relates well to people, is self-confident and independent, and who has a good memory of his or her childhood. So we're in the memory-building business; you can't build memories unless you have time."
>
> —Dr. Don Shifrin, associate clinical professor of pediatrics, University of Washington

Sometimes, however, parental intuition is based upon information or past experiences from your own childhood. For example, some of your intuitive feelings about parenting might be based upon the good experiences you had as a child. You may know how to show your unconditional support for your child because your parents expressed these wonderful feelings in words and actions when you were a young child. On the other hand, your remembrance of being routinely spanked for misbehavior might factor into the automatic feelings that launch you into action as a punishing parent when your own child misbehaves. You must sometimes step back and take a good look at those past experiences to evaluate whether they are consistent with how you want to raise your child now that you are a parent. You can choose to change your approach and be true to your values as a good parent.

Find Professional Support and Advisers

Every chief executive officer of a major corporation has many advisers and support personnel whom she relies upon to fulfill her responsibilities to her employer. You should fulfill your responsibilities to your child and family in a similar way. You may indeed be the boss, but you don't have all the answers. You will find you need advice, consultation, and outside information from time to time to do your best. Just like a

CEO, you have tremendous authority to pick and choose advisers with whom you can work. You can include professional advisers as well as friends and relatives who will help you out of love and compassion for you and your child.

Professional Advisers

Choose wisely. Find an obstetrician (for good prenatal care), a pediatrician, and a pediatric dentist that you trust, admire, and with whom you can work well. Find a good doctor (and counselor if needed) who can help take good care of you. Consult other medical or mental health specialists as needed for your child. Consult with child care providers, teachers, tutors, learning specialists, and other professionals as problems occur. Some of these specialists may be needed only to offer you short-term assistance or information.

Build a Support Network for Yourself

Every parent needs friends and family members to talk out the issues that come up in raising a child. A good working relationship with your spouse is invaluable in solving child-related problems as they occur. But not everyone is so lucky, and particularly if you are a single parent, make an effort to talk with valued friends about the parenting challenges you face. Choose your support system with the same care that you would give to selecting trusted, valuable professional consultants. Not every friend will have the experience, insight, or interest needed to help you with parenting problems. Talk with friends whose lives reflect the values and beliefs that you admire and respect. Find friends who "walk the walk" of good parenting, rather than "talk the talk" of good intentions. Remember, too, there is a wealth of wisdom and perspective in friends of an older generation who have successfully raised their own children.

Find a Balance

One critical skill of parenting is finding and maintaining a balance in your life—making your child your top priority, pursuing your career, spending time with your spouse, and finding time to rest and relax. This juggling act is one of the most difficult aspects of parenting because everything about your life is in constant flux. Just when you get the hang of how to discipline your toddler effectively, he progresses to another plateau, which seems to require a fine-tuning of your parenting skills. Just when you establish a reasonable work schedule that is compatible with the needs of your family, you get the flu and chaos reigns for a time.

> "Warmth and support yet steady discipline are really the solid keys to, and the essential ingredients of, effectiveness for parents."
> —Dr. Frank Furstenberg, professor of sociology and coauthor of *Divided Families: What Happens to Children When Parents Part*

Now that you are a parent, you must become adaptable because life is at its most unpredictable. You might as well expect change and disruption. What this means to me is that if I wait until the last minute to prepare for that radio interview I'm doing in two hours, it is just about guaranteed that one of my children is going to come home from school with strep throat or there will be some other minor catastrophe. Once you become a parent, you lose the luxury of counting on spontaneity to prevail in your work, your intimate relationships, and your time alone. These activities have to be planned in advance in such a way that mishaps can be allowed for.

Children Learn Best in the Everyday Moments of Life

Your son may begin to talk while you are in the grocery store, reaching for a jar of apple juice. He points and says, "Dooo." Your two children might discover how to write a poem under a fort made of blankets on a dreary Saturday morning in March. Your daughter might begin to learn to be brave when she is very young and experiences her first shot at the doctor's office. Your son may feel a profound sense of security while listening to you sing happily as you rock him and feed him. Your daughter may start to learn math when she's in a preschool program by matching blocks of the same color and sorting them into piles. Your teenage son may fine-tune his problem-solving skills when he must resolve a conflict with a friend after the pep rally at school.

> "I think if you understand each developmental step, you can see the ingredients that go into it, and you can see your role as a parent more clearly."
>
> —Dr. T. Berry Brazelton, pediatrician, author of *Touchpoints* and *Going to the Doctor*

These everyday opportunities provide your child with a hands-on approach to learning. These are the opportunities you must look for and embrace. Most of the magic that happens in your life with children arises from ordinary moments. Or to put it another way, ordinariness is what's magical in the life of your child.

These opportunities exist every day of your lives together. They occur if you are at home full-time with your child, or if you work part of the day and return to your child in the late afternoon or evening. These opportunities occur in the morning, at noon, and at night. They require your openness to discovery, and your willingness to listen, slow down, and spend what precious time you have with your child giving your undivided attention to those moments of being together. These ordinary times create the rich tapestries of experience that help your child grow. These are also the beautiful moments that will live on in your memory long after your child has grown. These ordinary moments are your legacy to your child, and his gift, in return, to you.

Summary of Infant Stage of Development

Infant: Birth to Twelve Months

During the first year of your child's life, she will learn to control her body and begin to communicate. Newborn babies have use of all five senses from the very first days of life. Although each individual baby's development is on a schedule of its own, following are some general tips about learning during the infant stage.

How Infants Learn

- By careful observation and listening
- Through play, experimentation, and repetition
- Through imitating what you do

Developmental Milestones

- First smile: six to eight weeks

- Watches and follows moving objects (vision): three to four months
- Bonds emotionally with parents and caregivers: ongoing
- Turns head to follow sound (hearing): three to four months
- Grabs for objects purposefully: four to six months
- Babbles, laughs, and squeals with delight: four to six months
- Rolls over: four to six months
- Develops good hand-eye coordination: four to six months
- Sits up alone: six to eight months
- Creeps on all fours: eight to twelve months
- Crawls: eight to twelve months
- Pulls himself up to standing position: eight to twelve months
- First attempts to feed herself: eight to twelve months
- Imitates gestures: eight to twelve months
- Understands and responds to no: eight to twelve months
- Walks, holding onto furniture: eight to twelve months
- Walks, unassisted: ten to fourteen months

Summary of Toddler Stage of Development

Toddler: Twelve Months to Two-and-a-Half Years

Toddlers are motivated to move about and explore, making a busy life for themselves and their parents. Toddlers are not capable of understanding which things are dangerous, so parents must baby-proof their homes and continuously supervise their toddler. Although each toddler develops on her own schedule, here is a general timeline of developmental milestones occurring during the toddler stage:

> "Love means...spending time and paying attention to children. It means family rituals. Children like structure and they like to have things they can count on happening."
>
> —Marion Wright Edelman, founder/president of the Children's Defense Fund

How Toddlers Learn

- By careful observation and listening
- Through play, experimentation, and exploration
- By imitation and repetition
- By testing the limits

Developmental Milestones

- Walks, unassisted: twelve to fourteen months
- Points to identify objects: twelve to fourteen months
- Talks one word at a time: twelve to sixteen months
- Responds to no: twelve to sixteen months
- Imitates activities: twelve to twenty-four months
- Picks up tiny objects with fingers: twelve to sixteen months
- Can push and pull a toy: fourteen to sixteen months
- Waves bye-bye: fourteen to sixteen months
- Scribbles with crayon: fourteen to sixteen months
- Can follow one-step verbal commands: fourteen to sixteen months
- Speaks in two-word phrases: fourteen to sixteen months
- Increasing ability to express and interpret feelings
- Plays/stacks blocks: sixteen to twenty-four months
- Runs: sixteen to twenty months
- Begins to show defiant behavior: sixteen to twenty-four months
- Climbs stairs: sixteen to twenty months
- Uses fork and spoon: twenty to twenty-four months
- Speaks in sentences: twenty-four to thirty months
- Has vocabulary of fifty words: twenty-four to thirty months
- Can throw a ball: twenty to twenty-four months
- By the end of this stage, toddlers can identify and categorize similar objects by color and shape. For example, they can distinguish one kind of animal from another.

Summary of Preschool Stage of Development

<u>Preschool Child</u>: **Two-and-a-Half to Four Years**

Preschool children have already mastered a great deal of control of their bodies, so they work to refine these skills. They are also learning to imagine, think, and question, to invent and discover. They are learning to get along with other children. Although each preschooler develops at his own individual pace, here are some milestones that typically occur during the preschool stage.

How Preschoolers Learn

- By careful observation and listening
- Through imitation and repetition
- By testing the limits
- Through imaginative and creative play
- Through experimentation and exploration
- By asking questions

Developmental Milestones

- Masters use of hands and fingers: holds pencils, turns pages in a book, draws pictures
- Recognizes most common objects
- Understands most sentences
- Uses five or more words in sentences
- Can tell a story
- Can identify colors, shapes, and like objects
- Begins to count
- Understands the concept of "two"
- Develops empathy; learns what "hurts" other children
- Learns to take turns in games
- Desires to make friends
- Can understand the concept of mine and yours
- Learns through fantasy and imaginative play
- Begins to remember simple rules of behavior
- Understands concepts of same and different
- Expands ability to express and interpret feelings

Summary of Elementary School Stage of Development

<u>School-Age Child</u>: Five to Ten Years

The early years of school are marked by many intellectual, social, and emotional milestones as well as a fine-tuning of physical

"Sometimes we focus so hard on all the things we're supposed to do that we forget to enjoy. And children are only with us for a very short time!"

—Judy Ford, family therapist and author of *Wonderful Ways to Love a Child* and *Wonderful Ways to Love a Teen*

development. This is a stage in which children are very much venturing out into a world beyond the family and establishing friendships, as well as learning how to work hard and fit into the group setting at school. Although all children develop at their own individual pace, here is a list of challenges that children meet and master during the elementary school years.

How School-Age Children Learn

- Through hands-on experimentation and exploration
- Through imaginative and creative play
- By asking questions
- Through trial and error
- By testing the limits
- Through reading and studying

Developmental Milestones

- Understands the concept of time: present, past, future
- Learns to get along in a group setting: to take turns, etc.
- Begins to grasp abstract thinking and applying logic
- Develops a good memory for detail
- Masters sports that require a high level of coordination
- Works to express emotions and control behavior
- Can remember and choose to follow rules
- Desires friendships
- Expands mathematical thinking
- Understands and practices concepts of honesty, courage, responsibility, and compassion
- Learns nuances of social rules of communication—at school, at home, and with friends
- Begins to learn to manage schoolwork
- Begins to develop work ethic
- Learns to negotiate and cooperate with others
- Understands cause and effect

Summary of Preteen Stage of Development

<u>Preteens/Early Teens</u>: **Eleven to Fourteen Years**

Preteens are beginning to use reasoning to explore and question the world in which they live. They have mastered a high level of everyday independence, which makes them feel grown-up and competent. However, preteens still need parents' involvement, nurturing, and limit-setting in order to flourish. Although every child develops at his own individual pace, here are some of the many challenges that preteens face and work to master during this stage of development.

How Preteens Learn

- Through hands-on experimentation and exploration
- By asking questions
- Through trial and error
- Creative thinking and problem solving
- By testing the limits
- Through reading and studying

> "I can't think of anything else that any human being can do that is more important than starting another being off successfully in the first year of life. There is no other work that I can imagine that's basically more important."
>
> —Dr. Burton White, educational psychologist and author of *The First Three Years of Life* and *Raising a Happy Unspoiled Child*

Developmental Milestones

- Uses language to express complex thoughts, ideas, and feelings
- Applies logic and reason to argument
- Works to express emotions and control behavior
- Grasps cause-and-effect relationships and anticipates consequences
- Refines problem-solving skills
- Maintains friendships
- Feels and expresses empathy and compassion
- Controls feelings and behavior
- Daydreams about future plans
- Organizes school projects, manages workload
- Develops life skills

- Learns to break large challenges into smaller steps
- Sets goals and works toward them
- Uses questioning and pondering as tools for discovery
- Learns to negotiate and cooperate with others
- Understands and practices concepts of honesty, courage, responsibility, and compassion
- Learns nuances of social rules of communication—at school, at home, and with friends

Summary of Teen Stage of Development

<u>Teens</u>: **Fifteen to Nineteen Years**

Teens seem to know instinctively that they are preparing to live on their own. They may alternate between excitement and anxiety at the prospect of growing up and becoming self-reliant, between maturity and immaturity in their behavior. In every case, teens still need their parents' love, guidance, time, and attention. Although each teen matures and develops on her own schedule, here are some of the many challenges faced during the teenage stage of development.

> "I think children are a constant. I think their needs are the same. We, of course, perceive differences. We say, 'Gosh, they know so much more than I ever knew when I was a youngster. And oh, aren't they bright, aren't they sophisticated, aren't they smart.' Scratch all of that away and underneath you'll find a child who's asking the same questions as were asked forty years ago, probably four hundred years ago, probably in ancient Greece. 'Who am I?' 'Am I loved?' What has changed is our system for answering those questions and meeting those needs."
>
> —Bob Keeshan, TV's Captain Kangaroo and author of *Good Morning, Captain*

How Teens Learn

- Through hands-on experimentation and exploration
- By asking questions
- Through trial and error
- Creative thinking and problem solving
- By testing the limits
- Through reading and studying
- By setting goals and striving to achieve them

Developmental Milestones

- Uses questioning and pondering as tools for discovery
- Refines problem-solving skills

- Learns to express feelings and control actions
- Applies logic and reason to thinking
- Learns to evaluate consequences for actions in advance
- Daydreams about future plans
- Organizes school projects
- Learns to break large challenges into smaller steps
- Sets goals and works to achieve them
- Learns to negotiate and cooperate with others
- Understands and practices concepts of honesty, courage, responsibility, and compassion
- Maintains friendships
- Learns to turn feelings of empathy into actions
- Questions values
- Learns to respect the ideas, feelings, and needs of others
- Practices skills of everyday living and independence

"Throughout the four-million-year history of humans living together in families, parents have had two jobs with children—to protect their children and to socialize their children. And, all of a sudden, in America I think those two jobs are at odds with each other."

—Dr. Mary Pipher, clinical psychologist, author of *Reviving Ophelia* and *The Shelter of Each Other: Rebuilding Our Families*

chapter two

Getting to Know Your Child

Jeremiah was a keen observer of life. He seemed to have an extra dose of curiosity about how things worked right from the beginning. When he was three years old, he became fascinated with watching his grandfather repair clocks in his workshop. Jeremiah watched quietly without asking many questions, paying unusual attention to each small detail of the repair. When he was ten years old, his grandfather gave him his own small desk clock to work on. In his quiet manner, Jeremiah disassembled and reassembled the clock and used it that same night in his room.

Every child is unique, with a special look and personality all his own. It is this unique odyssey of finding your way with your own child that is the greatest journey of parenting. The process of getting to know and understand your child happens quietly, over time, through your daily routine with him. It is what makes you the expert on *your* child.

All children need the same basic ingredients of good parenting. Each child in your family needs your love, commitment, nurturing, encouragement, guidance, and discipline, and all the other essentials for good growing. But added to

> "Temperament is just another word for nature's contribution to our personality. And the best take that you can get on who your child is as an individual is by studying and looking at his or her temperament."
>
> —Dr. Stanley Turecki, child and family psychiatrist, author of *The Difficult Child* and *Normal Children Have Problems, Too*

these essentials, your child needs you to respond to the individual needs that are in part driven by her personality and temperament. Any parent raising more than one child knows that those individual personality differences make parenting each child a separate challenge. Your son, for example, may be inherently more defiant than your daughter. Perhaps your oldest son is more flexible by nature than your youngest son. Your daughter might have been born more aggressive than her older brother. These individual differences require you to provide the basic essentials to your child in a tailor-made way that considers her temperament and personality.

Your job is to help your child accentuate the many positives that seem to come naturally to him and help him learn behavior that compensates for his shortcomings or individual difficulties. A seemingly aggressive child can learn behavior that allows others to have a vote that counts. A child who tends to be withdrawn can learn behavior that helps him interact with other children and express his opinions and needs. This kind of individualized parenting must be undertaken for each child throughout all of childhood.

The more you know and understand your individual child's personality and temperament, the more effective you will be in your daily role as a parent. Your child has a deep emotional need to be understood and appreciated by you. The time you spend getting to know your child speaks volumes about the love and appreciation you feel for your child. You can watch her personality unfold. You share a deep sense of personal history with your child from the first day of her life. Indeed, you help shape your child's history by the way you live each day together.

Getting to Know Your Child

Some parents say they recognize distinct personality characteristics of each child in the family from the first moments and weeks of life. For some parents, however, many years pass before they are able to piece

Discovering Your Unique Child

Think of yourself as a "master of observation" in your child's life. Part of your job is to help your child make his way in the world, taking into account his strengths, talents, and shortcomings. The strengths can be accentuated and the shortcomings minimized with the consistent guidance of loving, observant parents.

Job Description for a "Master of Observation"

1. Become a quiet observer. Who is this child that you have brought into the world? You have the capacity to know your child better than anyone else in the world. Combine your intuition with your intelligence to appreciate your child's unique personality.

2. Become a good, thoughtful listener. Make yourself available to listen to your child's thoughts, feelings, and recollections each day throughout childhood.

3. Apply what you know about your child to each parenting challenge and problem that arises. Take time alone to brainstorm with pencil and paper in hand as parenting challenges present themselves.

together the early signs of their child's emerging personality, temperament, and interests.

The process of getting to know your child happens as you observe and listen to him. As you spend time with your baby during the first year of life, you will notice many details about your child that make him unique. For example, you may notice what he does when he is curious. You may notice that he plows ahead and tries something new with no hesitation, or that he hangs back to observe before he takes the tiniest new step forward. You might notice that your son likes things quiet and calm, or perhaps he thrives on high-energy excitement in the household.

> "You know your child better than anybody else. You are the expert with your child!"
>
> —Dr. Charlotte Thompson, pediatrician, director of the Center for Handicapped Children and Teenagers in San Francisco, and author of *Raising a Handicapped Child* and *Single Solutions*

The Birthday Letter

One way to honor your child and record your thoughts and perceptions as your child grows is by writing a "birthday letter" each year of your child's life. This letter is a special, personal letter to, for, and about your unique child and her growing years, a way to say, "I know you."

Each year, sometime around your child's birthday, reserve half an hour of time alone to write a letter that reflects your child's current life. This is a letter about your child's strengths, not weaknesses, so make these letters positive, not critical.

The birthday letter is a way to trace your child's journey through childhood as seen through the eyes of a loving parent. Save these letters, give them to your child when he is grown or years later when he is about to become a parent himself. These are your "snapshots" of your child's journey through childhood.

In later years you may notice that your child delights in being center stage and "performing" for others, or perhaps becomes paralyzed at the thought of presenting a book report before the entire class. Armed with these many insights into your child's personality, you will be able to help her develop her positive qualities and overcome obstacles and compensate for shortcomings.

Become a Good Observer

As parents we are given hundreds of opportunities to observe our children in action—at home and out in the world. Here are some tips designed to help you become a good observer:

1. Spend time with your child and pay attention as she communicates her likes, dislikes, and interests.
2. Unobtrusively watch your child in the action of playing by himself. (Many parents make important observations about their children while reading the newspaper and watching their child at play.)

3. Casually observe your child at play with other children without interfering with them. You will notice the following:
   a. How does your child express herself to others?
   b. How capable is she at empathizing with other playmates?
   c. How long will your child play or work at a task?
   d. What happens when she becomes frustrated? Is she able to persevere or regroup or move on to another activity?
4. Talk with other adults who care for your child to hear their observations about him.
5. How does your child react to new situations? New people? New places? New experiences?
6. How does your child express her anger? Her delight? Her enthusiasm?

"I think the parents' job—and you can't rely on the schools to do this—is very early on to help the child find out what he is interested in. I think children should be taken not just to art museums but to markets, to band concerts, to hardware stores, to car repair shops, and to pet shops, because every place they go can be a learning place."

—Fredelle Maynard, author of *Raisins and Almonds*

Use Your Understanding of Your Child in a Positive Way

Don't label your child. (For example: "He's a difficult child," or "She's a shy child.") Labeling is limiting rather than encouraging.

Don't confuse getting to know your child with excusing problem behavior. Understanding your child is not an open invitation to spoil your child and force the world to cater to all her whims. As unique and wonderful as your child is, she must still find a way to fit into the world. If, for example, your child has a tendency toward aggressive behavior toward others, help her find a way to alter her behavior rather than making excuses.

Don't compare children. Comments like "I wish you could be outgoing like your sister" or "Your brother never seems to give up on a problem. Why can't you be more like him?" are destructive and will only hurt your child's self-esteem.

Observe your children throughout all of childhood. You will continue to gain new insights into your child even during the preteen and teen years. You will also see indicators when something is troubling your child along the way.

Making Time

Getting to know your child means finding time to spend with him. Parents have busy lives with many demands competing for their time. Here are some practical ways to make time for your kids each day:

- When you are overwhelmed, serve an easy meal—healthy sandwiches and fresh fruit for dinner, for instance—to find extra quiet time to spend with your child.
- Let the answering machine catch your calls each evening and return calls the next workday.
- Limit television viewing in the family. Spend time reading to your child, or reading alongside your child while she plays.
- Take one child with you for errands, while your other children are at home with your spouse or a baby-sitter.
- Shift to a more relaxed pace on weekends to allow for long brunches, lunches, and lingering in the kitchen sharing a snack and chatting.
- Make time for family dinners on a regular basis.

Become a Good Listener

We all think that we are good listeners. After all, we listen to conversations, radio, television, and all the sounds around us each day. Our days are so busy that we are often rushing from one task (such as cooking dinner) to the next (doing laundry) and trying to fulfill our commitment to our career as well.

Listening to children requires a different pace from some of the household or office responsibilities that nip at our heels each day.

Children don't always get to the point of what they're thinking or feeling in a linear or methodical fashion. They may drift around from one subject to the next. Your son may begin to tell you about the pizza he made with his teacher in kindergarten today and eventually get around to the episode of hitting a classmate and getting punished by the teacher. Your thirteen-year-old daughter might begin to tell you about the volleyball game after school and eventually mention that her best friend is no longer speaking to her.

> "We are all wonderfully temperamented when things are going our way. It's when we encounter anxiety, frustration, and disappointment that unfortunately our true temperamental style is unveiled."
>
> —Dr. Don Shifrin, associate clinical professor of pediatrics, University of Washington

The first rule for listening to your child is to make yourself available every day by finding a quiet moment and a place for listening where other pressures don't compete. It also sometimes requires you to adopt an easygoing, got-all-the-time-in-the-world-to-chat-with-you attitude, when in truth you have only twenty-five minutes until you must bathe your youngest child and put him to bed.

Applying What You Know About Your Child

The insight that you gain about your child is like a transparency that must be placed on top of the various theories and guidelines of raising children. You will probably find yourself using a different approach with each of your children based upon the insight you have into each one. You know, for example, that all children need their parents to set limits, to establish consistent guidelines for behavior, and to follow through with consequences for misbehavior. But it is *your* understanding of *your* child that will help you figure out the most effective and compassionate way to set and enforce limits.

> "Some children are extremely difficult. Some children are shy and...it's all right to be shy. We don't create a child. In fact the important thing...is to help the child find out who he is...and that is a very exciting and wonderful and thrilling job!"
>
> —Dr. Jeree Pawl, clinical psychologist and director of the Infant-Parent Program, University of California/San Francisco

Some of the problems and challenges that arise in your family life might best be solved by spending some time alone and jotting down not only the problem at hand, but also specific

"Parents are usually wonderfully intuitive. As parents enjoy their everyday interactions with their babies and children, and do things that come naturally, they actually foster the baby's growth and development to a far more significant degree than trying to read about the latest new-fangled educational toy or the latest way of academically stimulating their children."

—Dr. Stanley Greenspan, clinical professor of psychiatry and pediatrics at George Washington University School of Medicine, and author of *The Growth of the Mind, Building Healthy Minds, Playground Politics,* and *The Challenging Child*

information you have about your child. For example, let's say there's a problem with your child adjusting to her new school and new classmates. Take a look at what you know about your child. Does she do better with one-on-one friendships than large-group play at recess? Does she wait for others to initiate friendship because she fears rejection?

By identifying what you know about your child, you can start brainstorming effective solutions. Perhaps you might decide to encourage your child to invite one classmate over during the weekend in order to establish a friendship that will carry over at school.

When your child becomes a preteen, and later a teen, your insight into the child will be especially important as you guide him into new learning experiences and away from disaster. It will take a special understanding of your child to package and deliver your suggestions in a style to which your teenager is open. Whatever your child's age, it is your knowledge of who she is that will lead you to strong, creative solutions to your parenting challenges.

Everyday Opportunities for Discovering Your Unique Child
Birth through Teen Years

Getting to know and understand your child is a process that begins the day she is born and continues throughout all the years of childhood. You will discover new information about your child throughout the stages of childhood.

Daily Opportunities to Learn

- Spend time alone with your child.
- Observe your child at home and interacting with others.

- Observe how your child approaches problems.
- Talk with teachers and child-care providers about your child and her activities and temperament.
- Spend quiet time alone reflecting on what you know about your child and apply this information to problem solving.
- Be available, and listen to your child's thoughts, feelings, and problems.
- Express your pride, appreciation, and wonder for the uniqueness of your child.

"We talk a lot these days about the genetics of behavior and how much genes contribute to who we are and how we behave. But the fact is that more of our limits most likely come from the environmental side of the nature/nurture equation than from the genetic side."

—Dr. Stanley Greenspan, clinical professor of psychiatry and pediatrics at George Washington University School of Medicine and author of *The Growth of the Mind*, *Building Healthy Minds*, *Playground Politics*, and *The Challenging Child*

• • • • • • • • • • • •

chapter three

Nurturing and Establishing Security and Stability

Lisa and Jim were brand-new, first-time parents. The first six weeks with their new baby, Christopher, were woven with ecstasy and anxiety. Everything about their daily lives was unfamiliar: the schedule, the lack of sleep, the caring for their newborn baby. But there was magic in these moments too. When their tiny, fragile child cried, Lisa and Jim were very often able to settle him down just by holding him close, rocking him, and talking in a quiet soothing voice. In these magical moments, Lisa and Jim conveyed a powerful language of affection that their baby understood.

Security is one of the most critical ingredients your child needs to develop and thrive. Each child needs a foundation of security and stability in order to go about their business of growing, learning, exploring, and blossoming into the person he or she was meant to be.

The amazing thing about your job of providing security to your child is that it is expressed in such simple, everyday ways. Daily acts of nurturing routine form a framework of love and commitment. These caring deeds that you undertake for your child also teach her the concept of cause and effect that will later apply to her intellectual development. She learns that when she cries, you pick her up and hold her. When she is wet or uncomfortable, you make her feel dry and fresh again. Later when she babbles, you chatter back to her. These early lessons provide a wonderful, warm, secure feeling for your child, setting the stage for all that comes later.

The Essentials of Security

Parents provide security in two important ways: through consistent nurturing and affection and by providing a predictable family routine.

Nurturing

Children can feel a sense of security from the nurturing of their parents during the very first days and weeks of life. Imagine for a moment what it might feel like to be a tiny newborn child just born into this strange new world. Your head is wobbly, you feel wet and hungry and uncomfortable part of the time. You are hearing an assortment of loud and puzzling sounds all around you—blenders whizzing, doors slamming, hammers banging, children screeching, engines roaring. You see a whirl of color and shapes moving before your eyes, and the bright lights startle you. You feel wind, rain, or sunshine against your face, but you don't recognize these sensations. Almost nothing feels or seems familiar to you in the early moments and days of your life.

And then, through this bombardment of new and unpredictable sounds, sights, and sensations, you begin to recognize those firm, strong arms lifting you up, supporting your head, and cradling your body. Then, too, you recognize that melodic, soothing voice speaking softly to you—your mother or father! Now a feeling of calm comes over you and you begin to feel settled and safe.

Newborn babies have many ways of showing their contentment. Their small tense arms

> "Even the tone of voice with which we talk to a small baby conveys to that baby how we feel about him. Whether we feel loving, whether we're appreciative of the little movements, the ability to start sitting or crawling or gurgling or holding a bottle. Those things are critical even at those very young ages because a child begins to feel appreciated or not appreciated, loved or not loved, held in a way that is loving or not loving, right from the beginning."
>
> —Dr. Debora Phillips, behavioral therapist and coauthor of *How to Give Your Child a Great Self-Image*

and legs relax as they are cuddled or sung to. They coo when they are being fed. Their eyes stare into yours and follow you around the room.

> "Studies have shown that kids that are securely attached to parents come out of infancy with this feeling of solidarity between them and their families, and are the kids that are most likely to be obedient and respectful and to follow family rules later on."
>
> —Dr. William Damon, developmental psychologist and author of *The Moral Child*

The need for security is just as strong in older children. A happy toddler will talk to himself and sing as he plays alone with his toys and blocks when you are standing nearby doing your chores. Your nearby presence, and occasional chatter and hugs, allows him to feel secure. School-age children also need to feel secure, but they need your nurturing packaged and delivered in a variety of different older-kid ways. For example, hugs at bedtime and snuggling up together to read a story will likely be an enjoyable and appropriate way to convey your affection to your school-age child at home.

"Mushy" remarks, hugs, and kisses from Mom or Dad when other fifth- or sixth-grade friends are present might be embarrassing to your child. Your ever-expanding job description as a parent requires you to change your language approach to nurturing as your child moves closer to becoming independent. You want to convey solid feelings of support and love without undermining your child's own feelings of competence and independence.

Many parents overlook the important need for security and stability essential in the life of their seemingly independent and disinterested teenager. Your fifteen-year-old son, for example, might appear to be big and capable, but underneath he undoubtedly still appreciates sitting with you on the couch and reading the paper or watching a movie, or whatever your particular routine may be. Some teens who resist spending time with their parents suddenly become enthusiastic when that time is framed around an activity that is fun, exciting, or adventurous. For one child a day spent golfing with Mom or Dad might be a thrill, for another canoeing or taking a trip to a neighboring city for a day of shopping (with a long drive for listening and chatting along the way) might be exciting. The key is to remain accessible, available, and interested.

Parents' Role in Providing Security and Stability

As a parent, you provide one of the most essential ingredients your child needs to grow and thrive—security. It is like the fertile soil that holds the roots of a tender young plant. By creating and maintaining this foundation, day in and day out, your child will have the environment she needs to do her job of exploring and developing.

Job Description for "Head of Family Security"

1. Provide daily nurturing and affection to your child throughout all of childhood.

2. Establish a daily family routine. Work to make the morning routine, after-school routine, and mealtime and bedtime routines manageable, orderly, and predictable.

3. Spend one-on-one time reading to your child each and every day. Even school-age children and preteens will enjoy this special parent time if you select lively books or articles geared toward your child's interest, maturity, sense of humor, etc.

4. Regularly express your love and commitment to your child during quiet moments. Update these messages as your child moves from one stage of childhood to the next.

"As soon as the baby is born you can share a book or nursery rhyme. You can share language with her in a way that is beautifully ordered and organized in a book."

—Amy Cohn, children's literature specialist

Creating Stability through Your Daily Routine

All children are dependent upon grown-ups to provide them with food, clothes, and a warm, safe place to live. Because they are in this vulnerable position, they need to know that their parents are in charge and will provide for them. This message can be delivered loud and clear by the daily routine that you provide for your child. Creating and maintaining an orderly daily routine where dinnertime, bath time, and bedtime happen in a predictable way is one of the most important jobs of being a parent.

Children need to know that dinner will be provided each night, that there will be lunch money on the kitchen counter each day, and that Mom or Dad will be a part of their day. In addition, younger children may thrive on knowing that they have a predictable evening routine—dinner, quiet time, bath, and bedtime story—day after day. This simple framework translates into tremendous stability for children.

> "What I really argue is...in the '90s, if you just let the culture happen to your family, if you take in everything and don't do some protecting and shelter of your family...you sort of end up awash in consumer goods within no time!"
>
> —Dr. Mary Pipher, clinical psychologist, author of *Reviving Ophelia* and *The Shelter of Each Other: Rebuilding Our Families*

Even older children need a dependable routine to function at their best. School-age children will ask, "Who's going to pick me up after school today? When is my teacher coming back to school? Am I staying at Mom's house or Dad's house next weekend?" They need to know what to expect.

Of course there are some times in your family life that are more chaotic than others. Perhaps you are moving to a new city or home or starting a new job. Perhaps you have recently separated or divorced. Perhaps a close family member is ill or has died. It is especially during these times of emotional upheaval that an underlying sense of security is most important. How can this be conveyed? In very simple ways. You may snuggle in the rocking chair and read a short story to your child for a few minutes in the evening. You may sit up a half hour past normal bedtime with your teenage child to chat over a cup of hot chocolate. These simple acts, established in the everyday routine, are soothing when a crisis strikes. They convey the important message that even when everything is turned upside down, the love and commitment you feel toward your child remains.

Parents need routines as well. By having a predictable bedtime routine, for example, both you and your toddler know that he will be in bed at eight o'clock each night, which gives you a little "off-duty" time afterward. As a parent, you also need to know what to expect and when you will have time to recharge your battery or enjoy some peace and quiet.

> "It takes time to establish traditions, to establish an economy, and to establish some laws. But once they're in place in the family, then it's a little like putting a family on autopilot. Certain things are there; they happen routinely. Kids get security from that, and as a result, the job of parenting actually becomes easier."
>
> —Richard Eyre, coauthor (with Linda Eyre) of *Teaching Your Children Values* and *Three Steps to a Strong Family*

Creating Stability: Making the Morning Routine Manageable

Mornings are typically hectic. There's so much to do in so little time. You have to get up, get dressed, have breakfast, and get to work. Your children must get up, get dressed, have breakfast, brush their teeth, round up their books and belongings, and get to school.

Here are a few suggestions that will help establish a smoother, more predictable start of the day:

1. Plan ahead so that you always have the necessary ingredients for school and work lunches. If your children are in grade school or older, encourage them to make their own lunches the evening before.

2. Make each school-age child responsible for rounding up the following items before bedtime each evening:
   a. Clean clothes for tomorrow
   b. All schoolbooks and needed supplies
   c. Any special projects, school notes, etc.
   (You should round up all items needed by your young children headed for day care in the morning.)

3. Allow a realistic amount of time to get going in the morning. If an hour is not enough time for your family to get in gear, try an hour and twenty minutes. (You may want to wake up thirty minutes earlier than your kids just to have a quiet and gradual start to the day.)

4. School-age kids wake up in a more pleasant mood when awakened by an alarm clock rather than a nagging parent. Buy an inexpensive alarm clock for each of your children. Help them learn to set it each evening.

5. Encourage your kids to "do-for-themselves." This approach makes

everyone a winner. You will feel less pressured, and your kids will feel competent and self-reliant. Even a five-year-old may be able to dress himself each morning after several practice sessions.

> "Something as simple as reading a bedtime story to your child should not be viewed as only a learning activity. It is also a social and emotional activity. It's a time when the child is receiving your care, nurturance, and love by sitting in your lap, by having your focused attention."
>
> —Dr. Jerlean Daniel, assistant professor of child development and child care, University of Pittsburgh

6. Make your kitchen "kid-friendly." Have unbreakable bowls, cups, and plates stored in a low cupboard in the kitchen so even your youngest children can get breakfast on their own.

7. Always have healthy and easy breakfast foods in the pantry, and encourage your kids to get their own breakfasts. Store cereal in low cupboards too.

8. Buy half-gallon containers of milk and juice rather than the heavy one-gallon size. These containers are manageable for children six years old and up. You may want to have small plastic bowls half-filled with milk, with a lid in place for your three- or four-year-old child. These bowls are ready to be filled with dry cereal.

9. Don't engage in important or controversial family discussions about curfew, spending money, homework, etc., in the morning when you are pressed for time. When your kids clamor for a discussion about these issues, calmly set a time for a discussion later in the day when everyone is on a more relaxed schedule and ready to listen.

Set up your environment and morning routine so that your children can succeed in doing for themselves. This is a great opportunity to practice independence.

Creating Stability: Daily Transition to Child Care/School

The transitions to and from your child's day-care center or school have the potential to be rocky. Here are a few suggestions designed to help smooth out this part of your day:

1. Check and double-check to see that you have that special blanket or stuffed animal your child relies upon to keep her company at the day care center.

2. Post a note on the refrigerator listing the items your child must take to school each day and you must take to work. Provide a space on this note for extra things that you'll need from time to time. Check this list each night before bedtime and update it whenever necessary.

3. Work out a standard good-bye ritual for your small children so you can say good-bye each morning in a predictable way. Perhaps you can give your child a hug once inside the day care center and walk past a designated spot outside to wave good-bye before you get back in your car to head off to work.

4. When picking up your children after a long day at work and school, provide some apple slices or other fresh fruit for everyone to munch on in the car. These healthy snacks will take the edge off everyone's hunger and allow you to begin making dinner without cranky or hungry children buzzing around the kitchen clamoring for food.

5. You may want to postpone dinner preparation by thirty minutes and spend the first thirty minutes of the evening regrouping with your children. Small children in particular make this daily transition better if you take fifteen to twenty minutes to rock in the rocking chair and read a few stories together. (That fruit snack will help keep the hunger at bay so everyone can settle in for a little snuggly time together.)

> "You know what people tend to forget is that when a baby cries he's not trying to disturb your sleep. That's the only way he has to communicate."
>
> —Dr. Peter Weiss, obstetrician, gynecologist, and assistant clinical professor of OB/GYN at UCLA School of Medicine

Creating Stability: Making the Bedtime Routine Manageable

Bedtime is when most kids will test your authority (and patience!). What makes bedtime especially volatile is that the kids are tired, and you are often frazzled too.

Here are some tips:

1. Set a specific bedtime for each of your children based on your child's age and sleep needs. Let each child know his bedtime schedule.

2. Work to establish a predictable pre-bedtime routine for your children. Reading or telling a bedtime story is a great way to shift gears. Read the story in the same place each evening. Set a definite amount of reading time. Let your kids know ahead of time that you will read one story—or two short stories—for fifteen minutes, for instance.

> "We need enough nurturance for a good baseline; there's got to be enough chicken soup there: enough caring, security, and limit-setting. But within those broad parameters we have to then tailor them in a unique way for each and every child."
>
> —Dr. Stanley Greenspan, clinical professor of psychiatry and pediatrics at George Washington University School of Medicine and author of *The Growth of the Mind*, *Building Healthy Minds*, *Playground Politics*, and *The Challenging Child*

3. For older children, you may consider encouraging your child to read to herself in bed each evening before bedtime. Some families like to have twenty to thirty minutes of reading or drawing time for each child as a wind-down time in bed. Start the clock twenty to thirty minutes before their actual lights-out deadline.

4. Allow your child to get one drink of water sometime during this wind-down period, before he or she gets settled into bed. Make this rule clear to each child in advance and repeat it periodically.

5. Allow your children to have a night-light on if they choose.

6. Don't engage in confrontational or argumentative discussions with your child at bedtime. Simply and calmly say, "We can talk about that tomorrow after dinner." (And then make good on this promise.)

7. If your older child is misbehaving at bedtime and fussing to stay up longer or scrapping with her sister, simply and calmly say, "I can see that you are overtired and can't cooperate at bedtime. This tells me that you need more sleep. If you can't settle down immediately, you will go to bed one hour (or half hour) earlier tomorrow so you'll be in a better mood."

Create a Nighttime Routine for Preteens and Teens

While your teenage child is independent enough to manage his bedtime routine of showering, brushing his teeth, and reading on his own, there's still room for a short time to regroup with him at the end of the day. Invent a routine that the two of you might share each evening—a cup of decaffeinated tea, soda, or hot chocolate shared at the end of a busy day is a quiet way to reconnect with your teenage child in a peaceful transition to bedtime.

Everyday Opportunities for Security and Stability
Infant: Birth to Twelve Months

Babies do not understand your spoken words, but they do understand your loving actions and daily care as the language of security. Here are some of the many small but significant ways that you can create a sense of security for your baby:

Nurturing

- Hold and rock your baby whenever you have an opportunity.
- Carry your baby in a safe front-pack baby carrier while doing light chores indoors. (Most babies love this feeling of closeness.)
- Respond to your child's cries when she is wet, hungry, or uncomfortable. (Don't worry that you will spoil your baby with too much attention in the first months of life.) A tremendous sense of security is conveyed to your baby through the simple acts of feeding and diapering.
- Read to your baby each day; he will love the rhythmic cadence of reading.
- Sing to your child softly. Sing your favorite songs so your child hears the enjoyment in your voice.
- Chat with your baby when she is awake. She will not understand your words, but will enjoy your soothing voice and your attention.

Begin to Establish a Stable Routine

- Help your baby distinguish nighttime from daytime by making his middle-of-the-night feedings as brief and uneventful as possible. Keep the lights low and save your lively chatter for the daytime feedings.
- As the weeks and months go by, help your baby establish a predictable feeding and sleep routine. This schedule will provide a sense of stability and security to your baby and family.

> "Reading to babies is a great idea. There's no such thing as too early."
>
> —Dr. Elizabeth Bates, professor of psychology, professor of cognitive science, and director of the Center for Research in Language at the University of California in San Diego

Safety Issues

You must make your child not only feel secure but also actually be safe from harm. Protect your baby from falls and injuries, and later, when she crawls, protect against drowning, accidental poisoning, and electrical hazards. Create a safe, baby-proof home.

Evaluating Your Family Routines

Sometimes the harmony in your daily routine unravels because of a change in circumstances or stress in the family. It may be necessary to sit down with pencil and paper in hand and take a look at your daily routine and lifestyle. This evaluation process will help you identify where your life has become frayed around the edges. Is everyone fussy the hour before dinner? Are your children stalling at bedtime, making you angry each night? Are your older children watching violent or frightening television programs in the evening and becoming insecure and scared at bedtime? Are there tears and short tempers every morning as you rush to get your children dressed and fed and off to the sitter? This chaos can set the stage for crabbiness (or insecurity) in the family. Be a problem solver! First try to pinpoint what is not working—rushing too much in the morning, consistent whining and stalling at bedtime, and so on—then devise a plan of action or put a new routine in place to improve the situation.

> "Emotional and intellectual development are completely bound up with each other. A baby needs a parent's security and encouragement. Children can learn from a loving parent that the world is beautiful, exciting, and also safe. Parents provide the emotional security; the base from which a child explores the world."
>
> —Dr. Ann Barnet, professor of neurology and pediatrics at George Washington University School of Medicine and author of *The Youngest Minds: Parenting and Genes in the Development of Intellect and Emotion*

Toddler: Twelve Months to Two-and-a-Half Years

Toddlers understand your words and actions. Toddlers clamor for independence in one breath and cling to your leg in the next. Toddlers need a lot of love and nurturing and benefit greatly from a predictable routine.

Nurturing

- Make time every day for cuddling, snuggling, and reading to your child.
- The daily care you provide by feeding, bathing, and diapering your toddler is the nonverbal language that conveys security.
- Toddlers understand much more than they themselves can express in words. Chat with your child, and use your words to express your love and appreciation for your child every day.

Establish and Maintain a Stable Routine

- Allow time for breakfast together each day before you begin your workday.
- Make your evening together predictable: dinner at home or at a restaurant together, quiet time for your child to play or an evening walk, followed by bath time, story time, and bedtime at a similar time each evening.
- Your calm and firm reaction to your toddler's temper tantrum helps define a sense of order in your child's world. Anticipate toddler temper tantrums. Many tantrums can be prevented by scheduling your day to avoid fatigue. Don't push your luck by going to a busy supermarket with your child right before nap time or when your child is hungry. When your child does lose control with an occasional temper tantrum, remain calm, in control, and decisive.

Safety Issues

You must make your child not only feel secure but actually be safe from harm. Provide vigilant protection against household injuries and poisoning by making sure your home is toddler-proof every day.

Preschool Child: Two-and-a-Half to Four Years

Preschool children are typically great adventurers and pretenders. They are beginning to observe the world around them with greater appreciation and interest in imitating.

Nurturing

- Spend one-on-one time snuggling, cuddling, and reading to your preschooler every day.

> "I'm a firm believer in touching. I think the baby responds very well to being held by mom or dad. It helps build the relationship both between the baby and the parents."
>
> —Dr. Peter Weiss, obstetrician and gynecologist and assistant clinical professor of OB/GYN at UCLA School of Medicine California in San Diego

---

Children's Stories about Feelings of Security

Young children love to hear stories about other children. They also love story themes that strike a chord with issues in their own lives (even if unspoken), such as making mischief and getting in trouble (*Curious George*), adventure (*The Tale of Peter Rabbit*), and feeling snuggly and secure (*Good Night Moon*).

Here are some tried-and-true books that hit a chord with infants, toddlers, and preschoolers on a theme near and dear to their own hearts—feeling loved best of all and being secure.

1. *The Runaway Bunny* by Margaret Wise Brown
2. *Good Night Moon* by Margaret Wise Brown
3. *Where the Wild Things Are* by Maurice Sendak
4. *Blueberries for Sal* by Robert McCloskey
5. *Make Way for Ducklings* by Robert McCloskey

- Preschoolers still like to rock in the rocking chair with you. This is a good way for children and parents to unwind after a busy day!
- Take regular walks together; hold hands or carry your child in a sturdy child backpack on occasion.
- Preschoolers will entertain themselves happily with blocks and safe toys if you are working nearby and taking notice of their play from time to time. This fosters a feeling of security and encourages independence at the same time.
- Use words and hugs to express your delight in and love for your child every day.
- Don't let your child watch violent and frightening television programs that undermine his sense of security.

Create and Maintain a Stable Routine

Preschoolers like to know what is planned for their day.

- Maintain a loosely structured daily routine, with evening mealtime together and playtime, bath time, story time, and bedtime scheduled. Give your child advance notice several minutes before bedtime each evening so that she can begin to get geared down for sleep time.
- Set clear limits for your child. Preschool children need to know that you are in charge in order to feel secure.

> "Children learn to trust others when adults respond to their needs promptly and when adults tune in to their feelings."
>
> —Toni Bickart, coauthor of *Preschool for Parents* and *What Every Parent Needs to Know about 1st, 2nd and 3rd Grades*

Safety Issues

Provide vigilant protection against household and traffic accidents. Also, because preschool children have vivid imaginations, your child may need extra reassurance about scary thoughts and concerns.

<u>School-Age Child</u>: Five to Ten Years

School-age kids are beginning to venture out into the world, primarily through school. They need a home base filled with security and stability in order to be confident enough to move beyond their home and family.

Nurturing

- Your school-age child still needs your hugs and snuggles on a daily basis to reinforce a sense of security.
- Curl up and read together for a few minutes each day.
- Eliminate access to violent and frightening television programs and movies that undermine your child's sense of security.
- Regularly express your appreciation for your child and your delight that he is part of your life and family. (Be creative and express your heartfelt feelings in language that reflects your style and your child's age.)
- Be available and accessible to your child each day. Schedule one-on-one time with your child each day.

> "I think security really is the foundation of all that follows for children. It starts in the very first days and months of life as a child comes to learn that he or she has a safe place and will be cared for. And that continues right on through all of development."
>
> —Marti Erickson, developmental psychologist and director of the Children, Youth and Family Consortium at the University of Minnesota

Create and Maintain a Stable Routine

- Continue a predictable family routine that includes dinner together, an evening walk, or a hobby that you might share from time to time.
- Bedtime continues to be an important part of your older child's daily routine. Stick to a firm weekday bedtime and predictable pre-bed routine. (Even school-age kids like their parents to read interesting or lively bedtime stories.)

Safety Issues

- Your school-age child is more aware of the dangers of the world. She will hear about crime, disaster, and tragedy from her peers and in the media. Stay in touch with your child and be available to listen to her fears and offer reassurance on a regular basis.

- Be sure your child is trained in basic issues of safety. Arrange your life so that your child not only feels safe but is safe—at school, after school, and at nighttime.

Preteens/Early Teens: Eleven to Fourteen Years

Despite your child's size and maturity, he still needs security. As a matter of fact, a sense of security is a prerequisite for spreading his wings of independence. Your maturing child needs to see that you love him, believe in him, and will help him as he grows. Following are some ways that you might convey a continuing sense of security.

> "A lot of parents pull back in terms of affection and praise during early adolescence because they think their child doesn't want it or doesn't need it anymore. It's very important to hang in there and continue to let your child know that you're there!"
>
> —Dr. Laurence Steinberg, professor of psychology at Temple University and coauthor (with Ann Levine) of *You and Your Adolescent*

Nurturing

- Make yourself available and accessible. Find time to chat, go to a sporting event, play sports (golf, canoeing, fishing, skiing, and so on), or shop together regularly.
- Express your heartfelt pride, appreciation, and love for your child. Find a way to express these feelings that is consistent with your style and your child's age and sensitivities.
- Allow time to listen to your preteen's concerns, worries, insecurities with peers, and other important issues. Spend three times more time *listening* than lecturing or criticizing your teenager.
- Establish rules to limit viewing of violent and frightening television programs and movies that undermine your child's sense of security.

Maintain a Stable Routine

- Part of your preteen's shifting sense of security rests in her belief in herself. Help her feel capable and competent. Your child knows she will be out on her own in the future. Help her begin to prepare to meet the challenges that lie ahead. If she has deficiencies in school, work, money management, or relationships that create problems, help her find ways to make concrete improvements to boost her confidence.

> "Children always need to know that there is a place of security that they can touch base with throughout their development."
>
> —Marti Erickson, developmental psychologist and director of the Children, Youth and Family Consortium at the University of Minnesota

- While a predictable family routine may not always be possible with preteens' school and sports schedules, try to ensure your family eats dinner together frequently each week. Schedule these family dinners on the calendar if necessary. Be flexible. If the best time for your preteen to spend an hour with you in the summer, for example, is during your lunch hour, meet for lunch.

Safety Issues

Continue to set firm limits about those issues that truly affect your preteen's safety, such as curfews, after-school rules, parties, etc.

Teens: Fifteen to Nineteen Years

Your teenager may be a head taller than you, with a grown-up–sized foot to match, but he still derives his foundation of security from your love, commitment, and involvement in his life.

Nurturing

- Spend one-on-one time sitting and chatting with your teen each day.
- Hug your teen and let her know how proud you are of the way that she is growing up. (Tell your teen, "You may not need a hug from me, *but I need a hug from you!*")
- Show with your actions (and time) that you are interested in your teen's life: continue to attend sports events and school, music, and theater productions, and so on.

Maintain a Stable Routine

- Your teenager still needs to know that you are available and involved in his life. *Be available regularly.*
- Have dinner as a family as frequently as possible.
- Plan extra Saturday or Sunday brunch or lunch dates to spend with your busy teen as frequently as possible.
- If schedules conflict, arrange at least one family dinner night where the family cooks and dines together. Make this family time a high priority.
- Your teen draws conclusions about the world around him from the information he gathers. Try to limit the routine viewing of violent television programs (which undermine your child's sense of security) and encourage positive, creative, and constructive evening activities.

Safety Issues

- Continue to exert control over safety issues such as driving, curfew, sexually transmitted diseases, parties, and alcohol.
- Help your child assume responsibility for her actions and safety. Encourage her to be a smart thinker who "thinks for herself."
- Discuss safety precautions related to late-night travel in your city and elsewhere.

• • • • • • • • • • • • •

chapter four

Encouragement and Recognition

Amy was nine months old when she took her first steps alone. She would take one tiny step, then teeter and fall. Her mom always said the same words, "You're such a big girl now! Good job!" Each time she fell, Amy would glance at her parents, who would laugh lightly and say, "Come on, let's try again. I know you can come over here to me." And without shedding a tear or showing alarm, Amy would push herself up and try again. The focus was on the tiny successful steps alone rather than the many falls that Amy experienced. And each expression of encouragement seemed to reinforce the idea that she was doing something very special indeed.

As a parent, you are afforded a special place of honor in your child's eyes right from the very beginning. You feed her, make her comfortable, give her affection, and provide her with a sense of security. She knows instinctively that she can depend on you. This is the beginning of a beautiful relationship!

As you continue to care for your child each day, his dependence upon you grows into a deep emotional bond with you. You become very special people (parents) with a tremendous ability to encourage his growth and development.

Your enthusiasm adds fuel to his natural desire to learn and progress. Throughout his childhood you will have thousands of opportunities to encourage your child to grow and develop in every way.

What to Encourage

> "We know that people who are successful in life are people who have a positive desire to achieve rather than a fear of failure."
>
> —Dr. Ron Smith, sports psychologist and coauthor (with Frank L. Smoll) of *Way to Go Coach*

The first order of business is to decide what it is that needs to be encouraged. Let's take a look at what's important to your child.

The big picture is that you must encourage your child to develop to her full potential—emotionally, intellectually, physically, spiritually, and socially.

Parents' Role in Encouragement and Recognition

There are two prerequisites for this job: You must believe in yourself as a parent and believe in your child. You must be confident about your intentions and commitment as a parent even if you lack practical experience. Your encouragement plays itself out in the ordinary moments of every day, every week that forms your life together as a family.

Job Description for "Conduit of Encouragement"

1. Believe in your child. Show her with your words and behavior—adopt an "I know you can do it" attitude about your child.

2. Focus on her successes; ignore minor failures and setbacks.

3. Praise your child's efforts every day throughout childhood.

4. Show up for and be supportive of events that are significant to your child (even later when your teen seems indifferent).

5. Live *your* life in an optimistic, can-do, problem-solving way—your child will imitate your behavior.

6. Show pride when your child makes progress in overcoming obstacles and improving behavior.

7. Help your child take note of his progress in every aspect of his life.

You must encourage him to be a whole and complete human being who makes the most of his talents, intelligence, and inner strength to live a good life. You do this in small steps each and every day of your lives together. When you see his attempts at learning, understanding, and doing in each area of his life, you must show your recognition of his progress.

For example, your child's social growth occurs in subtle steps over the entire span of childhood. You will notice your toddler observing another toddler playing alongside her. She may even show a spontaneous act of kindness in the sandbox by handing a small shovel to her playmate without saying a word. Her actions show that she is aware and somewhat interested in befriending her playmate during fleeting moments of play. Later, when she is a preschooler and school-age child, your daughter is able to show concern purposefully for a favorite playmate with both her words and her actions. She can ask her friend to share her toys, play a game, and split her cupcake. Years later, when your daughter is a teenager in high school, you will see many daily examples of her loyalty and compassion for her friends. She may come home from school one day and announce that her best friend's family must move away to a distant city and ask if her friend might live with your family (and share her room) in order to finish out her senior year at high school.

Your Child's Self-Esteem

Because your appreciation and encouragement are so critical to your child, your response to him helps shape his self-esteem. When you believe in your child, and let him know that he is an important, valuable, and capable person, he will begin to believe this about himself. Your reaction to him is like a mirror; you are reflecting

"Early in our research, we were visiting an athletic field to do some observations. Two children came along as they were leaving a baseball game. They were about eight years old. We said, 'Hi, how did things go today?' to them. One child said, 'Oh, it went okay. We lost.' I said, 'Oh, what was the score?' He said, 'I don't know.' The other child said, 'It was six to five.' I replied, 'Well, how did you remember that and he didn't?' He answered, 'Because that's the first thing my dad is going to ask me when I get home. What's the score?' When a child comes home, say: 'Hey, did you have fun? Was it a good game? Did you enjoy yourself? Did you play a good game?' Those are the kinds of things that we should do."

—Dr. Ron Smith, sports psychologist and coauthor (with Frank L. Smoll) of *Way to Go Coach*

Phrases of Encouragement

Kids can spot a phony a mile away. While kids want your recognition, they do not want false praise or praise that is exaggerated. Be attentive—use words of encouragement when heartfelt and appropriate to the situation. Here are some examples:

- "I knew you would do a great job."
- "You really stuck with this big project. You should feel very proud of your work."
- "I was very proud of the way you helped the smaller children at the party today."
- "You are such a great help to me. Thanks for straightening up the house today."
- "I am so proud of the way you are growing up. You are doing such a fine job!"
- "You are a hard worker!"
- "You are a great problem solver."
- "You have really made progress!" (And talk about specific skills your child has learned.)

Secrets of Encouraging Good Behavior

- Catch your child doing something good or behaving appropriately and compliment his efforts.
- Stack the deck for success in social situations; talk with your child ahead of time about what is expected when going to a restaurant, concert, play, party, or wedding. Rehearse good behavior with small children, and stay only an appropriate length of time for your child's attention span and age.
- Children need gentle reminders—create a chart on the refrigerator to encourage good behavior at bedtime, helping with chores, homework responsibilities, and so on. Give stars for each day of success with these tasks. (Stars can be traded in at the end of the week for special privileges—going to play miniature golf, going to a movie, and so forth.)

back to him a profound message about his value. As you encourage the efforts he makes to sit up, crawl, walk, make friends, share, study, and so forth, you are also encouraging him to appreciate all the things he's learned, his talents, his hard work, and his accomplishments, and to hold himself in high regard. The more competent he becomes, the more confident he feels. Self-esteem does not arise so much from well-intended parents giving constant praise, but from your child's belief in his own competence and worth.

> "So, in many, many small ways in the daily relationship with a child, you're constantly saying to the child, 'I know you can do it, I know you can do it!' It's like *The Little Engine That Could,* which we used to talk about on *Captain* for many years."
>
> —Bob Keeshan, TV's Captain Kangaroo and author of *Good Morning, Captain*

Encourage your child to pat herself on the back for a job well done. You can be a good role model by expressing your pride for your own job well done from time to time too.

Encouragement Is the Foundation of Effective Discipline

The consistent encouragement and positive attention you give to your child is also an important building block for effective discipline. Because your child thrives on your encouragement, it will mean more to him when you are less than pleased with his behavior. Your most effective power in establishing guidelines and setting limits throughout your child's life rests upon the foundation of your loving relationship with him. This does not mean that your child will happily aim to please you at every turn and therefore will never engage in disruptive or inappropriate behavior. But it will give you more influence.

Everyday Opportunities for Encouragement
Infant: Birth to Twelve Months

During the first year of life, your baby will learn your language of encouragement. She will come to recognize and be motivated by the delight expressed in your face and your voice as she interacts with you.

> "Every time there's a guest who comes to your house for dinner and your child shows respect and eats nicely...you say afterward, 'Oh, I was so proud of you. You were terrific at dinner tonight. Just beautiful manners...good for you!'"
>
> —Letitia Baldrige, author of *Letitia Baldrige's More Than Manners*

> "If you go to a shopping mall and you watch families walking through, the child who is getting the attention is inevitably the child who is misbehaving! The child who is doing just fine and behaving himself is getting ignored. The lesson we have to learn as parents is that children will gain your attention however they can. I mean, the praise should come when the child is doing the right thing, when he's behaving. It's this kind of praise that will motivate long-term good behavior far more than the punishment."
>
> —Richard Eyre, coauthor (with Linda Eyre) of *Teaching Your Children Values* and *Three Steps to a Strong Family*

What to Encourage

Encourage all of your baby's efforts to master new skills: following objects with his eyes, listening carefully, smiling and laughing, grasping toys, rolling over, chattering, attempting to imitate your speech, sitting up, scooting and crawling, cruising and walking, saying simple words, communicating, being curious, exploring, and making things happen!

How to Encourage Your Infant

Encourage your baby with your loving words, delight in her actions and activities, your smiles, your chatter in response to hers, your encouraging tone of voice, and your time and undivided attention.

Toddler: Twelve Months to Two-and-a-Half Years

Toddlers are able to understand the meaning of your words even though their own speech is still limited to short words or phrases. Express your delight through conversations with your child every day.

What to Encourage

Encourage all of your toddler's efforts to master new skills: walking, his ability to pick things up, to push and pull toys; his expressive language, his curiosity, his efforts to create; his attempts to do for himself, feeding himself, drinking from a cup, putting his hat on; his attempts to be gentle with others; his attempts to play and share with others; his attempts to browse through books; his efforts to use the potty.

How to Encourage Your Toddler

Give your undivided attention. Express your delight with your voice and face and an encouraging word, such as, "You can do it!" With your smiles and laughter, engage in conversations that include your toddler; express pride about your toddler's progress to others (to be overheard by your toddler); help him take a nap when he is overtired and frustrated by saying, "We'll try again later after your nap."

> "Very rarely can we see what our own sense of possibility is without somebody on the outside helping us to see that."
>
> —Jim Thompson, author of *Positive Coaching: Building Character and Self-Esteem through Sports*

Preschool Child: Two-and-a-Half to Four Years

Preschoolers understand your words, tone of voice, body language, and other subtle methods of communicating emotions.

What to Encourage

Encourage all of your preschooler's efforts to master new skills: her curiosity and imagination; all of her efforts to do for herself; all of her efforts to help others and contribute to family chores; her creative efforts; her efforts to cooperate and share; her efforts to resolve conflicts with others; her physical development—running, kicking, riding a tricycle; her efforts to use her words to express feelings (rather than taking angry action).

How to Encourage Your Preschooler

Encourage your preschooler with your praise for all efforts and jobs well done, specific compliments for small acts of kindness, your smiles and laughter, your conversations that include your child, your display of work and creations placed on the refrigerator, the words and attitude that say, "You can do it," a "progress chart" with brightly colored stars for each day when bedtime goes smoothly, and special privileges because she is competent and trustworthy. Encourage your preschooler to pat herself on the back for a job well done.

School-Age Child: Five to Ten Years

Your school-age child is extremely perceptive about your emotions and picks up on your moods, feelings, and approval. Choose your words carefully and try to use positive ways to encourage rather than voicing complaints and criticism.

What to Encourage

> "And it's the nod of recognition and the smile and the response of the parent that indicates to the child, sometimes even without words, the parent's belief in the goodness of the child."
>
> —Dr. Robert Coles, child psychiatrist and Pulitzer prize–winning author of *Children of Crisis* and *The Moral Life of Children*

Encourage your school-age child's efforts to master new skills: all efforts to do for himself and help with chores, learning at school, making friends, cooperating, sharing and caring for others, finding solutions for problems, sticking with a task until completion, making creative projects, behaving appropriately, using manners, learning to control his temper, and showing patience.

How to Encourage Your School-Age Child

Spend time with your child, show up for all important activities, help your child succeed, teach her to break large jobs into small steps, praise your child's efforts and accomplishments, express your pride about your child to others in conversation, help your child learn to take a break from a project that is overwhelming and tackle it after a good night's sleep, recognize special accomplishments with a family celebration, make your child's favorite dinner or dessert, send some of your child's creative projects to grandparents, and give special privileges when your child has taken on extra responsibility. Encourage your child to give herself pats on the back for a job well done.

> "My parents raised me as a child a long time ago when girls really weren't encouraged to go into the working world at all in executive positions. My parents always treated me the same as my brothers. They gave me the same aspiration in education. We all reached for good colleges. There wasn't the money, but we reached for it because our parents inspired us. I was very lucky to have parents who knew about the strength of the women's movement before anybody else did!"
>
> —Letitia Baldrige, author of *Letitia Baldrige's More Than Manners*

Preteens/Early Teens: Eleven to Fourteen Years

Don't be fooled by your preteen's seeming nonchalance toward you. Preteens still want and need your encouragement, acceptance, and understanding. And they do care to please you.

What to Encourage

Encourage all your preteen's efforts to master new skills: finding solutions to problems, completing schoolwork and projects, all creative activities, acts of kindness and caring for others, academic, sports, music and arts activities, self-control skills, teamwork and cooperation, responsibility for chores, caring for smaller children, perseverance, and courage.

How to Encourage Your Preteen

Stay involved in your child's daily life; express appreciation for your child each and every day; be available to say, "You can do it," at appropriate times; extend special privileges for extra responsibility; establish limits that will help your child succeed (for example, limits on weeknight TV viewing); praise his efforts; encourage your child to give himself pats on the back for a job well done; display his artwork; celebrate special accomplishments with a special family dinner; bake his favorite dessert; and when you feel it, say, "I am so proud of how you are growing up!"

> "Make it a point to compliment your child often. Tell her what a good kid she is. Give her a hug often. Send her a card in the mail or put a card under her pillow or at the breakfast table that tells her how special she is. When she's going to bed at night, remind her of what she has to offer others. Make her feel like there's a lot that she is successful at, that she has a lot to offer others. Kids just love to hear these things. It makes them feel so good and…those things are just going to enhance their self-esteem."
>
> —Robin Goldstein, child development specialist and author of the *Everyday Parenting* book series

Teens: Fifteen to Nineteen Years

Your teenager may be a head taller than you, but she still wants and needs your acceptance and understanding. Because she is beginning to think about going out into the world soon, she also sometimes feels uncertain about her capabilities. Your child needs heartfelt enthusiasm and encouragement from you.

What to Encourage

Encourage your teen's efforts to master new skills: his academic efforts; sports, music, art and theater performances; responsibility at work; cooperation; care for others (including small children); finding

> "Always reward them, even more than you criticize them. Help them along."
>
> —Letitia Baldrige, author of *Letitia Baldrige's More Than Manners*

solutions to problems; tackling long-term projects; pursuing school and work opportunities; respect for family rules; good judgment in social settings; all creative efforts; self-control; financial responsibility; courage; and perseverance.

How to Encourage Your Teen

Stay involved in your child's life; express your appreciation for your child each day; extend extra privileges for extra responsibility; continue to show up for all important events and activities in your child's life; be available to say, "You can do it," at appropriate times; delight in your child's unique personality and talents; honor your child's accomplishments and milestones with a family celebration or special outing; encourage your teen to give himself pats on the back for a job well done.

Be a good role model: live your life with a "can-do" attitude!

chapter five

Guidance and Discipline

Four-year-old Remy knew that he wasn't allowed to color on the walls. But he was mad at his sister, Alex, so he got a box of markers and scribbled all over the wall behind the door in her bedroom. As soon as he finished the deed, he had a terrible feeling—his mom and dad would see what he had done, and he would be in very big trouble.

Children need your help in learning to behave. You have some powerful influence to help in your job of guidance and discipline, but you also have some sticky challenges that change with the age of your child. Before jumping ahead to the nuts and bolts of *how* to discipline your child in the ordinary moments of life together, it is important that you understand your overall mission in the discipline department.

Long-Term Discipline Goal

The dictionary definition of discipline that best applies to children is "training that develops self-control." Your job in the long haul is not to police and punish your children, but to use effective parenting skills to guide your child toward self-control. The result that you are striving for is that your child will develop an inner mechanism that guides him to behave and act appropriately and effectively in all sorts of real-life situations. He will achieve this goal, with your help, in thousands of tiny installments throughout childhood.

> "Our children can make us angry, they can make us upset, and if you want to solve a problem for your child, you're going to need to be able to calm down yourself."
>
> —Dr. John Clabby, psychologist and coauthor (with Maurice J. Elias) of *Teach Your Child Decision Making*

For many parents, the task of disciplining their child is the most difficult part of parenting. This is true because unfortunately the way children learn how to behave appropriately is often by misbehaving and experiencing the consequences of their misbehavior. In the process of testing the limits and misbehaving, kids press a lot of your emotional buttons. You become angry or outraged, your authority seems threatened, and your confidence as the parent-in-charge is ruffled. Very often you must stay focused on controlling yourself and remembering what your goal is in the discipline department rather than just reacting from anger.

Parents want their children to love and approve of them as parents. Once you become a parent, you must get comfortable with the idea that you are the grown-up responsible to guide and discipline your child, and sometimes you're on the hot seat of unpopularity. In order to stick to your long-term goal of training your child to develop self-control and do so respectfully, firmly, and matter-of-factly, you must hold on to the confidence that you are doing the right thing for your child and keep your mission in the forefront of your mind.

> "It is a very strong, effective way of communicating to kids. Say what you have to say. Say it clearly and then say no more."
>
> —Dr. Anthony Wolf, clinical psychologist, author of *It's Not Fair, Jeremy Spencer's Parents Let Him Stay up All Night*

When Does Your Job of Discipline Begin?

During the first months of your child's life there is little need for discipline. Once your child reaches six months of age she may grab your glasses, pull your hair, or bite you, and you must respond with a firm "No, that hurts Daddy (or Mommy)," and put her down in a safe place for a moment without you

Parents' Role as the Instructor of Discipline

Job Description for "Instructor of Discipline"

- Clearly express to your child what is acceptable behavior in all sorts of daily situations.
- Establish firm rules and clearly, briefly explain them to your children. Don't make a million rules governing every little thing; instead, make and enforce a small number of important rules.
- Expect that your children will need to be reminded of rules over and over again.
- Expect some misbehavior at each stage of development.
- Tailor your discipline approach to your child's developmental age.
- Remember your mission statement to "train your child to develop self-control," and do a mental review to see that your discipline approach is consistent with this goal.
- Maintain control of yourself and your emotions to act effectively.
- Recognize your child's good behavior when you see it in action. (Misbehavior is often a misguided bid for attention.)
- Establish a routine to ensure you and your child are getting enough sleep each night so you are at your best the next day.
- Be a good role model for your children; solve problems nonviolently, communicate clearly, and take responsibility for your own actions.

as a consequence. Your child has no clue that her actions hurt you other than by your response. But she will begin to learn from your firm reaction that her actions are not okay.

Once your child is mobile and can explore totally on his own, you suddenly will be launched into a world that requires you to set limits and discipline your child daily. This is when your real day-to-day job of discipline and guidance begins, and it will continue for the next eighteen to twenty years.

Child Care Providers Are a Significant Influence

When selecting a baby-sitter or child care provider for your young child, make discipline a central issue in your evaluation. The same principles of effective discipline are essential for both parents and child care providers.

Ask these questions about discipline and handling of misbehavior when interviewing a prospective child care provider:

1. What do you do when a child misbehaves?
2. Do you spank? Use time-out?
3. What happens when one child hits or pushes another?

Very often your best information about misbehavior and discipline at a child care center comes from your own observations. To see the children and caregivers in action, plan to visit your child at her child care center for an occasional lunch date, if possible. Observe quietly and unobtrusively during your visit.

Establish a Foundation of Encouragement

Encouragement and discipline go together like peanut butter and jelly. Your child's natural desire to please you is your biggest asset in encouraging good behavior and discouraging misbehavior. (The rules of encouragement outlined in the previous chapter form the foundation of your effectiveness in guidance and discipline for your child.) Remember to include heartfelt encouragement for your child each and every day of your lives together. Compliment good behavior and hard work when you see it. When your child misbehaves, you need to show clearly that you disapprove of that particular behavior without expressing sweeping statements that sum up your child's character in a negative way.

This long-term goal and approach to discipline dovetails with many of your other jobs of parenting: encouraging responsibility and independence, compassion for

"The No. 1 limit, and it's a category—it's in a category of its own—is anything that could cause harm to them or to somebody else."

—Dr. Anthony Wolf, clinical psychologist, author of *It's Not Fair, Jeremy Spencer's Parents Let Him Stay up All Night*

Toddler Temper Tantrums

Many toddler temper tantrums can be prevented. Temper tantrums occur when your toddler is overwhelmed and feeling out of control, fatigued, hungry, or pushed beyond his limit. You can prevent a significant percentage of temper tantrums by paying attention to your child's need for sleep (naps) and regularly scheduled meals. Avoid going to the grocery store with your toddler right before mealtime or nap time.

When a Temper Tantrum Occurs

The first rule when your child loses control of herself is that you must stay in control. React to your child's temper tantrum in a firm, decisive but measured (calm) way. In the midst of a temper tantrum, some children respond well to your saying, "I see you are having a hard time now, come and rock with me in the rocking chair or snuggle up on the couch while I read you a short story." Other children do not regain their composure by your attempts to offer nurturing and reassurance, but instead need to be alone in the crib or bed, to live out the tantrum and perhaps fall asleep. In either event, you must try not to accelerate the tantrum by screaming or showing loss of control yourself. Let your child know that the tantrum behavior is not okay, but once she pulls herself back together she can rejoin you, the other family members, her playmates, and so forth.

others, self-esteem, problem-solving skills, and learning respect for self and others.

Establish Rules

Rules make kids of all ages feel safe. Rules create a framework of predictability in which kids can operate. Rules help a family run smoothly. When a small number of firm and important rules are established in your family, some of the debate will be eliminated.

The Biggest Factor in Effective Discipline

The single most influential factor in a parent's ability to handle misbehavior and discipline problems effectively and appropriately (especially with young children in the family) is sleep. When your child (of any age) is overtired, he is more likely to lose control of his feelings, challenge your authority, and disobey the house rules. Likewise, when you are overtired you are most likely to react purely out of anger and frustration to your child's misbehavior. Bedtime is often a volatile time because you and your child are close to your limit.

Accept this situation—make a good night's sleep (and rest and naps) a high priority in your family throughout childhood. Stick to a firm bedtime routine that affords your child adequate time to recharge her battery every day. Along these same lines, schedule time alone for yourself to relax and get relief from your heavy responsibilities as a parent. Your time to relax and your child's predictable bedtime routines are insurance policies so that you can do your best in the discipline department.

Exercise the creation and enforcement of rules wisely; don't make a million rules for every little detail of your child's life. Decide what issues are most important and establish unshakable rules surrounding these issues. Because one of your top priorities is ensuring your child's safety and protecting his well-being, many of the hard-and-fast rules will be related to safety. Each stage of childhood requires some different safety rules; for example, "You may not ever play with matches!" "Hitting another person in the family is not allowed." "Do not drink and drive; do not ride with a friend who has been drinking."

Express these and other safety rules firmly and clearly in advance. Use words that your child understands. For toddlers and preschoolers, keep your rules simple and to the point. Expect that rules will need to be repeated over and over again. When a rule is broken, follow through with appropriate consequences for your child.

All Children Need to Know What Is Expected

One of the consistent rules throughout all the stages of development is that children need to know in advance what is expected and which behaviors are unacceptable in any kind of real-life situation. For example, when going to a children's concert or play, preschoolers need to know what an auditorium is like, who performs, how long it will last, and also what is appropriate behavior for members of the audience. Parents must help stack the deck for success by staying a specific, short length of time—what is manageable for a young child's attention span, and be willing to leave early if a child's behavior and attention span clearly aren't up to the event.

> "Some of the early training is: What are the boundaries? What's okay and what's not? What's appropriate and what's not? What's your space and what's mine? A lot of kids in that second year will pinch their parents' faces. They'll pull their hair. They do all kinds of little things like that and then they'll stop and look and see what happens. That's one way the patterns of discipline start. It's important for parents not to get too mad, but to very quickly, kindly, firmly set a boundary and say, 'I'm not one to be pinched. That hurts.' Put the child down right away and maybe even walk away and say, 'I'm not willing to be with you when you hit.'"
>
> —Dr. Tim Jordan, pediatrician

Even preteens need clearly identified expectations: "We are going to Aunt Susan's birthday party at three o'clock today. We will likely stay for at least three to four hours. You are going to be the only teenager there. What books or activities would you like to take to keep yourself busy? Would you like to take your homework and work after dinner in a quiet room at Aunt Susan's house?" Letting your child know what is planned in this way may help prevent misbehavior that stems from boredom or a desire to act out to get attention.

Good Children, Bad Behavior

When your child misbehaves, you must show clearly with your words and actions that you disapprove of his specific behavior without judging him to be a "bad boy." This is especially true because you want your child to take responsibility for his actions and seek solutions that improve the situation. If you send a clear message to your child—"That behavior is unacceptable"—he then has the option to change or improve his behav-

Tips for Using a Time-Out for Discipline

Sending your child for a time-out is a good way to force an immediate stop to misbehavior and allow your child a chance to regain her composure.

Rules for Effective Time-Outs

In clear, simple language let your child know his behavior is cause for a short time-out: "You hit Sally, now you go to the couch for a time-out."

Select a time-out place that is uninteresting and away from the family excitement.

Initiate time-out immediately after the misbehavior so your child associates her misbehavior with being sent for a time-out.

Keep the time-out short; it's intended to force a break in the bad behavior. Two to three minutes is sufficient to accomplish this goal for toddlers. Five minutes for preschoolers. Fifteen minutes for school-age children. (Use a timer to keep track of time.)

After the time-out is over, quickly restate, "It's not okay to hit." Then help your child find a positive activity to get involved in, such as a different toy to hold his interest.

"If the child brings away the message that goes something like this: It's wrong to hit other people because it hurts them, you can expect that the kid will avoid hurting people whether or not the parent is around. That's the part you want to have prominent in the kid's mind. The actual harm that he's caused and not the fear of punishment."

—Dr. William Damon, developmental psychologist and author of *The Moral Child*

ior to gain your positive attention. On the other hand, if you say, "You are a very bad boy," there doesn't seem to be a solution to the problem; he feels unlikable and helpless to change the situation. This same principle holds true throughout all of childhood. For example, if your teenage daughter breaks the family rules about curfew, show your disapproval for her misbehavior and follow through with appropriate consequences (restriction, loss of use of the family car, and so on), but do not sum up your daughter's character as being hopeless.

Be very clear with your child throughout all of childhood that you disapprove of certain behaviors, then lead the way through encouragement for her to find ways to change and improve her behavior.

Tailor Your Discipline to the Developmental Age of Your Child

The overall goal of discipline is the same throughout childhood, but the specific best approach varies with the age of your child. It's helpful to have a general idea of how your child views the world at each stage of development for you to be most effective with discipline.

Toddlers and preschoolers, for example, have a very short attention span and need a lot of reminders of what is expected in the behavior department. Toddlers also have almost no judgment whatsoever, so that even the most basic sense of danger is missing from their consciousness. Preschoolers are only slightly more aware of how their actions can cause serious consequences to their own safety and that of others. Both ages need repetitious reminders of what behavior is okay, what is hurtful to others, and what is dangerous.

School-age children, on the other hand, have ventured into the world of school and peers but don't have much experience in the fine points of getting along with other children and negotiation. They learn by doing and making mistakes along the way.

Preteens are quite sophisticated at questioning their parents' rules and actions and are pursuing independence in a big way. One of the ways they develop good judgment and responsibility is by making small decisions, some of which are faulty.

Teenagers are full of themselves, which is in part a positive develop-ment; they believe they know more than their parents and are fully

> "You have to remember that reason and logic do not usually work for preschoolers. You say the rule, you tell them exactly what you need them to know, and then you stop. You can repeat yourself a couple of times. And if a child asks you a question, go right away and answer it....Here's how I do it: you hit; you sit! That's it. A nice simple rule. We've broadened it in my classroom to you spit; you sit, and you bit; you sit. These are easily remembered rules. And, believe me, after the first few months, the children are saying it. They don't need you to say it anymore!"
>
> —Patti Greenberg Wollman, preschool teacher for over twenty years and author of *Behind the Playdough Curtain*

equipped to make any manner of decisions on their own. Sometimes they miscalculate, don't think through their actions, and behave disrespectfully to adults as they experiment with more independence.

Your goal at each stage is to help your child learn to control herself. You must factor in her age and maturity in order to help her succeed in this important aspect of growing.

Ineffective Discipline Techniques

> "One of our most positive discipline skills that people sometimes don't even think about, because it's just so natural, is instead of punishing let kids know how we feel. Simply say, 'I don't like that! That makes me very angry. That is unacceptable. I won't have one person I love hurt another person I love!'"
>
> —Nancy Samalin, author of *Loving Each One Best* and *Loving Your Child Is Not Enough*
> *Shelter of Each Other: Rebuilding Our Families*

Many of the off-the-cuff, reactive approaches to discipline just don't work to improve your child's behavior. These approaches often undermine a good parent-child relationship as well. As parents we sometimes fall into the trap of disciplining our own children in the same way our parents responded to misbehavior when we were small without evaluating the effectiveness of these responses. At other times we are not using effective parenting skills to discipline because of extreme fatigue. Evaluate what you are doing and saying to your kids under the umbrella of discipline. Fine-tune your approach whenever necessary.

Here are some discipline techniques that do *not* achieve the two principles above of "training your child to develop self-control" and maintaining a positive parent-child relationship:

- *belittling*
- *ridiculing*
- *hitting*
- *screaming*
- *humiliating*
- *spanking*
- *nagging*
- *threatening*
- *name-calling*

Tips to Discourage Whining

Most preschoolers go through a whiny stage in which many of their wants and needs are expressed in a whining, irritating tone. It's important to nip this behavior in the bud so that it doesn't become a habit throughout all of childhood.

In order to discourage whining, it's important that you have the same conditioned response to your child's whining every time it occurs. When your child approaches you whining or demanding something say, "I cannot understand you when you whine. If you want to ask me nicely, I will listen, but I cannot understand your whining." Then immediately turn your attention to something else or walk away to another room, if necessary, but do not listen or respond to the whining request.

If your child comes back momentarily and makes his request in a normal speaking voice, listen attentively and respond, "You may not have three cookies, but you may have one." If your child whines again, restate clearly and simply that you cannot understand whining, but when he can talk in a nice way you will listen, and walk away again.

Discipline Often Calls for a Parental One-Two Approach

In many real-life situations, you are required to give a one-two approach to a behavior problem. One, you must respond immediately with an appropriate response to misbehavior; and two, you must give a follow-up response later to encourage good behavior when your child is back in the game trying to behave appropriately.

For example, when a toddler is angry and hits her playmate while you are

> "We use words for sharing knowledge; we use words for expressing emotion. We know that with little preverbal children who are angry or frustrated when they don't have words, they cry, they hit, and they have to give physical expressions. But when they have some words, and when a parent says, 'I see you're upset...use your words, I will listen,' the child can say, 'I'm angry,' or, 'I'm jealous,' or, 'My toe hurts,' or, 'I hate green beans.'"
>
> —Priscilla Vail, learning specialist and author of *Emotion: The On/Off Switch for Learning* and *Words Fail Me*

Tips for Using "Restriction"

Restriction, a concept similar to time-out, can be effective for preteens and teens who have broken family rules or engaged in significant misbehavior.

Restriction is based upon the premise that children must earn the special privileges of television, playing video games, having friends over to visit, movies, going out with friends, talking on the phone, and so on. These privileges are earned by appropriate behavior and respecting important family rules. Put simply, responsibility earns these privileges; irresponsibility cancels these privileges.

Here are five rules for using restriction as a discipline technique:

1. Explain the concept of restriction clearly to your child.
2. Have a written list that explains what privileges will be canceled when and if your child is put on restriction, so there will be no debate or negotiation later.
3. Use restriction wisely, for significant misbehavior or irresponsibility only.
4. Enforce restriction for a realistic (short) length of time—one day or for a weekend. For extreme violations of safety rules, etc., increase the time to one week.
5. Help your child remember she is on restriction with a simple reminder: "Remember you are on restriction today. When you get home after school there will be no television, no telephone calls, no visiting friends," and so forth.

nearby, your most effective response is to say immediately in a firm, disapproving voice, "It is not okay to hit someone. That hurts Kelly. You may not be in the room with Kelly or me when you are going to hit," and remove your child to her room for several moments. When you go into her room to retrieve her, follow up with a firm, "You may come back into the living room with Kelly and me if you can play nicely and not hit." When she joins her playmate, encourage and compliment her cooperative behavior by saying, "I like to see you playing together so nicely. It makes me proud of you two children." If your child hits again, respond quickly with the same message of disapproval, and remove her to a time-out alone for several minutes again. She will eventually get the message that she has the free will to control her behavior.

Everyday Opportunities for Guidance and Discipline

Infant: Birth to Twelve Months

During the first several months of life, babies do not need discipline but they do need a lot of love and encouragement.

From about six months to twelve months, when babies are beginning to scoot, crawl, and perhaps walk, they are capable of getting into mischief and danger.

Daily Opportunities to Learn

- Baby-proof your home; make it a safe place for your infant to explore. This eliminates the need for you to say *No! No!* at every turn as your baby scoots about.
- Anticipate small mishaps as your infant is beginning to explore his world.
- When visiting a non–baby-proof home for a short visit, keep your child safely with you. Do not allow your infant to poke or pull on pets, who might react with biting or scratching.
- As an experiment, your baby may pull your hair or poke or bite other children or you. Send a clear, firm disapproving message when this occurs to *begin* to shape your child's behavior. ("No! That hurts Susan!")
- Select child care providers who follow these same guidelines for safety and limits with your baby.

> "Too many restrictions threaten the bond on which discipline depends in the long run. One should choose carefully the areas in which very strict rules that can never be transgressed are laid down, so that when you say no, very firmly, the child knows that you mean business."
>
> —Dr. Sophie Freud, professor emerita at Simmons College, Boston, and author of *My Three Mothers and Other Passions*

> "I think it's really important to stress to parents that they are the boss. You want to be your children's friend, but you are not their friend; you are their parents. Teenagers love some structure and some real, honest, good rules."
>
> —Dr. Charlotte Thompson, pediatrician, director of the Center for Handicapped Children and Teenagers in San Francisco, and author of *Raising a Handicapped Child* and *Single Solutions*

Toddler: Twelve Months to Two-and-a-Half Years

Toddlers are driven to experiment and explore. Because they are quick and curious they can get into mischief and dangerous situations in the blink of an eye. You can begin to set limits and encourage good behavior, but don't expect instant results. Toddlers forget quickly; you must always watch over them and be patient about minor behavior mishaps.

Daily Opportunities to Learn

- Toddler-proof your home so that it is a safe environment in which to explore and experiment.
- Do not overuse the word *no*. Use it when it matters most; otherwise, your toddler will ignore you.
- Expect some minor mischief and misbehavior.
- Distract your toddler's attention when he's determined to do something "off limits" and redirect him into another interesting and safe activity.
- Clearly and simply express rules to your toddler: "Do not hit; that hurts Billy!" Clearly show your disapproval with your voice and facial expression.
- Give older toddlers alternatives: "You may not play in the refrigerator, but you may play in the pots and pans drawer while I make dinner."
- Expect to remind your toddler of important rules over and over again.
- Recognize your child's frame of reference and capabilities. For example, parental logic and reasoning falls on deaf ears with a toddler.
- Remember that your toddler cannot yet use language to solve his problems or express emotions.

Preschool Child: Two-and-a-Half to Four Years

Preschoolers are imaginative and curious. They live in the moment and do not think about the repercussions of their actions. As with toddlers, you must set limits with regard to safety issues when dealing with your preschool child.

> "You know, we don't have to make a federal case out of every instance of misbehavior...sometimes just remind kids. As adults, we have litter signs that remind us about a rule that we should already know, and once in a while children need reminders."
>
> —Dr. Marilyn Gootman, professor of early childhood education at the University of Georgia and author of *The Loving Parents' Guide to Discipline*

Daily Opportunities to Learn

- Make your home a safe place for your preschooler to explore.
- Establish clear safety rules, and express them in simple, understandable language: "You may never play with matches!"
- Be creative; make short behavior rules that are easy to remember: "You hit, you sit!" (time-out). "You spit, you sit!" (time-out). "You bit, you sit!" (time-out).
- Teach preschoolers to use words to settle a disagreement with a playmate or sibling, not hitting.
- Use a time-out as a break from preschool misbehavior. (See "Tips for Using a Time-Out for Discipline," page 64.)
- Have realistic expectations about mastering manners at the dinner table; this is a long-term project. Translate modest expectations into preschool language that is easily remembered. For example, your rule "Don't touch the food on the platter unless you want to eat it" becomes "You touch it, you take it, you eat it all up!"
- Long lectures and explanations are worthless with preschoolers.
- Remember, rules make children feel safe. Establish firm safety rules and some behavior rules, but don't go overboard with a million rules.
- Sharing is a difficult skill to master. Give concrete instructions: "Now it's Peter's turn to play with the truck." Recognize progress when you see it in action: "I'm proud to see you playing nicely with Daniel!"

> "There are two fundamental ways that small children learn about the world around them. The first way is through play, exploring objects in an imaginative way. The second way is one that we often overlook, and that is through their misbehavior."
>
> —Dr. Peter Williamson, clinical psychologist and author of *Good Kids, Bad Behavior*

School-Age Child: Five to Ten Years

During the early school years, children are trying to get the hang of getting along with others, developing friendships, and interacting with other nonfamily adults (teachers, coaches, etc.). School-age children have the ability to remember rules (with gentle reminders) and remember what behavior is expected.

Daily Opportunities to Learn

- Clearly identify important rules. Don't make rules for every little thing—stick with those safety and behavior issues that are most significant.
- Establish a firm house rule for "No hitting."
- When children misbehave, let them experience logical consequences for their actions. For example, if your child smashes a toy in anger, she loses the privilege of playing for a time.
- Use a time-out to provide a break from misbehavior. (See "Tips for Using a Time-Out for Discipline," page 64.)
- Ignore minor verbal squabbles between siblings; encourage children to resolve their own conflicts wherever possible.
- Encourage siblings to use their words to settle arguments—no hitting!
- Separate siblings when they cannot get along (give each a time-out; don't ask, "Who started this argument?").
- When you catch your children behaving well, remember to compliment the good behavior.
- When your child engages in verbal attacks, screaming, or disrespectful behavior, say, "You may not scream at me (or call me names, etc.)." Send him to his room without engaging in any debate. Later, let him know that screaming, name-calling, and so on will not be tolerated, but will be treated with a time-out whenever they occur. (And follow through as often as needed.)

Preteens/Early Teens: Eleven to Fourteen Years

Preteens are quite capable of using debate and reasoning to attempt to bend the rules and in general challenge your authority on a frequent basis. Like other children, preteens need rules to feel safe and give order to their lives.

> "We need to give children clear messages that they are good and lovable and valuable people even as we let them know that sometimes their behavior isn't so good."
>
> —Marti Erickson, developmental psychologist and director of the Children, Youth and Family Consortium at the University of Minnesota

Daily Opportunities to Learn

- Clearly establish rules that hitting, threats, and bullying are not acceptable behavior in your family.
- Continue to let your child know what behavior is expected in new situations that arise.
- Use logical consequences for misbehavior whenever possible. For example, if your preteen is purposefully engaging in obnoxious or crude behavior at the dinner table, he will be immediately excused from dinner.
- Stick with a calm but clear reaction to minor sibling squabbles: (1) encourage your children to resolve/negotiate minor disagreements on their own; (2) send both siblings to their rooms when disagreements escalate to force a break in the situation.
- Use restriction as a consequence for significant misbehavior or breaking of important rules. (See "Tips for Using 'Restriction,'" page 68.)
- Don't take the bait from your child when she is looking for an argument; it takes two to tango.
- Set clear expectations about respect. When your child calls you names or screams, simply say, "I don't like being treated in this way," and remove yourself from the room (and refuse to consider the request or discussion under way until your child can speak respectfully at a later time).
- Even preteens need your attention. Continue to give positive attention for cooperative behavior on a regular basis.

<u>Teens</u>: **Fifteen to Nineteen Years**

Teens are striving for a high degree of independence, but they still need rules and guidance from you.

Daily Opportunities to Learn

- Discuss issues with your child, listen to her viewpoints, and find mutually agreeable solutions to teen concerns when possible.
- Set clear, firm rules on important issues of teen safety and well-being.
- Clearly establish rules that hitting, threats, and bullying are not acceptable behavior in your family.
- Use restriction as a consequence for significant misbehavior or breaking of important rules. (See "Tips for Using 'Restriction,'" page 68.)
- Wait up for your teen when he has been out on a date or with friends.
- Establish a clear no-questions-asked plan, in which your teen may call you anytime, from anywhere, for a ride, if she finds herself in an unsafe situation (especially regarding drinking and driving, problems with dates, and so forth).
- Set firm rules that your teen may not visit unsafe teen hang-outs and violence-prone areas of town.
- When a discussion with your teen turns disrespectful and insulting to you, leave the room and refuse to consider the request or continue the conversation until your child can calm himself down. (Try to remain calm yourself.)

Be a good role model for your child: resolve all family conflicts without hurting, hitting, or humiliation.

thinking and learning

chapter six

Experiencing and Exploring

Sixteen-month-old Chase was enthralled with every ball he encountered—beach ball, tennis ball, soccer ball, or basketball, it didn't matter. Each Saturday he went to the park with his father and played "ball." What he loved best of all was kicking the ball and watching it roll down a small hill. After each kick, he stood watching intently until the ball came to a complete stop; then he laughed with delight and ran to the ball to kick it and watch it roll again. Every Saturday was the same routine of chasing, kicking, and squealing with delight.

The learning that takes place in the first several years of your child's life sets the stage for all later learning at school, yet it occurs in the simplest of settings and without great fanfare. It is through the ordinary routine of life, under your guidance and with your encouragement, that your infant and toddler begins her education, and you are your child's first and most important teacher.

How Children Learn

Your child's brain is actually growing throughout all of childhood. The everyday experiences to explore and discover turn on the learning mechanism in your

Parents' Role in Child's Exploration and Learning

While much of the learning children experience comes through their own exploration and discovery, parents have a tremendous role to play in facilitating their child's learning. First and foremost, you must provide a sense of security to your child so that she can go about her business of exploring.

Job Description for "First and Most Important Teacher"

1. Provide a safe home environment in which your child can explore and discover on her own (provide supervision but let your child lead the way to discovery).
2. Provide safe, age-appropriate toys and materials for play.
3. Encourage hands-on play and discovery throughout childhood (even for your older child).
4. Give your child your undivided attention for moments throughout his day. Respond to his world and his interests and activities.
5. Provide a household in which music, conversations, and ideas abound.
6. Respect the fine line between encouragement and hurrying. Recognize that your child will learn on a timeline all her own as long as you provide the daily opportunities to learn along with heartfelt enthusiasm.
7. Encourage your child to be a problem solver early in life, looking for solutions for everyday dilemmas. "How can we build a roof on this fort?" "What can you add to the poster to make it look like a cloud?"

child's brain and help it grow. There are two essential ingredients that you provide to your child's learning throughout all of childhood: daily opportunities for hands-on learning and your attention and response (encouragement) as your child tries to master new skills and understand new concepts.

When your seven-month-old baby sits up straight and nudges a plastic truck along the floor and sees it roll away, your response, "Look at the truck go! Let's do that again," puts a high value on his learning. You've given the message, "Look what you can do. It's important and worthy of my attention."

When your eight-year-old invents a song with words all her own and records it on her cassette player to share with her friends, it is in part your enthusiasm and pride at her creation that help cement the idea that learning and doing are good.

When your sixteen-year-old son builds an elaborate model of an imaginative dream house of the future, with energy-saving features incorporated into each room, he is continuing his exploration and learning with his mind and his hands, and of course his creativity. And although he prefers to think of himself as a young adult, his desire to learn is reinforced when you respond with genuine interest and enthusiasm.

> "In the early years, get down on the floor and join your child in pretend play. Do what we describe in *Playground Politics* as floor time. That's a foundation for everything."
>
> —Dr. Stanley Greenspan, clinical professor of psychiatry and pediatrics at George Washington University School of Medicine and author of *The Growth of the Mind, Building Healthy Minds, Playground Politics,* and *The Challenging Child*

Much of the learning that goes on throughout childhood is sequential. What she learns during the infant stage of development paves the way for learning in the toddler stage. Toddler-stage learning paves the way for pre-school learning, and so on throughout all of childhood. The individual components of learning are sometimes minuscule. But when added together over weeks, months, and years of childhood, the accumulated knowledge, skills, and understanding add up to profound learning.

Early Learning

Right from the start, newborns use all of their senses—smell, taste, sight, hearing, and touch—to learn about themselves and the world all around them. They learn through observation and listening, through experimentation, and through imitation and repetition.

> "Play is serious work for children and we ought not interrupt it."
>
> —Bob Keeshan, TV's Captain Kangaroo and author of *Good Morning, Captain*

Much of the miraculous learning that takes place during the first twelve months of life revolves around your child's mastering the use of hands, body, and voice, so that he can do for himself and interact with the world around him.

Learning to walk is a fascinating example of just how infants go about the business of learning.

Your baby begins the process of learning to walk long before she takes her first steps alone. In the first six months your child discovers her toes. While lying on her back in her crib, she wiggles her toes and puts them in her mouth. At eight months, when she is in her high chair or stroller, she kicks and flexes her legs in a purposeful way. Simultaneously, she is learning to use her hands and arms with repeated trial-and-error activities. All of these experiences occur over and over again in your baby's days and weeks before she actually walks.

At around six or eight months of age, she slides and scoots across the floor on her belly. She is thrilled to be moving. Your delight makes her progress all the more exciting; it motivates her to try again and again to perfect her scooting. Next, she crawls backward and forward; again she notices the excitement and encouragement in your face and your voice. (More motivation!) Shortly thereafter, she pulls herself up by the couch and cruises from one chair to another around the room. When she runs out of furniture to steady her steps, she improvises—she's back on the floor crawling to her destination.

Finally, to your delight and amazement, she takes that first step alone. By the look on her face when she walks and plops on the ground, she is as surprised and proud as you are.

This amazing process of walking started many months before those first steps. Each experience paved the way for the next. This learning was accomplished through experimentation, repetition, and observation. His natural motivation to learn and do was also fueled by your enthusiasm. And this walking is just the beginning. In the next two years, he'll run, skip, and hop and later pedal a bike and jump rope with his strong legs and steady balance. While

> "We typically refer to early childhood education as…birth through age eight, but what is pronounced about that period is that children in that age range learn best when they have opportunities to have hands-on experience. They learn best when they feel connected to the adults who are their teachers and caregivers, when they feel some sense of trust and know that the adult really cares about them."
>
> —Dr. Jerlean Daniel, assistant professor of child development and child care, University of Pittsburgh

this particular learning involved a physical accomplishment, other types of learning occur in the same sequential manner, built with layer upon layer of experience.

Older children also learn in this way—mastering one skill only to move on to another, which builds upon past learning. When your school-age child first learns to print letters, she has little concept of what those symbols mean. But as time goes by, she comes to understand that the letters connect to make words. The words join together to make sentences. These sentences express her own original thoughts and feelings in a new magical way. She can eventually write songs, stories, school papers, poems, letters to friends, scientific principles, mathematic concepts, and notes to organize her school and soccer activities. All these many layers of learning develop from the humble efforts of those inexperienced hands trying to hold a chubby pencil.

Learning through Play

Throughout all of childhood, your child learns through playing. In his crib, at four months old, he plays with his hands to discover what they taste like, how they move, and what they can do. Several months later, he will become skilled at playing purposefully with toys that make sounds and movement. In later years the play is moved to the school playground, the neighborhood swimming pool, or the front walkway. This playing is the context in which your child makes many discoveries.

"I have a friend who is a professor of physics at MIT—a brilliant man. I once asked him whether his parents, when he was real little, used to teach him a lot about math, and he sort of laughed and said, 'No. As a matter of fact, I remember when I used to come home from school every afternoon my mother was usually busy.' He said, 'What I would do every single afternoon'—he remembered when he was in about the first grade, he would get out all of her flour canisters and measuring cups and sit there on the kitchen floor pouring back and forth between these. And I know now that he was developing math concepts. At the time it just looked like he was fooling around. I said that that woman must have been a saint because then every afternoon she came in there and swept up all that mess....But that's the kind of thing that happens when children are alone and left to their own devices. We don't have to race them around constantly to learning experiences. Try to poke in the stimulation; try to make them smarter. Put them on a computer and get more facts. That's not the kind of things that are going to build good brains for learning later on."

—Dr. Jane Healy, learning specialist and author of *Your Child's Growing Mind*

> "Well, there was a little boy who put a bean in his ear. He put it in so far that we had to call his father and get him to take the boy to the pediatrician to get it out. While we were waiting for the father to come, we said to the child, 'Why did you put that bean in your ear?' And he looked at us and very simply and truthfully said, 'Because I have no pockets.' And we looked, and, in fact, he was wearing sweat pants with no pockets. So we told his father, and from that day forth for the rest of the year, the child wore jeans."
>
> —Patti Greenberg Wollman, preschool teacher for over twenty years and author of *Behind the Playdough Curtain*

Toddlers are sophisticated explorers who can turn ordinary household objects into toys and experiment and play for hours using cooking utensils or a cardboard box. The goal of this play is to poke and prod, to bang and scoot. In short, to see what will happen if she tries this or that. This is the kind of open-ended play that helps develop thinking and problem-solving skills.

When your sixteen-month-old son gets out the pots and pans, wooden spoons, and plastic bowls from the kitchen cupboard, he experiments and learns that he can put one small pan inside the other big pan. He learns that the sounds he can make by beating on the bottom of the plastic bowl are different from those he makes when beating on the metal pans. He also learns that he can make himself a silly hat through his cleverness—tipping the bowl up and placing it on his head—these clever antics seem to make you laugh, which is a wonderful reward for his experimentation and learning.

Preschoolers play in a way that blends their newly discovered imagination with their well-established physical skills and competence. Four-year-old Seth might dress up in a Batman costume and pretend he *is* Batman. While in this pretend world, he will use his physical skills to craft and build a Batmobile out of a large cardboard box. He tries to bend and decorate the box. When one attempt doesn't work, he'll try something new—or perhaps change the box into a castle and pretend to be a king. This imaginative play helps pave the way for sophisticated problem solving and abstract thinking in later stages of development.

When children enter school at age five or six, it appears on the surface that the arena for learning shifts exclusively to the classroom. In fact the play and exploration your child experiences at home continues to be an important piece of the learning puzzle. Infants, children, and teens learn through hands-on activities and play—by touching and manipulating, by trying this and trying that, by failing at one task and trying again. These are the best conditions for learning. From the adult sidelines, "child's play" may appear more like fun than education, but indeed it offers a vast arena for learning, and it needs to be honored and encouraged throughout all of childhood.

> "Parents can keep this spirit of learning alive by example as much as anything else."
>
> —Dr. Jane Healy, learning specialist and author of *Your Child's Growing Mind*

If you have an older child in the family, a preteen or teen, don't fall into the trap of believing that learning must always be serious business that takes place in an academic setting. Of course the discipline of learning at school is essential, but so too is the spontaneous and self-directed learning that can occur in your backyard, at the beach, at the drawing table, and in the kitchen where curiosity can lead the way to new discoveries. Your own curious attitude and appreciation for the many new discoveries that your older child experiences outside of school help place a high value on a lifelong love of learning.

Everyday Opportunities for Experiencing and Exploring

<u>Infant</u>: Birth to Twelve Months

Babies use all of their five senses to learn about the world around them. During the first year, much of your baby's learning will focus on mastering the use of her physical being: control and use of her hands, rolling over, sitting, scooting, crawling, and walking. The other critically important learning in the first year involves communication.

Daily Opportunities to Learn

- Provide daily opportunities for your baby to listen to your voice, study your face, and smile. You are fascinating to watch and listen to.
- Provide simple, safe, bright, age-appropriate toys for your baby to play with and figure out; look for toys that help your baby discover cause and effect—toys that squeak, rattle, and so on.

> "There is nothing a child wants to do more than learn."
>
> —Dr. Jane Healy, learning specialist and author of *Your Child's Growing Mind*

> "It's kind of that inner wisdom that children have—an inner curiosity, their creativity, their spontaneity—their sense of wonder toward the world that every child is born with. I think there's a biological guarantee of this so that we can survive as a species, and the trick is how do we keep that alive as they grow."
>
> —Dr. Thomas Armstrong, learning specialist, psychologist, and author of *The Myth of the A.D.D. Child* and *In Their Own Way: Encouraging Your Child's Personal Learning Style*

- Many discoveries your child makes will happen through trial and error. Give him free time in his infant seat or crib to play with his hands, toys, and so forth, with you working nearby.
- Be openly enthusiastic about your child's small accomplishments; remember tiny discoveries lead the way to profound learning over time.
- Talk to your baby as you go through the day caring for her—during feeding, bathing, diapering, and so on.
- Read to your baby to expose him to the rhythm of reading and bright, colorful pictures.

Toddler: Twelve Months to Two-and-a-Half Years

Toddlers are natural-born explorers. They are driven by an intense curiosity that requires your supervision to ensure their safety.

Daily Opportunities to Learn

- Provide a safe, toddler-proof environment in which to explore and move about freely.
- Provide age-appropriate toys and allow your child free time to investigate and experiment with playthings on his own.
- Be enthusiastic about your child's curiosity and accomplishments and minimize her defeats.
- Encourage your toddler to play alongside you as you do chores in the kitchen; provide a toddler-accessible cupboard with safe pots, pans, and bowls to play with.
- Get down on the floor and play with your child whenever you have the time and patience.
- Have conversations that encourage your toddler's participation.
- Toddlers learn through repetition. Be patient with requests for the same story or activity over and over again.
- Read to your toddler each day.

Preschool Child: Two-and-a-Half to Four Years

Preschool children thrive on discovering their own imaginations and putting their physical mastery skills into action in their play.

Daily Opportunities to Learn

- Provide a safe home environment in which to play and explore.
- Provide age-appropriate toys, blocks, and materials to build with and everyday odds and ends for imaginative play.
- Supervise your child and provide clear limits. Kids need a sense of security along with the freedom to explore.
- Be enthusiastic about your child's play. Help her get started with play and toys when necessary, but then bow out and let her lead the way.
- Engage your child in conversations. Listen to his stories and ideas.
- Read to your child each day. Select stories tailored to your child's interest and attention span.
- Be a good role model: live a life that shows you are a lifelong learner. Read, create, invent, and seek out creative solutions.

> "When a toddler finally learns how to do something, they need to do it again and again and again. We need to give them those opportunities to master their bodies and to master the skill that they've just acquired."
>
> —Sandi Dexter, preschool teacher and author of *Joyful Play with Toddlers*

School-Age Child: Five to Ten Years

Going off to school is a huge milestone in your child's development. While much learning will go on during each school day, important learning, discovery, and play will still take place at home.

Daily Opportunities to Learn

- Provide age-appropriate and interesting toys, games, and materials for your child's play; set aside time for your child's unstructured, creative play.

> "Children who believe that intelligence is something that you're just born with tend to be less motivated. On the other hand, children whose parents teach them that intelligence is something that you can improve, that you can grow and improve your brain, tend to be more motivated overall."
>
> —Dr. Jane Healy, learning specialist and author of *Your Child's Growing Mind*

- Provide books tailored to your child's interest and reading ability. Go to the library and bookstores regularly.
- Continue to read to your child even though he can read alone. He will be interested in and understand stories far beyond his own reading level.
- Let your child know with your words and actions that you value learning and doing.
- Include your child in conversations and ask for her opinions and ideas.
- Encourage your child to be a brainstormer and problem solver as daily problems and challenges present themselves.
- Show support for school learning and keep abreast (in a friendly way) of what's going on at school.
- Limit television viewing (replace it with active learning).

> "When we take our cues from the children about what they're curious about and provide those opportunities, then you get real growth spurts."
>
> —Dr. Jerlean Daniel, assistant professor of child development and child care, University of Pittsburgh

Preteens/Early Teens: Eleven to Fourteen Years

Although your preteen is a sophisticated learner in school, he also learns effectively with hands-on play and activities. He can see what works and why through everyday projects and activities.

Daily Opportunities to Learn

- Help your child develop organizational skills that will facilitate and enhance her learning.
- Be enthusiastic about your child's learning and accomplishments that occur outside of school.
- Go to the library or bookstore with your child on a regular basis. Encourage your child to select books and magazines geared to his interest.
- Help your child learn the skills necessary to build and create. Teach tool and equipment skills and safety in the workshop,

kitchen, sewing room, and so on.

- Engage your preteen in conversations. Listen to her thoughts and ideas. Accept her need to debate and express her opinions within a framework of general rules for family discussions.

- Encourage your child to explore the natural world around him; seek out learning and adventure field trips to enjoy together.

- Find magazine or newspaper articles in your preteen's area of interest and read them to her.

> "Little children, like the rest of us, are trying to figure out what makes things happen. Well, if we use language, we can explain the machinery of cause and effect to small children. And if we don't take the time to make these explanations, they're left on their own and they have only what they see, what they hear, what they smell, and what they touch. They can come to us with some really weird ideas."
>
> —Priscilla Vail, learning specialist and author of *Emotion: The On/Off Switch for Learning* and *Words Fail Me*

- Limit television and other passive entertainment and instead promote active, hands-on learning.

- Let your child see that you tackle new challenges and continue to learn in your adult life.

Teens: Fifteen to Nineteen Years

Teens are learning all about the world around them through a new, almost grown-up perspective. This is a time for self-discovery and experience during the last fleeting moments of childhood.

Daily Opportunities to Learn

- Encourage your teen to read magazines and books tailored to her interest. Offer to take her to the bookstore and library frequently.

- Seek out opportunities for outdoor adventure and learning tailored to your teen's interests.

- Help your child identify what learning is most exciting and find new opportunities for this learning.

> "Let's take the newborn for example. When parents say to me, 'I can understand talking to my child, but reading? He doesn't even understand what I'm reading.' Well, he doesn't understand what you're saying either, but you continue to talk!...So I recommend as soon as possible start reading aloud to the child."
>
> —Jim Trelease, author of *The Read-Aloud Handbook*

- Encourage your teen to be a real-life brainstormer and problem solver and recognize his good solutions.
- Expose your teen to careers where learning is an essential ingredient and where she will find mentors of all ages who have a love of learning.
- Have conversations with your teen on important issues and listen to and honor his ideas and suggestions.
- Help your teen break down large projects into small steps.
- Provide materials and encouragement for hands-on projects that build, invent, and create.
- Let your child see that you tackle new challenges and continue to learn in your adult life.

Be a good role model: show that you are a lifelong learner!

● ● ● ● ● ● ● ● ● ● ●

chapter seven

Creativity and Curiosity

The two preschoolers, Kyra and Dax, pulled out the pots and pans from the kitchen cupboard. Next they brought in the box of silk scarves and hats and gloves. Within minutes, they had created a cast of characters as they played. There were knights in armor, queens and kings, and a mean old pirate who sailed his ship up the moat. The castle was built next, using a huge assortment of wooden blocks, so that the moat would lead to the castle. Finally, when the knights became tired and hungry from defending their empire, the marshmallows and raisins were brought out to create a tasty feast for the brave queens, kings, and warriors.

Children are born with a remarkable sense of curiosity and imagination. It is through their natural curiosity that children learn about the world around them. They observe and ponder, they touch, they feel, they taste, they listen, they babble.

Creativity is the ability to mix curiosity and imagination with reasoning to make new discoveries that change the world around us. Some people mistakenly think creativity is just for artists, writers, dancers, musicians, and actors. In

"Imagination is one of the most fun things you can engage in with your child....It is a way of coming together, of feeling closeness.... You have an opportunity to do a tremendous amount for your child just by those few minutes of shared make-believe or shared storytelling."

—Dr. Jerome Singer, professor of psychology and child study at Yale University and coauthor (with Dorothy Singer) of *The House of Make-Believe*

truth, creativity is a very important, yet underestimated, ingredient of human survival. It is through creativity that humans sustain or improve their lives with new ideas, inventions, and solutions to threatening problems. Curiosity and creativity are also ingredients in every medical breakthrough, technological advance, and conflict resolution or negotiation. It is also through our creativity that we can bring joy, humor, and delight into the lives of others.

All children need to be curious and creative. Children who are encouraged to be curious and creative develop valuable problem-solving skills that enhance their play, their education, their relationships, their emotional lives, and their (later) careers.

How Do Children Incorporate Creativity into Their Lives?

All children start out with a fabulous natural sense of curiosity and a longing to create. Children master creativity and incorporate its

Why All Children Need Creativity in Their Lives

1. To imagine their dreams and learn how to shape these dreams into reality
2. To learn how to brainstorm to find creative, constructive solutions to their problems in play, work, and relationships
3. To express their thoughts, feelings, and ideas to others; to delight and entertain others
4. To feel the inner joy of creating
5. To satisfy their human need to contribute something good or interesting to the world

Parents' Role in Promoting Creativity

Job Description for "Promoter of Creativity"

1. Provide a safe environment for your child to explore and experiment throughout childhood. Offer guidance and set limits for safety as your child experiments and explores.

2. Demonstrate an attitude that encourages and values curiosity and creativity. Show heartfelt appreciation for your child's creations—put artwork on the refrigerator, send it to grandparents, save it in a special portfolio, or frame it.

3. Provide safe toys, blocks, and art materials for age-appropriate open-ended play where your child leads the way to discovery and invention.

4. Respect and encourage your child's quiet, reflective time in which he can dream, invent, experiment, doodle, or dawdle. (Be careful not to overschedule your child's life.)

5. Encourage your child to be a hands-on problem solver as she plays and creates.

6. Be a good creativity role model; put pizzazz in the way you live, look for opportunities for your family to be creative together, use creative problem-solving approaches to daily challenges in your family. *Your child will benefit greatly by the example you set.*

7. Engage in lively and creative conversations about the world around you with your child. Go for a walk in the woods, on the beach, or in your neighborhood, and observe, ponder, and chat.

principles into their daily lives through hands-on experience. They try this and that; they make a problem, then try to fix it. They start out with a sheet of paper and finger paints and begin to apply the paint gingerly with their fingers. They add yellow paint on top of green paint and create a new color right before their eyes. They spill too much water, then try to correct this problem with a lot more paint. They get paint on the

"Creativity is really the impulse to self-expression. Every child, every living person, longs to be able to communicate his thoughts, his feelings, his capabilities, to put his thumbprint on the world and to say, I'm here!"

—Fredelle Maynard, author of *Raisins and Almonds*

newspaper that is lying underneath the white paper, and that gives them yet another new idea to run with.

Young children build, they make, they color, they erase. When your toddler makes colorful scribbles on a piece of paper for the very first time, a lightbulb goes off in his brain—"I did that!" Two or three years later, after much practice at manipulating materials like crayons, paper, paints, and markers, he takes what his hands have learned to do and applies it to a more complex mode of expression. He imagines the big oak tree with the tire swing at Grandma's house in his mind's eye, and he draws his rendition of it on paper. This is a tremendous milestone in his creative development.

Your twelve-year-old son might build a wooden go-cart with scraps of wood and bicycle wheels. In the process, he tries this way and that way to attach the wheels to the wooden platform. Some ideas flop, other approaches almost work, and finally he discovers a way to do it! When his project is finished, he will incorporate what he has learned into his next attempt to create something new. Even the mistakes made along the way toward invention provide valuable information about how things work.

Where creativity is concerned, one idea gives way to another. Some of these new ideas stall out or lead nowhere. Other ideas create a mini-explosion of three, four, and five other new ideas in rapid succession. Creative projects give children a context in which to live and feel the valuable lesson, "If at first you don't succeed, try and try again." These may be simply words when incorporated into a well-meaning parent's lecture. But creative projects give children a way in which to feel, and see and conclude, this lesson in a real, experiential way. And this real-life lesson has greater impact than a parent's words from the sideline, no matter how well intended.

"By having kids draw at home, freestyle or suggesting topics for them to draw, you're really helping to draw out that inner image, and that inner imagination."

—Dr. Thomas Armstrong, learning specialist, psychologist, and author of *The Myth of the A.D.D. Child* and *In Their Own Way: Encouraging Your Child's Personal Learning Style*

Children who are encouraged to create with words, ideas, jokes, art, music, and invention of one kind or another are often not afraid to fail. In fact, failure takes on a slightly new definition for children who are creative thinkers and problem solvers. These kids say to themselves, "That didn't work out right. Tomorrow I'll try adding more dye to the water and soaking the T-shirt longer." Or perhaps they say, "I don't think I'm going to build a rocket launcher after all....I'll use these wood scraps to make a maze for my race car to drive through in the backyard!" These are kids whose definition of failure has expanded beyond their years. They are more accepting of the gift of time—to try again, to try something new—and they take pleasure in the discovery process along the way, realizing that the product is not all that counts. (They are not as quick to say, "Boy, am I stupid; I couldn't build a wooden boat!")

> "One of the things that the creative arts do, no matter what, is that they give you a doorway into ideas and feelings and abilities and a way of seeing or hearing or showing that you wouldn't otherwise have a chance to unlock, and that's incredibly important."
>
> —Barbara Esbensen, children's poet and author of *Dance with Me* and *A Celebration of Bees: Helping Children Write Poetry*

There is an invisible, magical thread linking all your child's creative attempts and triumphs to one another. A lovely, playful song created by your six-year-old daughter may seem to be unrelated to the science project she makes five years later, but indeed there is an important invisible thread of accumulated creative problem-solving experiences tying one to the other.

The Parents' Role in a Child's Creativity

Parents play a critical role in defining and promoting creativity and imagination. For starters, parents set the standard for what is creative and what is not, for where creativity and imagination can exist in their family life. Creativity is not restricted to the art room, to the make-believe costume bin, or the room where music fills the air. Creativity can be found in the kitchen, during conversations in the car, in the spontaneous poems and riddles made up at the dinner table, the new board games invented on a dreary Friday evening.

Free Time and Daydreaming Foster Creativity

Honor your child's need for free, unstructured time to play, think, and day-dream each and every day! Here are some creative play and thinking activities that give your child an opportunity to dream and create:

- playing in the sandbox
- listening to favorite music cassettes while doodling or drawing
- playing with Play-Doh
- swinging on the backyard swing
- riding bikes
- drawing cartoons
- gazing at the stars from the backyard porch or tent
- skipping stones across the water
- chasing lightning bugs in the early evening
- chasing butterflies
- building forts indoors with sheets and blankets
- playing melodies on the xylophone or glockenspiel
- looking at picture books
- making designs on the driveway with chalk
- writing in a journal
- taking photos of your neighborhood environment
- dancing and singing to favorite music
- recording plays and stories on a cassette machine
- playing jacks or pickup sticks or solitaire
- building with Legos, Lincoln Logs, blocks, etc.
- looking at sports card, stamp, or coin collections
- looking at family photos
- looking at (past) artwork stored in the keeper-saver

When was the last time your child did any of the above activities?

If your child does not engage in freewheeling play each and every day, try to find the culprit and make changes that allow for daydreaming and play.

Parents must offer support and encouragement for their child's curiosity and creativity. They do this in part by the example they set that incorporates creativity into their own lives, conversations, and work. They also set the stage for creativity by having materials on hand that give children something to work with—ingredients for hands-on projects for young children as well as teens.

Parents can also ask questions that stimulate their child's problem-solving ability in all sorts of real-life situations. "How can you make that mountain stand up taller on the platform?" "Could you write your own homemade anniversary card for Grandma and Grandpa? You know they love those funny poems you invent." Sometimes a well-placed question to a child in pursuit of a new idea is all the help that is needed from a nearby parent. "What about those old wooden bolts in the basement? Could you use those in your science project in some way?" If you have an older child in the family, continue to drop in provocative questions about projects that are under way. "Remember that project you did for your world history class two years ago? Didn't you write a short story about a make-believe child in ancient Rome? Perhaps you can get some new ideas by rereading that story."

Many parents have an easier time encouraging their child's imagination while their child is young. We all know instinctively that little children love to pretend and to create. But older children, preteens, and teens need to use their imaginations and problem-solving capabilities as much as (or more than) young children do. It helps prepare them for devising creative solutions to life's many challenges that lie ahead. It also infuses a spirit of joy and accomplishment into their present lives that is a wonderful contrast to the sometimes heavy stresses of the teen years.

A wonderful but often overlooked place for experimentation is the kitchen. The creative projects

> "I tell children when we're writing poetry: 'You know what? This is hard work. It's hard work to write well and to get something that you really love. But I'm telling you now that you're going to get sweaty and when you're all done, you're going to have something on that page that's so good that you're going to think that you had a good time.'"
>
> —Barbara Esbensen, children's poet and author of *Dance with Me* and *A Celebration of Bees: Helping Children Write Poetry*

Creative Conversations

Having lively and interesting conversations with your child can begin in the first year of your child's life. She may not understand all of your words, but she will understand and recognize your emotions, enthusiasm, excitement, curiosity, surprise, anger, irritation, puzzlement, and delight through your conversations with her. She will begin to learn that we can communicate our thoughts, feelings, and ideas by using our voice.

Once your child is a verbal toddler or preschooler, he will be able to participate more in these conversations. Here are some ideas to stimulate some lively conversations at the dinner table with your children of all ages. Why is this important, you ask? Because it encourages creative communication, and it encourages children to work to express themselves in a way grown-ups can understand. It makes the family dinner table fun and lively. It focuses on the thoughts and feelings of the honored guests at the table—the family members. It sets an expectation that these dinners and conversations are fun and worthwhile.

- Initiate conversations about whatever interests your child (think small and specific: a small cup made today at the preschool, a game played outside at recess time, a speech given to the class, a movie or music your child just discovered, a neighbor who dropped by to visit, the family dog's visit to the vet, Grandma's cookies that arrived in the mail, or the birthday cake decorations at Aunt Sue's college graduation party).
- Encourage every member to participate in the family conversations. Make way for the tiny family members. Set firm rules of tolerance for older children to follow when others speak and ask questions.
- Include "what if" questions to stir imagination. What if the dog could go to school? What would he do all day at school? These conversations are whimsical, causing adults to see and hear what the perspective of the child is at this age, creating an atmosphere of fun and acceptance for imagination and reasoning skills, and help adults lighten up to reenter their child's world for the evening together after a fast-paced workday.

generated in the kitchen not only give short-term gratification of your child's efforts, but they also very often pay off in good taste too. Providing creative opportunities in the kitchen for your older child fosters imagination and resourcefulness, but it also helps your child become competent at cooking, which is an important life skill that all boys and girls alike need to master. (This message can be further reinforced if your children see the adult men and women in your family creating meals in the kitchen and on the grill outdoors.)

> "Sometimes we tend to overlook the importance of imagination. But imagination is the playground, or I should say school yard or schoolhouse, of learning to reason."
>
> —Dr. Stanley Greenspan, clinical professor of psychiatry and pediatrics at George Washington University School of Medicine and author of *The Growth of the Mind*, *Building Healthy Minds*, *Playground Politics*, and *The Challenging Child*

Most kids love pizza, tacos, or pasta. When your teenagers are given free rein to create these foods for family or teenage friends, they have a chance to put color and pizzazz into their cooking. They become comfortable with the tools and equipment in the kitchen. They quickly learn which parts of the recipe in the cookbook must be followed closely for good results and they learn how to improvise to make a recipe uniquely their own.

Creativity, imagination, and curiosity deserve your respect and encouragement throughout all of your child's life.

Everyday Opportunities for Creativity

<u>Infant</u>: Birth to Twelve Months

Curiosity is an ingredient of creativity. Your tiny newborn baby is attentive and curious about the world all around him. During the first three months of life, nurture your baby, read stories, talk, and sing to your baby. All of these bonding experiences bring you and your baby closer together and give you ordinary opportunities to teach your baby about the sights and sounds all around. During the later months of his first year, he will begin to grab and touch, then later push and pull to put his curiosity into action.

> "We all have music in us. We all have the ability to sing, the ability to move, the ability to manipulate an instrument."
>
> —Christopher Hepp, associate professor and director of the piano division at the University of Kansas and cohost of *How to Choose a Piano Teacher*

Daily Opportunities to Learn

- Observation and listening are two of the first elements of curiosity and creativity. Provide safe toys and baby-safe music boxes and mobiles to watch. Read and tell stories, sing lullabies, and go on walks together.
- When your baby is older and can sit up safely on her own, spend time on the floor together, rolling a plastic ball back and forth or letting your baby make things happen.
- Play music you enjoy in your home and car to expose your baby to the joy of music.

Toddler: Twelve Months to Two-and-a-Half Years

Toddlers wake up each day ready to go. Your toddler not only loves to observe but also to create. Toddlers are game to explore and try just about anything. This presents a wonderful opportunity for fostering creativity. But because toddlers have no judgment about safety, you must be diligent in monitoring their safety and encouraging curiosity simultaneously.

Daily Opportunities to Learn

- Provide toddler-safe materials for creating: crayons, paper, blocks, toys for open-ended play and experimentation, balls that roll, toys that scoot and make noise, toddler-safe music makers, and so on.
- Show your child that you value curiosity and creativity: take time to notice your child's drawings and creations, hang artwork on the refrigerator for all to see, incorporate special colorful artwork into a family calendar, or ask your child to make a special drawing for Grandma or Grandpa.
- Tell stories, make up songs to sing for your toddler, encourage your child to sing along.
- Take your toddler on regular short curiosity walks in the neighborhood. Gather colorful leaves, observe the butterflies, and touch the flowers.

- Save some of your child's earliest creations; put these precious heirlooms in a safe place to keep forever.

Preschool Child: Two-and-a-Half to Four Years

Preschoolers can use their hands efficiently to manipulate materials and create. They have a tremendous imagination and love to pretend. Preschoolers benefit tremendously from unstructured play and free time with creative materials and safe pots, pans, and blocks close at hand to use in their creative play.

Daily Opportunities to Learn

- Provide materials and supplies for "pretend" play.
- Have preschool-safe art supplies on hand: safe scissors, paper, finger paints, Play-Doh, markers, watercolors, scraps of fabric, kid-safe glue. Bring out the art box when you can supervise.
- Take your preschool child to short concerts designed for kids.
- Take curiosity walks with your child. Discover leaves, bugs, animals, shells, stones, pinecones. Talk about and listen to your child's questions and observations.
- Show your child that you value her creations: send artwork to grandparents, frame it, save it in your child's homemade portfolio.
- Make certain your child has plenty of unstructured time for thinking, daydreaming, and open-ended play.
- Encourage your child to "make music" with kid-safe musical instruments. Play musical tapes at home and in the car.
- Read to your child daily. Tell your child stories (that you create). When you are full of patience, encourage your child to tell you a story about a silly monkey, a huge elephant, a giant snowman, and so forth.

> "I look at children as experts on creativity! My trying to teach my children anything about creativity is like my trying to teach Nolan Ryan how to throw a fastball!"
>
> —Jim Borgman, Pulitzer prize–winning editorial cartoonist

"Children, for example, are exposed to a wonderful influence in their church experience, and churches that do a lot of singing, where there are choirs, even where there are children's choirs. This is a primary and wonderful first way for children to be exposed to music."

—Christopher Hepp, associate professor and director of the piano division at the University of Kansas and cohost of *How to Choose a Piano Teacher*

School-Age Child: Five to Ten Years

These are amazing years for creative expression. Your child is competent at using simple, safe tools; she is capable of translating ideas into action and expressing her thoughts and ideas in a multitude of ways.

Daily Opportunities to Learn

- Show that you value creativity with your attitude and actions. Be available to your child when he has something to show you or something to tell. Save and frame his artwork, listen to him sing and make music. Read the stories and poems that he writes and save these heirlooms for your child to look back on so he can savor the steps of his creative development.
- Give each child his or her very own personal art box (large fishing tackle box) with paints, brushes, glitter, beads, charcoal pencils, erasers, tape, scissors, and a lot of paper of all sizes.
- Bring out the blankets and sheets on cold and rainy days and let the fort-building begin—this is a perfect place for daydreaming.
- Encourage the oldie-but-goodie crafts project you loved as a child: papier-mâché, modeling clay, Popsicle-stick creations, chalk art, macaroni on paper plates (painted), and so on.
- Encourage your child to write stories and make up songs (provide a child-proof tape recorder and blank cassette tapes).
- Take your child to short music or dance concerts.
- Enroll your child in summer day camps with a creative theme: art, music, crafts, photography, or science.
- Read to your child each day. Select books tailored to your child's special interest and maturity.
- Make certain your child has plenty of free time to think, daydream, create, and listen to music.

Preteens/Early Teens: Eleven to Fourteen Years

By now you know your child well. You see her temperament and interest portrayed in much that she does. Expose your child to new and creative experiences that suit her personality: take her to a small jazz concert, go to the art museum, attend a play together, and so forth.

Daily Opportunities to Learn

- Save artwork in a special portfolio. Listen to spontaneous poems and songs that your child creates.
- Teach your child to be creative in the kitchen: bake bread, cookies, and gourmet pizzas; decorate pastries; and so on.
- Make certain that your child isn't overscheduled; respect and protect your child's need for free time to daydream, build models, play music, write, tinker, and draw.
- Let your child's interest lead the way to occasional or special creative opportunities:
  1. Take your child to age-appropriate concerts, dance recitals, and plays. Attend art exhibits, science museums, and buildings under construction.
  2. Find lessons, day camps, and summer camps that foster your child's special interest in science, music, art, photography, film, dance, theater, cooking, or creative writing.
- Attend your child's art exhibits, band recitals, school plays, and concerts.

Teens: Fifteen to Nineteen Years

Teenagers are in the process of fine-tuning their ability to reason. Many parents will compare these oratory skills to those of a highly polished trial lawyer. These skills can be put to good use in many creative projects that require critical thinking skills coupled with imagination. Encourage your child to keep his curiosity alive and channel all these skills into creative projects.

"Well, as many boys growing up in this country, I was taken to baseball games or certainly heard a lot about baseball. It wasn't broadcast on the radio very much when I was really young, but certainly I heard about baseball and Babe Ruth and people like that so I was quite quickly caught up in baseball and excitement. I made up an imaginary league with different teams and of course there was my favorite, which happened to be the New York Giants. I made up a whole set of players. Some of them have names a little bit like the real players of the Giants, but most of them were made-up names. I had an absolutely wonderful time. Sometimes I would draw the incidents from the games. I'd draw the box scores. But I would imagine this in my own mind and certain hero players who were particularly good.

"I still remember many of them and their adventures, and as a matter of fact, I never gave up that fantasy. I have plenty of other fantasies and other things in real life that I do, but often when I'm trying to put myself to sleep, I have usually lots of things on my mind I have to do the next day and so on, so it is easier just to go to sleep by imagining one of those old baseball games with my favorite players. The first batter gets up and he gets a single. The next batter tries to bunt and the next thing you know, you are fast asleep. You wake up and you've got a guy stranded on second base."

—Dr. Jerome Singer, professor of psychology and child study at Yale University and coauthor (with Dorothy Singer) of *The House of Make-Believe*

Daily Opportunities to Learn

- Show through your attitude and actions that you value curiosity, imagination, and creativity: attend your child's school plays, concerts, art exhibits, and listen to her poems and essays. Save her artwork, musical recordings, poems, and stories. These are precious mementos of your child's creative and intellectual development.

- Spend time engaged in lively conversations with your child. Initiate what-if conversations that require brainstorming to solve problems. Listen to your child's thoughts and ideas.

- Find opportunities for learning through camps, lessons, and internships that appeal to your child's special interests and talents.

- Continue to expose your child to new creative experiences: go to plays, concerts, dance recitals, and science and art museums. Look for special opportunities to sit in on a music recording session or theatrical rehearsal.

- Teach your child to cook. Encourage him to apply his creativity to making gourmet pizzas, breads, cakes, and cookies. Encourage color and flair while cooking.

- Help your child find summer jobs that teach hands-on skills: photography, building, landscape design, painting, and so on.

- Encourage your child to tackle large creative projects in the summertime: write or illustrate a short children's story, invent a new card game or board game, write a journal.

• • • • • • • • • • • •

chapter eight

Learning at School

At first glance, it didn't look like much of a science project. Six ten-year-olds were clustered around each table gluing uncooked pieces of pasta on sheets of colored paper to represent the bones found in a human wrist and hand. But as the children worked diligently at arranging and pasting the pasta, a lively conversation began. Peter asked why the wrist can turn around and around but the middle joint of the finger cannot. Somehow that led to a conversation about basketball players running and stopping and knees swiveling before they pass the ball. All of this learning was unleashed by the humble spaghetti noodles, a good teacher, and twenty-two curious minds ready to learn.

When your child goes off to school, your job description as "first and most important teacher" expands significantly. Now, your child will encounter other teachers who will help shape her education. Some of those teachers will be lively and motivating, others may have lost the luster and enthusiasm for learning somewhere over the years of teaching. Each will have an impact upon your child's education. But it is you who continue to be the most important person to oversee your child's education and an advocate for a childhood filled with learning.

Parents' Role in Child's School Education

You are your child's educational advocate throughout all of childhood. It is your job to oversee your child's education in the early years and during the school years. You will sometimes need to nudge your child into new areas of learning. You will sometimes need to hang back and let your child struggle and persevere as she learns. You will sometimes need educational assistants—friends who are teachers and guidance counselors or professionals you can hire on a consulting basis to help you in your job.

Job Description for "Educational Advocate" for Your Child

1. Maintain an attitude that values learning.
2. Keep your long-term educational goals in mind and assess your child's education as you go along.
3. Encourage your child to play and create. (Even older children continue to learn through their play.)
4. Encourage an inner motivation to learn; help your child discover and pursue his special interests and talents.
5. Expect problems along the way and work to find solutions.
6. Stay involved in your child's daily education; know your child's teachers, class subjects, projects, and schoolmates.
7. Help your child establish good study habits.
8. Attend all parent-teacher conferences; express a willingness to work with your child's teachers to resolve problems, and so forth.
9. Volunteer to help with field trips and school parties, join the Parent-Teacher Association at school.
10. Continue to have lively conversations at home and encourage your child's participation.
11. Give your child pats on the back for good thinking and good problem solving when you see them in action.

continued

Parents' Role in Child's School Education (continued)

Maximizing the Parent-Teacher Conference

1. Show up for all school conferences. (If you cannot attend because of a serious schedule conflict, request a private meeting with your child's teacher.)

2. Spend a few minutes thinking about your child's school year and learning style in advance and compile questions that will help you gather information about your child's progress at school.

3. Approach each conference in a cooperative manner. Use diplomacy to address shortcomings in the classroom that don't work well for your child.

4. Show the teacher you want to be supportive of your child's education and are willing to work with the teacher to help your child succeed.

5. Ask questions not only about academic progress but also about your child's willingness to participate in class, his ability to get along with others in class and on the playground, your child's special interests at school, and so on.

6. Ask your child's teacher when you can meet or chat again to monitor your child's progress in the areas discussed.

As a parent, you are there day to day, school year to school year. If you are observant, you will see how your child seems to learn most effectively and what problems need solving along the way. You will also see what activities and topics excite your child and activate the learning button in your child's brain.

Pinpointing Educational Goals

When added together, each child in the United States spends about 16,500 hours in school from kindergarten through high school—quite a significant amount of childhood.

> "So, what I'm suggesting is that parents consider shifting their role a little bit...rather than being a rescuer, but being someone who can facilitate independent thinking."
>
> —Dr. John Clabby, psychologist and coauthor (with Maurice J. Elias) of *Teach Your Child Decision Making*

> "I remember a teacher in the fourth grade who wrote every day a note, the same statement on the blackboard: 'Have a heart that never hardens, a touch that never hurts, a temper that never tires.' The author of those words was Sara Teasdale. And here I am, a man in my fifties, and I still remember that statement on the blackboard."
>
> —Dr. Robert Coles, child psychiatrist and Pulitzer prize–winning author of *Children of Crisis* and *The Moral Life of Children*

As educational advocate for your child, you want your child to receive an excellent education during these many hours spent at school. But there is one tremendously important question that you must consider on behalf of your child: exactly what constitutes an excellent education? Does it mean enjoying school, is it reflected in good grades and high scores, or do we only know that our child did indeed get a good education when she graduates high school and is accepted to a "good college" or lands a "good job"?

The answers you give to these question will help you develop a road map to refer to again and again as problems arise in your child's schooling. This road map will help you decide which problems are transitory or circumstantial and which call for action to resolve. Some problems, for example, may simply require lending an ear to your child's feelings and concerns about problems with friends on the playground. These fleeting problems don't affect your child's education and might prove to be opportunities for your child to learn to get along with other children. Other problems might prove to be threatening to your child's love of learning, his thinking skills, or willingness to work hard and may require you to step in. For example, if there is a bully terrorizing your child each day on the playground and your child now refuses to go to school, you will certainly want to put a stop to it.

You will want to make your own, tailor-made list of educational goals for your individual child. Here are some items you may want to consider.

It is important to me that my child:

1. Learns to be a good thinker
2. Learns to be a good problem solver
3. Has many opportunities for hands-on learning
4. Is exposed to a range of subjects and ideas that activate his own talents and interests

5. Develops an internal motivation to learn (he enjoys challenge and learning)
6. Learns skills and concepts in many areas of study that he can apply to his life and work
7. Becomes a hard worker and is capable of sticking with a difficult task
8. Accepts responsibility along the way, for his effort and his work
9. Learns to get along with others at school
10. Feels pride in his hard work and progress

Several of these goals need an explanation. Your child needs to learn to be a good thinker. She needs to learn to ask questions, gather information, apply logic and reason, use experience and emotion to identify problems, search for solutions, and form conclusions. She needs to know when and how to ask for help. She needs to learn whom to ask or where to go for reliable information. She needs to know how to make an informed decision. She needs to develop the ability to apply these thinking skills to her schoolwork and to her practical life.

Some teachers may encourage the development of good thinking skills along the way, others may focus on minutiae and rote learning. But the buck stops with you to ensure this most important of all learning skills.

Just how does your child turn into a good thinker? Very gradually and through dealing with everyday dilemmas that occur at school, in the family, with friends, and in your neighborhood—through conversations that you have with your child and brainstorming together as a family, the encouragement you give your child every time you see evidence of good thinking, and through the example you set whenever you tackle your own issues.

The funny thing about life, even the life of a young child, is that it naturally seems to present us with many diverse experiences that require us to brainstorm and solve problems and consequently to learn. When children are very young we must do much of the problem solving that occurs outside the arena of our child's play. We must figure out which pediatric dentist to go to, how to find a new baby-sitter since our

> "In doing the research for the new edition of *The Read-Aloud Handbook,* I kept stumbling across certain consistencies in the research. When I tied the research into the demographics and statistics of our society, I came up with this formula: the more you read, the more you know. The more you know, the smarter you grow. The smarter you grow, the longer you stay in school. The longer you stay in school, the more diplomas you earn. (Here's where it really gets up close and personal as the TV folks would say.) The more diplomas you earn, the more days you're going to be employed in a lifetime. In other words, the more money you earn,....the more diplomas you earn, the higher your own children's grades will be in school. And the more diplomas you earn, the longer you live. So, reading has to be the single most powerful factor that we have in our society today; it all starts with being read to."
>
> —Jim Trelease, author of *The Read-Aloud Handbook*

former sitter has moved away, and how to make bedtime more manageable. But once your child goes to school and out into the world on his own each day, he will encounter all sorts of small manageable problems that help develop good thinking skills.

Much of the good thinking your child develops will be applied to classroom assignments and projects at school. Often overlooked, however, are the many important instances in which your child will also use problem-solving and thinking skills dealing with peers on the playground, in the lunchroom, and on the school bus. These real-life scenarios give your child practice at being observant, asking questions, drawing conclusions, and learning when and whom to ask for help.

Your child also needs to be exposed to new subjects, topics, and concepts in order to discover her personal interests and talents. If your daughter becomes fascinated with the marine biology she is exposed to at school, you have now found a springboard from which your child might do all sorts of learning—meteorology, oceanography, botany, math, creative writing—all motivated by her desire to explore marine life. Her enthusiasm for this subject generates an internal motivation to learn. When you see these interests awakened in your child, fan the flames of learning! Work together to research topics of interest, go to the library, take a field trip, spend the day with a mentor who can expose the two of you to more hands-on learning in marine biology. Make up bedtime stories about a magical dolphin!

If your six-year-old son is enthralled with the dinosaurs he learned about at school, find ways to incorporate dinosaurs into your trips to the library, the stories you read at bedtime, and the creative projects you do together at home with art supplies or music. Perhaps a love of dinosaurs will be a great vehicle to learn the basics of looking up reference material in children's dictionaries and encyclopedias or accessing kid-friendly websites on the Internet together.

Helping Your Child Succeed at School

Success at school won't necessarily come naturally to your child. During the first several years of school, many children have trouble sitting still, waiting to take their turns, staying focused on their task (with so many interesting distractions), and containing their emotions. But beyond these typical transitional adjustments, your child will likely need your help to get the hang of participating in school, doing homework, tackling long-term school projects, and so forth.

One educational expert after another confirms that the most important thing you can do to help your child succeed at school is to stay involved in your child's educational life. This translates to regularly showing interest, being available to listen, to help brainstorm, to know who the teachers are, the subjects, the books, the projects, and the problems. This doesn't mean meddling or hovering, and it especially doesn't mean doing your child's homework for him. Instead, your involvement is achieved through spontaneous conversations at the dinner table, through one-on-one time just to chat, and through attending school meetings, conferences, and activities and listening to what your child wants to tell you.

Another important ingredient that you contribute to your child's school success is your belief in your child ("I know you can do it!") and in your attitude that hard work makes for success (rather than "intelligence makes for success"). Some parents mistakenly typecast their child— "Well, you know you're not that great at math or science. Your brother is better at English composition than you

> "The greatest learning takes place at the point of interest. So, when you suddenly discover that your child is interested in rockets or a caterpillar, that is the time you go to the library or bookstore and ask, 'Do you have any caterpillar books? Do you have any books about rockets?'"
>
> —Jim Trelease, author of *The Read-Aloud Handbook*

> "I remember, as a student in elementary school, beginning the day with a couple of songs. This was in a regular classroom. I think all children, if they had the opportunity of simply starting the day with a couple of songs, could activate that musical learning style and perhaps perform much more effectively during the rest of the day."
>
> —Dr. Thomas Armstrong, learning specialist, psychologist, and author of *The Myth of the A.D.D. Child* and *In Their Own Way: Encouraging Your Child's Personal Learning Style*

are, so just do your best." It's not your child's genes that make for school success, it's her hard work. Your child will actually build his intelligence through his hard work. And it's not her outstanding test scores alone that make for a brilliant education. Einstein would not have been the Einstein we know without hard work, creative thinking, and perseverance, no matter what his IQ! And it's safe to say that his hard work challenged and expanded his intellect.

Another ingredient for school success that requires your help from time to time is the development of good study habits. Your child doesn't automatically know how to organize her time, plan ahead, and find a quiet place to do her homework or organize her tasks. One thing that I find extremely helpful to older kids is a daily calendar to jot down class or homework assignments. Without one, kids must rely on memory to do their nightly homework in their five school subjects. They arrive home from school and say, "I can't remember if I was supposed to read chapter seven or ten in social studies." Or, "I know I wrote my math assignment down in class today but now I can't find the piece of paper I wrote it on. I tried to call Justine to ask her what the assignment was but she's at soccer practice." (And so she sits or perhaps gets anxious.) There aren't many grown-ups among us who could remember five different work assignments mentioned in passing—which are all due tomorrow—without our daily pocket planner!

You will need to help your child find a quiet time and place to do his homework. Give your child some room to help make these decisions. "Do you want to play outside after school, then buckle down to do homework later? Would you rather do your homework right after school and have your evening free to play or watch television?" (I believe strongly that parents need to limit television viewing, video and computer games, and surfing the Internet during the school week. These activities can indeed interfere with your overall, long-term educational goals for your child!)

Concentration is an important ingredient for school success. As a parent, you have influence over one of the ingredients needed for good concentration—a good night's sleep. Look at the table below, which gives the average hours of sleep needed at various ages throughout childhood.

> "If we want our children to write well, they have to see us writing letters, thank-you notes, a report, whatever. If we want them to read, they have to see us reading."
>
> —Dr. James Uphoff, professor of teacher education at Wright State University in Dayton, Ohio, and author of *Real Facts from Real Schools*

Typical Childhood Sleep Needs, by Age

Age of Child	Total Hours of Sleep per Day
Newborn	16 to 17
1 to 3 month	15 to 16
4 to 12 months	14 to 15
Toddler (12 months to 2 1/2 years)	13 to 14
Preschool (2 1/2 to 4 years)	11 to 13
School-age child (5 to 10 years)	10 to 11
Preteen (11 to 14 years)	9 to 10
Teen (15 to 19 years)	8 to 10

Monitor Your Child's School Progress

It is important that your child sees and hears that you are interested in what goes on during his school day, in regard to homework, projects, and peers. It is also important that you stay involved so that you can monitor your child's progress, become aware of problems, and help find solutions. Here's how to monitor your child's progress at school:

1. Talk with your child informally and spontaneously each day about the happenings at school and assignments given.
2. Establish a working relationship with your child's teachers.
3. Attend all school conferences and Parent's Day at school; volunteer to help with field trips, school parties, and so on.

4. Meet with your child's teacher, guidance counselors, and principal to gather additional information about your child if significant problems arise.

Talk with other reliable parents about school activities and teachers.

Everyday Opportunities to Learn in Child Care
Infant: Birth to Twelve Months

Your child is far too young to go to school, but he may go to a day care center for part of his day sometime during this first year. Below are some daily opportunities regarding learning in the child care setting.

Daily Opportunities to Learn

- Select a sitter or child care center that is well staffed and safe.
- Look for a child care situation that places a high value on learning through the ordinary experiences of play and exploration.
- Select a child care provider who gives your baby a lot of positive attention, nurturing, and encouragement—all prerequisites to infant learning.
- Continue to provide opportunities for your infant to learn at home through everyday activities, safe toys to touch and shake, soft music to listen to, and encouragement for learning to master use of her body and experiment with babbling.

Everyday Opportunities to Learn in Child Care/Preschool
Toddler: Twelve Months to Two-and-a-Half Years

If your child spends time at a child care center, preschool, or play group, you must play an ongoing role of overseeing her care while she is away each day.

Daily Opportunities to Learn

- Select a child care situation that provides a safe environment to explore and play in, with toys appropriate for encouraging exploration and learning.

- Select a sitter or child care provider who gives loving attention to your child and responds with enthusiasm to her efforts to learn.
- Establish a good relationship with your child's care provider or sitter; talk with her frequently to learn what your child is doing and learning each week.
- Provide your child with a safe home environment that encourages his play and exploration. Show enthusiasm and interest in your child's daily efforts to do for himself and make things happen.
- Read to your child each day.

> "Little brains need quiet time to consolidate that learning and make those connections. Sometimes I wonder if our kids today are having enough of it."
>
> —Dr. Jane Healy, learning specialist and author of *Your Child's Growing Mind*

Everyday Opportunities to Learn at Preschool

<u>Preschool Child</u>: **Two-and-a-Half to Four Years**

Preschoolers are fascinated by other children their own age; a good preschool center can provide many opportunities to explore and play with other preschoolers. Here are some guidelines for ensuring that your child is in a good learning environment:

Daily Opportunities to Learn

- Select a preschool program that is safe and well staffed, and one that places a high priority on playing and exploring.
- Look for a preschool that has interesting and engaging toys: blocks, water and sand tables, toys that encourage "pretend" play, and safe materials for creative play.
- Look for the setting of appropriate limits and the use of appropriate discipline such as brief time-out periods for misbehavior.

> "Emotions, it turns out, are the key experiences that stimulate and foster the mind's growth. Now what we're finding is that emotions are responsible for our traditional cognitive skills like doing math or physics as well as our ability for social reasoning and our ability for having a sense of morality. Emotions underlie everything."
>
> —Dr. Stanley Greenspan, clinical professor of psychiatry and pediatrics at George Washington University School of Medicine and author of *The Growth of the Mind*, *Building Healthy Minds*, *Playground Politics*, and *The Challenging Child*

- Look for a program that incorporates music, storytelling, and dance and movement for creative expression.
- Look for a preschool that encourages the development of social skills: sharing, cooperation, and negotiation among playmates. This learning is important during the preschool years.
- Stay in touch with your child's teachers; request regular information about how and what your child is doing each week.
- Provide your child with a safe home environment that encourages his play and exploration. Show enthusiasm and interest in your child's daily efforts to do for himself and make things happen.
- Read to your child each day.

Everyday Opportunities to Learn at School

School-Age Child: Five to Ten Years

"Parents and kids who read together are going to have a much better linguistic experience and a better parent-child experience."

—Dr. Jean Berko Gleason, professor of psychology at Boston University and author of the college textbook *The Development of Language*

When your child begins school, she ventures out into a world beyond her family, with new friendships, teachers, and a different structure for learning. This new arena for learning is continually changing; there will be new teachers, subjects, classmates, and expectations. Continue to provide security and a predictable routine at home to create a safe place to return to at the end of each school day to maximize her learning.

Daily Opportunities to Learn

- Encourage your child to be a good thinker and problem solver; praise these efforts whenever you see them in action.
- Look for your child's areas of interest—baseball, ballet, dinosaurs—and explore these interests together with reading, conversations, and field trips.
- Support his efforts to learn to read and write, spell, and do math. Find ways to work these activities into your at-home time together; count similar items in the pantry, read labels, and so on.

- Begin to encourage your child to develop good study habits.
- Assume the role of "homework consultant"; be available to assist in a secondary, supporting role, but let your child do the homework.
- Supplement any weak areas in your child's schooling with learning and thinking activities at home: creative projects, brainstorming, music making, physical activities, and sports.
- Have lively conversations that include your child and encourage her participation and opinions.
- Give your child pats on the back for hard work.
- Be available as a good, steady listener for concerns and problems with school and peers.
- Be committed to intervening to solve significant school problems that interfere with your child's educational goals.

> "If you read to your child, the child understands that 1) reading is good and 2) that there are words on the page. And of course it helps maintain your relationship with your child and it helps introduce your child to new worlds."
>
> —Dr. Jean Berko Gleason, professor of psychology at Boston University and author of the college textbook *The Development of Language*

Preteens/Early Teens: Eleven to Fourteen Years

Schoolwork, homework, and peer pressure intensify during the preteen and early teen years. Even though your child is quite competent, he still needs your daily involvement in his life.

Daily Opportunities to Learn

- Encourage your child to be a "good thinker" and "good problem solver." (Praise these efforts whenever you see them in action.)
- Stay involved in your child's education; know her teachers and subjects. Attend all parent-teacher conferences.
- Find a few minutes each day to talk with your child about his school day, peers, and so on.
- Help your child establish and maintain good study habits.
- Set rules about homework; give your child some freedom to set the schedule—either after school or after dinner.

- Some preteens need more sleep than elementary school students; enforce firm bedtimes during the week and give more freedom for later bedtimes on the weekends.
- Encourage your child to use a daily pocket calendar for school and homework assignments.
- Encourage your child to read books, magazines, and newspapers related to her individual interests.
- Expose your child to many subjects and interest areas; look for summertime learning opportunities at camp, and so on.
- Help your child learn to break large school projects into small manageable pieces.
- Be a good role model who continues to learn.

<u>Teens</u>: Fifteen to Nineteen Years

Teens still need your help and guidance regarding school and setting limits despite their size and relative maturity. Continue to remain interested in your child's daily life and studies.

Daily Opportunities to Learn

"I think the school board is probably the most important elected office in the country....People should really take seriously school boards; go out and run for elective office or run for the school board."

—Marion Wright Edelman, founder/president of the Children's Defense Fund, author of *The Measure of Our Success*

- Give your child recognition for his hard work, perseverance, and effort with schoolwork.
- Encourage your child to use a daily planner to keep his life and school assignments organized.
- Set limits when necessary to ensure your teen is not overloaded with too many extracurricular activities in addition to her schoolwork.
- Encourage your child to be a brainstormer and problem solver.
- Encourage your teen to read for pleasure.
- Help identify specific school problems, and work with your child and teachers to find solutions.
- Encourage your teen to explore summer learning opportunities through camps and work/study programs.

- Help your child begin to set long-term educational goals and evaluate her true interest areas in preparation for college.
- Encourage your teen to pursue creative projects of his own invention.
- Be a good role model who enjoys lifelong learning.

"Emotions are the engine for learning."

—Dr. Ann Barnet, professor of neurology and pediatrics at George Washington University School of Medicine and author of *The Youngest Minds: Parenting and Genes in the Development of Intellect and Emotion*

chapter nine

Problem-Solving and Decision-Making Skills

Justin and Scott were both fourteen-year-old boys who loved to experiment. Sunday afternoon, while their parents were away, they decided to use a small funnel to fill up balloons with water and food coloring and drop them off the second-story balcony to make designs on the pavement below. When they couldn't find food coloring, Justin said, "Let's use paint," which seemed like a good idea at the time. The green paint they found was oil-based and it did indeed make quite a splash of color all over the pavement. When they went downstairs to hose the paint off the driveway before the parents returned, they realized the paints would not come off with water. Scott said, "Justin, we have a real problem here—and here comes my mom's car!"

Most anyone of parenting age has figured out by now that life presents each of us with many challenges and problems over the course of a lifetime. When we peer from the outside into the lives of glamorous personalities, it seems as if their lives are golden. But the glossy photos in a magazine hardly portray the depth of real-life human experience that includes disappointment, heartache, and trouble that visit us all at some time.

If you were to survey a hundred parents with the question, What are the most important wishes you hold for your child? their "wish list" might read something like this:

I want my child to

1. Be healthy
2. Be happy
3. Have a successful life
4. Have high self-esteem
5. Be loved and loving
6. Have a strong sense of faith
7. Find fulfilling work
8. Have financial security

> "We want every child to feel like 'I am capable, I can prevail.' And that comes about with moms and dads encouraging their children's sense that they can handle things on their own; even things that are as ordinary as, 'Who should I sit next to on the bus, or who should I talk to at recess?'"
>
> —Dr. John Clabby, psychologist and coauthor (with Maurice J. Elias) of *Teach Your Child Decision Making*

But there are two important wishes missing from this list that have a significant impact upon all of these other good wishes: (1) I want my child to be a good decision maker, and (2) I want my child to be able to resolve problems.

It's reasonable to assume that even our dear children will be faced with challenges and problems of assorted flavors, sizes, and colors when they grow up and flee the nest. Making sound decisions and solving problems are the keys to their health, happiness, personal fulfillment, self-esteem, relationships, work, finances, and faith and spiritual development. If your child never learns to evaluate a situation and make sound decisions, or doesn't know how to find solutions as problems crop up in her life, she will suffer for it in all of these areas.

Accepting that our children will face assorted challenges and troubles is at odds with our deep desire to protect them from the troubles of the world. And in fact there are a multitude of problems that are our responsibility to solve or ease. But another part of our responsibility is to prepare our children to deal with their own problems.

Parents' Role in Child's Decision-Making and Problem-Solving Skills

The culmination of many of our goals in parenting is to help our children become seaworthy so they can eventually navigate their own course in life. In order to navigate, your child must become a good problem solver and decision maker. You are her guide, and the ordinary ups and downs of childhood provide the arena for learning.

Job Description for "Counselor for Decision Making and Problem Solving"

1. Make all bottom-line decisions regarding your child's health, safety, and well-being throughout all of childhood.

2. Allow your child opportunities to make age-appropriate choices and decisions in his daily life.

3. Help your child brainstorm about possible solutions to daily problems.

4. Help your child think through the consequences of her decisions.

5. Encourage your child to be a question asker and information gatherer.

6. Praise your child when you see good decisions and solutions in action.

7. Anticipate mistakes in choices and solutions; provide an emotional safety net for your child along the way.

8. Don't overreact to mistakes, or your child might become so fearful of failure (and disappointing you) that she'll be reluctant to make future choices or find solutions.

Where Do Problems Come From?

Although there's no easy answer to this question, it's useful to think about it, because it leads to a better understanding of how decision-making and problem-solving skills enhance your child's life.

We have all experienced firsthand the heartache and trouble that arises from circumstances beyond our control—natural

"Some children somehow intuitively pick up skills on how to solve problems, but most children need some assistance. It's important to teach children because their success in getting what they want...will be dependent on their problem-solving ability."

—Elizabeth Crary, parent educator and author of *Kids Can Cooperate*

disasters, tragedies, accidents, and illness, for example—but there are many problems in life over which we do have some influence.

Now that you are a parent, you can take much of what you have learned about life—through your many ups and downs—and put this wisdom and life experience to work to help your child. You can help train your child to be a good problem solver and good decision maker.

- Good decision making can prevent problems and help your child choose the right path that moves toward happiness and fulfillment.
- Problem-solving skills are damage-control skills to turn bad circumstances into better circumstances.

This is a one-two approach to trouble that may help your child achieve the good wishes you hold in your heart for her.

How Children Learn to Be Good Decision Makers and Problem Solvers

Learning problem-solving and decision-making skills is much like other kinds of learning that take place in childhood. It is built through experience—trial and error, layer upon layer—over time. Like other kinds of learning, problem-solving and decision-making training requires many daily opportunities for learning how to solve problems and make sound decisions.

Problem Solving

Somewhere along the line, the little grievances and small problems of childhood creep into your child's life. These are not life- or health-threatening troubles. These normal ups and downs are wonderful learning opportunities for decision-making and problem-solving skills, with you alongside to offer guidance and a safety net.

> "We tend to be a society of instant gratification. We need to start talking about futuristic issues with our daughters and our sons. This is one of the points that studies have shown around the issue of teen pregnancy prevention. A girl who can project into the future and understand the consequences of her actions today is far less likely to become a teen parent."
>
> —Mindy Bingham, educator and coauthor (with Sandy Stryker) of *Things Will Be Different for My Daughter*

When seven-year-old David's best friend got mad because David ruined his favorite baseball card, a real-life problem presented itself. When sixteen-year-old Molly wanted to go to the school dance despite her commitment to work at the Dairy Queen, she had to make a decision. When twelve-year-old Matt planned to sit next to James on the long bus ride to the band competition but his neighbor Jeffrey claimed this seat, he had to decide how to handle this.

> "One of the things I've learned as a therapist is that when people don't have options, they don't see a way out. That's pessimism. If you sit with them and you generate ten, fifteen, or twenty new options, it gives them hope. It gives them a way to then proceed. It gives them a sense of power. That's what we need to do as parents."
>
> —Dr. Dale Olen, clinical psychologist and author of *Self-Esteem for Children: A Parent's Gift That Lasts Forever*

In small steps, your child must begin to take the reins of life firmly in her hands and steer this way and that way, speed up, slow down, make decisions, and solve problems in her everyday life.

Parents must pick and choose which problems kids are equipped to deal with and which are beyond their capability. In matters of safety, parents must ride roughshod over their kids throughout all of childhood, making the bottom-line decisions. In matters that pose little serious risk to a child's safety, stability, or well-being, parents should pass the torch of responsibility for problem solving to their child in small doses along the way and serve as their "brainstorming consultant" if needed to help get the ball rolling on possible solutions.

One way for you to determine which problems your child can really tackle alone and which he cannot is to imagine worst-case scenarios. You must expect mistakes as your child is learning to make decisions. So, in the situation at hand, what's the worst-case scenario if your child makes a poor decision? Will he suffer serious consequences, such as getting expelled from school, hurt, or injured, or will he simply have a friend mad at him for the weekend with some possibilities available to smooth things over later if he chooses a less-than-wonderful solution to his immediate problem?

To analyze the anatomy of good problem solving, imagine that you are a figure skater who can do beautiful turns and jumps on the ice, but has suddenly found herself in the unfamiliar role of teacher. You have an eager young skater who wants to skate just like you. Your first step would be to break down what you do naturally and effortlessly into its small components. You have to think to yourself, "Now is the blade of my skate turned inward or outward? Is my left shoulder pulled back or forward? Am I bearing my weight predominantly upon my left foot or right? Do I lead with my right hand or left?" And in this way you are able to explain how to skate to your student.

Likewise, guiding your child toward becoming a good decision maker and problem solver involves breaking down the process into steps.

Here is the basic anatomy of solving a problem:

1. Identify the real problem (sometimes this requires breaking a problem down into smaller parts or understanding why a problem occurred).

   For example, you flunked the driving test. Now, exactly why did you flunk the test—got nervous? Didn't practice at all? Didn't study? Didn't understand the written test? Your vision is bad and you couldn't read the speed limit signs?

2. Brainstorm a list of possible solutions, drawing upon the knowledge or experience you've gained in the past under similar situations.

3. If you need help, figure out whom to ask.

4. Imagine what the impact of each of these possible solutions might be.

5. Figure out how to implement the solution you decided upon.

6. Be willing to try another solution if the first one didn't work (which means evaluating this new solution, deciding whom to ask for help, and figuring out how to implement it).

I find this anatomy of problem solving helpful to keep in mind, but I translate it into child-friendly language when I'm dealing with a child:

"Well, let's brainstorm about what you might do to solve this problem." Or, "Let's think about what might happen to you if you do push Jenny in class next time she calls you a name."

Practice at Decision Making

Children as young as two-and-a-half or three years old are old enough to begin to make small decisions about their daily lives: "Do you want apple juice or grape juice?" "Do you want to go to the playground now or read a story?" "Do you want to invite Gloria over or Sharon?" These decisions will help your young child pause for a moment and think, then make a decision and see what the consequences will bring. He may decide on the apple juice, then while drinking it wish he had the grape juice. He might go to the playground, find it too cold, and wish he'd picked the story, but find that your lunch hour is over. In this way, he will begin in very small, harmless steps to see what the consequences are for his decisions. (He will also feel as though he is entitled to make personal choices in his life, which is important for everyone to feel. Even tiny children—or especially tiny children—who have so much done and decided for them by grown-ups need to feel like they can make choices for themselves.)

Older children are capable of making decisions that are in the near future. "Which friend would you like to invite to come along to the beach next Saturday?" "Do you want to join the soccer team or tennis team this spring?"

School-age children, preteens, and teens can also begin to learn to make some financial decisions. You might say to your fourteen-year-old son, "I will give you one hundred fifty dollars to spend on some new spring clothes this weekend. You can make your own choices, but when the money is spent, the bank is closed for the rest of the spring." Or, "I will give you a generous allowance each week but you must pay for

> "One study was done, for example, at Harvard that followed people for about forty years and found that everyone…had hard things to deal with in their lives. But the adults who did the best could problem-solve. I think that during the preschool years is the time when we begin to teach problem-solving techniques."
>
> —Ellen Galinsky, president of the Families and Work Institute and author of *The Six Stages of Parenthood*

> "It is so critically important that children have a variety of tools; that they know how to bargain, that they know how to ask, that they know how to wait, that they know how to involve the other person in finding a solution that works for both of them."
>
> —Elizabeth Crary, parent educator and author of *Kids Can Cooperate*

all your monthly entertainment with your friends (movies and so on), snacks, and presents for your friends' birthdays." These are great ways to encourage children to learn to make financial decisions under your protective wing and live with the consequences of poor ones. There's no better way, for example, to teach your school-age child to become a savvy consumer than to let him spend his own money (perhaps from his allowance) to make purchases. When that inexpensive toy truck falls apart with one hour's use, or when the game wasn't as cool as the pictures looked, he learns a valuable lesson about choices and consequences.

Decision making involves many of the same components as problem solving and a few extras as well. Here are some of the ingredients that go into making sound decisions, and these too are only something for a parent to keep in mind.

1. Gather information from reliable sources about the choices you are considering.
2. Think through the strengths and weaknesses of each choice.
3. Try to think through the possible consequences of your decisions; weigh the pros and cons of each choice.
4. Be ready to brainstorm solutions to any potential problems that could be consequences of essentially sound decisions.
   For example, you've decided to move away to a college that is an excellent choice for your chosen field, but you won't see your aging parents as frequently because of the distance. Brainstorm workable solutions to this newly created problem.
5. Draw upon any firsthand experiences of the past that are relevant.
6. Use your intelligence and your feelings to make decisions. Factor in information you have about yourself, what's most important to you, and so forth, so that these decisions are in harmony with you and you can live with them in a way that truly honors your identity and your values.

Everyday Opportunities for Problem Solving and Decision Making

Infant: Birth to Twelve Months

Your infant cannot yet verbalize his wishes or make choices. But he can begin to build the thinking skills that are needed to make choices and solve problems later.

Daily Opportunities to Learn

- Encourage play that helps your child discover cause and effect. When she shakes a rattle, she makes a noise.
- Praise your child's efforts to make things happen.
- Show with your voice and your actions that you are confident in her ability to grow and develop.

> "I would say that creative play actually helps children learn great life skills that will serve them their whole life long: how to become problem solvers, how to become risk takers. They learn to build on what they already know and learn that there isn't just one way to do things."
>
> —Sandi Dexter, preschool teacher and author of *Joyful Play with Toddlers*

Toddler: Twelve Months to Two-and-a-Half Years

When a toddler plays, you can almost see the gears of his mind turning; he spends considerable time trying to discover how things operate. This toddler method of figuring things out is a wonderful step toward problem solving and decision making.

Daily Opportunities to Learn

- Encourage play that engages your child's curiosity and experimentation: blocks, stacking cubes, balls, and activity boxes that make noise and make objects move, and so on.
- Provide toddler-size wooden puzzles to encourage your child to try this piece and that and toys that require your toddler to make choices about which button to push, wheel to turn, and so on.
- Read interactive storybooks to your toddler.
- Give your toddler simple choices whenever appropriate: "Which sweater do you want to wear today, the red or the blue?" "Would you like to read *Goodnight Moon* or *Pat the Bunny?*" "Do you want a banana or a pear?"

Preschool Child: Two-and-a-Half to Four Years

Preschool children love to make their own choices about everyday activities in their lives. They are also capable of brainstorming about consequences. "If you hit Robert, how would he feel?" Or "What might happen if you take Valerie's favorite doll away from her?"

Daily Opportunities to Learn

- Continue to make bottom-line decisions regarding your child's health, safety, and well-being.
- Begin to talk with your child about consequences as problems arise: "How did you feel when Steve said he was not your friend anymore?" "How do you think Arlene felt when you said you weren't her friend anymore?"
- Begin to teach your child how to brainstorm a list of possible solutions to problems that arise. Listen to all his suggestions and steer him toward dreaming up positive solutions.
- Praise your child when you see good problem solving in action.
- Encourage creative play that lets your child try this way and that way to see what works best.
- Be a good problem-solving role model—let your child see you in action solving simple problems at home and thinking out loud about possible solutions.
- Give your preschool child opportunities to make choices. At this stage, children understand the concept of events taking place in the near future: "Pick a game you'd like Daddy and me to play with you after dinner." "Would you like to take your bath first or read our story first tonight?" "It's your turn to pick a restaurant tonight, here are the choices..."

School-Age Child: Five to Ten Years

School-age children enjoy being great brainstormers, and they have a good grasp of the basic idea of consequences.

Daily Opportunities to Learn

- Establish clear limits on all matters of safety and well-being.
- Allow your child to make many small choices that reflect her tastes, interests, and wishes.
- Be available to listen and help your child brainstorm and evaluate a list of possible solutions to problems.
- Help your child become an information gatherer, one who asks questions, thinks through consequences, and asks for help.
- Expect mistakes as your child begins to solve problems and make small decisions—she'll learn through trial and error.
- Praise good decision making and problem solving when you see them in action.
- Give your child a small allowance and let him manage it for discretionary purchases.
- Be a good problem-solving and decision-making role model.
- Since children of this age can think about the future and anticipate consequences, you can broaden the choices you provide to decisions such as: "Which sport, musical instrument, or hobby would you like to try?" "Which friend would you like to take to the state fair?" "What camp or summer vacation plan would be most fun for you?" "You may pick out your own shoes and clothes with this money."

"One of my favorite stories is about a little boy who was almost four years old and became very frightened of snakes. He had seen a nature program on TV and saw that snakes could be very mean and could bite you. At night time, he became convinced that there were snakes. His mother tried something rather creative. She wrote a sign that said Snakes Stay Out. It worked for one night. The next night, the little boy had trouble and couldn't sleep because of thoughts of snakes. His mom came and said, 'Why can't you sleep? The sign is up and it says Snakes Stay Out.' And the boy said, 'I've been thinking about it, Mom, and I don't think snakes know how to read.' So sometimes our preschool children can be a combination of incredibly sophisticated knowledge and logic and at the same time have fears that have nothing to do with logic."

—Dr. Harold Koplewicz, director of the Child Study Center at New York University School of Medicine and author of *It's Nobody's Fault: New Hope and Help for Difficult Children and Their Parents*

> "Give them choices that don't cost you anything, and don't be surprised at these really interesting rejections of things they want to do because they're more interested in the power and the pleasure of rejection than in the activity or the ice cream!"
>
> —Dr. Burton White, educational psychologist and author of *The First Three Years of Life* and *Raising a Happy, Unspoiled Child*

Preteens/Early Teens: Eleven to Fourteen Years

Preteens discover they have many personal tastes and interests that are quite separate from yours. They also can be very creative and logical thinkers—a winning combination for good problem solving and decision making.

Daily Opportunities to Learn

- Stick to your guns on important issues regarding the health, safety, and well-being of your preteen.
- Encourage your child to make choices about his everyday life and routine.
- Be a good listener when everyday problems arise; help your child brainstorm possible solutions.
- Encourage your child to write down the pros and cons of each choice from her perspective; round out the list with a few that you might have thought of.
- Help your child think through repercussions or consequences for his possible decisions as real-life dilemmas arise.
- When solutions for friendship problems are identified, role-play with your child to rehearse putting a solution into action.
- Expect mistakes as your child is learning through trial and error—don't overreact. Instead, provide encouragement to try again.
- Praise good problem solving and decision making when you see it in action.
- Be a good problem-solving and decision-making role model.
- Your preteen may be ready for the following decisions: "Which clothes should you buy to stay within your budget?" "Which music, hobbies, sports, and interests do you want to pursue?" "When do you want to do your homework—before or after dinner?" "How do you want to spend your weekly allowance?"

Teens: Fifteen to Nineteen Years

Teens are capable of reasoning things out, looking ahead to the short-term future, and understanding the consequences. They still, however, need reminders from you to shift into the problem-solving mode and help in making decisions manageable.

Daily Opportunities to Learn

- Continue to make bottom-line decisions regarding your teen's health, safety, and well-being.
- Allow your teen to make many choices about everyday matters but set modest limits: "When we go to Aunt Valerie's birthday party, you may not wear your ripped jeans."
- Be available to listen as problems arise; help start the brainstorming process with your child.
- Encourage your child to write down the pros and cons of possible decisions.
- Help break down big decisions into smaller parts. Find compromise decisions when necessary.
- Help your child think through the repercussions of his decisions: "If you go to the community college, will you be able to transfer your credit to the university next year?"
- Encourage your child to pay attention to her true interests and desires as she makes big decisions so that she'll be able to live with them.
- Expect mistakes as your child practices decision making and problem solving.
- Be a good decision-making and problem-solving role model.
- Consider allowing your teen to make decisions in the following areas: managing money on a daily basis; which friends, music, clothes, hobbies, sports, jobs, classes, or college to choose (unless issues of safety and well-being arise or family finances conflict with choices).

inner strength and character

chapter ten

Learning to
Persevere

Cassidy was a lively six-year-old boy who had never been ice-skating before. On this bright, wintry day, he and his mom headed for the outdoor skating rink at the city park nearby. He laced up his skates and gingerly walked along the ice, then fell. He got up and shuffled along a short distance and fell again. Each fall made his pants and gloves a little wetter. After nearly an hour, his mom was ready to go home. Cassidy was just getting the hang of gliding, rather than walking, and begged to stay "just a little longer." His mother was cold and wet and ready to go home, but she also respected her son's determination to learn, so they stayed for another two hours of skating. By the end of the afternoon, Cassidy was skating confidently and making plans to skate again tomorrow with his best friend, Michael.

Perseverance develops in the face of challenge. It is the ability to stick with a task or goal despite inexperience and difficulty. Perseverance is a critical ingredient in your child's development of inner strength and stamina, in her ability to pursue goals and hang tough through all sorts of ups and downs in childhood and adulthood.

> "What we do when the children are very young is we encourage them to try it again and again and again. And we do it by… encouraging effort but also ignoring failures."
>
> —Jack Youngblood, educator and coauthor (with Marsha Youngblood) of *Positive Involvement: How to Teach Your Child Habits for School Success*

Perseverance can be the one critical distinction between success and failure in many scenarios of life. The old saying, "The difference between the man who failed and the man who succeeded was five extra minutes of hard work," is a simple but telling example of what a difference perseverance can make in your child's life. It's not only the effort your child puts forth in mastering a challenge, but sometimes it is his staying power that matters most.

Because children are faced with new challenges nearly every day of their lives, they have repeated opportunities to fine-tune this important component of inner strength and stamina. In fact, because perseverance will be an important trait to your child after he grows up, it is something that should be mastered during childhood.

Parents' Role in Encouraging Perseverance

While your child may discover the basic idea of perseverance on his own through trial and error, he will need your encouragement to maintain his ability of "sticking with it" through many of the challenges he faces.

Job Description for "Facilitator of Perseverance"

1. Provide your child with age-appropriate challenges and the opportunity for safe, challenging play.
2. Be available to help your child clearly identify his goal.
3. Help your child break a larger goal into small steps. Give your child support and praise for efforts along the way.
4. Help your child pace himself: take a break when needed, relax, and recharge his battery when overwhelmed.
5. Encourage your child to ask for help when she is perplexed.
6. Show your pride and appreciation not only for the goal achieved in the end but for his ability to "stick with it."

Perseverance underlies many of the other important ingredients of childhood: exploring and learning, problem solving, creativity, and the development of courage and optimism. All of these ingredients work in harmony with your child's perseverance as she grows and develops to her full potential. These other aspects of your child's life give her a context in which to practice perseverance.

> "I think that the best way kids can learn is through modeling. If they see their parents, their teachers, other significant adults, and older kids in their lives persevering at something, not discouraged by setbacks and mistakes, but keeping at it and seeing something through to completion, I think that's going to have a big impact."
>
> —Teresa Amabile, professor of business administration at Harvard University and author of *Growing up Creative*

How Children Learn Perseverance

Perseverance is a concept your child learns quite naturally, through her own discovery process. The idea is this: "If I keep at this task and try again and again, perhaps try something a little different, I can succeed." Children begin to grasp this concept through experimentation and play during the first months of life. When your baby is about three months of age, through his sheer determination and perseverance, he will discover he can roll over from his back to his side. He discovers this by trial and error and sticking with his goal. When your two-year-old daughter tries again and again to stack wooden blocks, then finally succeeds at making a tall tower that doesn't fall, a giant beam of recognition flashes in her brain. She may not articulate this idea to you with words, but she has learned that if she tries over and over again, she is likely to achieve her goal.

Your thirteen-year-old son may decide to build a complicated radio-controlled car from a kit, assembling transmission, shocks, and all the inner workings of the car with no prior experience. Along the way, he will likely experience doses of frustration that he must manage. He may have to struggle with disappointment and mistakes. He will try this way and that way to attach the steering mechanism. And he will certainly have to look at the photo on the box showing what the car should look like when finished to help keep his goal squarely before him. All of these efforts combined will help him persevere.

> "I think this idea that winning is how you respond to adversity rather than the final point-score is a big idea!"
>
> —Jim Thompson, author of *Positive Coaching: Building Character and Self-Esteem through Sports*

When your teenage daughter tries surfing for the first time during her summer vacation, she will likely wrestle with inexperience and defeat. But if she perseveres, in the end she will master the challenge of riding a wave, reinforcing the value of perseverance.

The Presence of Challenge

There are a number of factors that seem to help children embrace the attitude of "try and try again" in their play:

1. They have a clear goal in mind (building a tower with blocks).
2. They observe others to see what is possible.
3. They learn to manage feelings of frustration and keep going.
4. They apply flexibility to their task: a "try-this-try-that" approach to meeting their goal.
5. They rebound from mishaps and failures along the way without feeling emotionally devastated.

All of these attitudes can play an important part in every challenge your child faces.

> "Young people today can't just say, 'Oops, that's as far as I go.' If they had a tough class, they have to have the self-esteem to say, 'I can figure this out! It may take me a while, but I'm going to struggle through and I can get where I want to go. I can realize my dreams.'"
>
> —Mindy Bingham, educator and coauthor (with Sandy Stryker) of *Things Will Be Different for My Daughter*

Everyday Opportunities to Learn Perseverance

Infant: **Birth to Twelve Months**

Babies begin to learn how to persevere during their first year of life. They are faced with tremendous physical challenges as they attempt to gain control of their bodies.

Daily Opportunities to Learn

- Provide daily encouragement for your child's attempt to gain control of her body and communicate her needs.
- Provide your baby with a good sleep schedule and quiet time for sleeping to help maintain his stamina as he attempts to master new skills.

- Be close at hand and watchful, but provide your baby with some short moments of time alone in a safe crib, baby seat, and so on so she can begin to feel comfortable experimenting with her hands and her body's movement outside your protective arms.

Toddler: Twelve Months to Two-and-a-Half Years

Toddlers naturally find opportunities to try their hand at new endeavors, but they also sometimes suffer a meltdown from frustration.

Daily Opportunities to Learn

- Observe your baby (quietly) when she is immersed in play and activity; get to know her tolerance for frustration and her attempts at problem solving.
- Provide toys that challenge his physical and intellectual development.
- Don't rush in to rescue your child at the slightest sign of bewilderment when she's playing; let her learn to manage small doses of frustration on her own.
- When appropriate, be a facilitator; make brief suggestions that encourage him to "try something different" to solve his dilemma while he's playing.
- Help your child move on to another activity when she's truly overwhelmed or overtired.

Preschool Child: Two-and-a-Half to Four Years

Your preschool child is quite happy to play independently for short spurts of time. During this imaginative play he is likely to try this and try that, which will lead the way to discovering important components of perseverance.

Daily Opportunities to Learn

- Provide age-appropriate toys that challenge physical and intellectual development.

- Encourage your child's creative play and efforts to make discoveries on her own.
- Observe your child quietly in action; watch how he approaches new challenges.
- Don't rescue your child at the slightest sign of frustration.
- When appropriate, be a facilitator; make brief suggestions that encourage her to "try something different" to solve her dilemma while she's playing.
- Step in when your child is truly overwhelmed by a challenge and help him move on to another activity, take a break, or look at the challenge from a fresh perspective.
- Praise your child's efforts to "stick with it".
- Encourage play that takes a "try-this-try-that" approach to problem solving.
- Read stories with the theme of perseverance woven into them—for example, *The Little Engine That Could*.

School-Age Child: Five to Ten Years

Your school-age child is old enough to recognize frustration in action and engage in a conversation about what frustration feels like.

Daily Opportunities to Learn

- Encourage your child to tackle play, activities, and sports that provide age-appropriate physical and intellectual challenges.
- Help your child break big projects down into manageable steps.
- Encourage your child to recognize what frustration feels like when it occurs and to react with a remedy:
  1. Take a break to relax.
  2. Relieve stress with some physical exercise.
  3. Ask for help.
- Brainstorm with your child about creative ways to approach her project or challenge.

- Praise effort and determination along the way.
- Celebrate the finished project or goal accomplished.

Preteens/Early Teens: Eleven to Fourteen Years

Your preteen will be faced with many intellectual, emotional, and physical challenges. Help him learn the specific skills that factor into persevering on a project or challenge.

> "That's one of the great things about sports. There's always another day."
>
> —Dr. Ron Smith, sports psychologist and coauthor (with Frank L. Smoll) of *Way to Go Coach*

Daily Opportunities to Learn

- Encourage your child to see each challenge as an opportunity to grow and learn.
- Help your child identify her specific goal and break large goals into smaller steps.
- Encourage your child to use good problem-solving skills infused with a can-do attitude when tackling a challenge.
- Provide encouragement, not criticism, along the way.
- Help your child learn to recognize signs of frustration and discouragement as they occur and respond with:
    1. A break from the challenge to gain new perspective or rest
    2. A request for help from a good resource person
    3. A good night's sleep and physical exercise to release anxiety
- Celebrate your child's accomplishments.

Teens: Fifteen to Nineteen Years

Teens face many emotional, social, intellectual, and physical challenges in the normal course of their routine.

> "One of the big things that comes from sports is the idea that persistence pays off. I have a little slogan: *S = E/T*, which stands for success comes from effort over time."
>
> —Jim Thompson, author of *Positive Coaching: Building Character and Self-Esteem through Sports*

Daily Opportunities to Learn

- Encourage your child to be involved in sports, music, art, theater, debate, writing, photography, and other activities of interest that challenge him, and discuss the effort and discipline needed to pursue these interests.

"Their work is to be children. And that means exploring, trying things out, making all kinds of mistakes—regressing, advancing, regressing, advancing—I always tell parents life is a spiral. It goes forward but then it falls back. And when children fall back, it seems as if everything falls back to ground zero, but things never do. It spirals. It's just the back side of the spiral. You just stay with kids through that, and they will keep advancing."

—Dr. Dale Olen, clinical psychologist and author of *Self-Esteem for Children: A Parent's Gift That Lasts Forever*

- Offer much more encouragement than criticism.
- Be available as a resource, brainstormer, and assistant problem solver, but don't take on your child's challenges for her.
- Help your child learn to recognize frustration, stress, and overload and respond with a remedy: take a break, get sleep, get physical exercise, get help, or plan a different approach.
- Help your child develop a can-do attitude, where mishaps and mistakes are opportunities for learning.
- Help your child realize that hard work is an important ingredient for success.

• • • • • • • • • • • •

chapter eleven

Discovering Courage

Patrick was only four years old, but he already had practice at being brave. He had chronic ear infections for the first three years of his life and finally had surgery to put tubes in his ears to relieve the problem last year. His parents said Patrick was a "brave soldier" for being so strong before and after the surgery. Today, he was going to the pediatrician's office with his dad to get a childhood booster shot. On the drive over, Patrick was very quiet. His dad asked him what he wanted to do for a special treat when his shot was over. Patrick said, "I want to go where all the other soldiers go when they are brave—to get ice cream!"

Courage is a quality of the grown-up world that has its humble beginnings in childhood. With a little luck, your child may be buffered from situations that test his courage in serious or threatening ways while he is young. But once he is an adult, there will likely be many scenarios in which he must stare trouble in the eye and muster up the courage to respond. There may be times when he must have the courage to stand up for what is right, to protect his health, his loved ones, and the principles in which he believes. He must also have the quiet courage to speak up about his feelings with important people in his life.

Parents' Role in Child's Development of Courage

Courage can't be forced; it is learned ever so slowly throughout life. Your child will have many small opportunities to practice being brave and strong in his daily routine.

Job Description for "Mentor of Courage"

1. Provide your child with a good understanding of what courage is.
   a. Have conversations about people who are "strong on the inside."
   b. Read and tell stories about girls and boys, men and women, who were and are courageous.
   c. Editorialize about courageous acts that start with good thinking.
2. Be supportive of your child's way of trying to be brave during her ordinary routines—at the doctor's or dentist's office, school presentations, and so forth.
3. Find time to talk with your child about fears as they develop. Help him make concrete plans for mastering those fears.
4. Crying is a normal part of childhood. Don't confuse a suppression of feelings with courage.
5. Support your child's efforts to try new activities without a tremendous fear of failure.
6. As a parent, have realistic expectations; recognize that courage develops slowly, in the tiniest of ways, throughout childhood.

How Children Learn Courage

"I think fear is an intrinsic part of being human. If we didn't have the capacity for anxiety and fear, we probably wouldn't last very long."

—Dr. Jeree Pawl, clinical psychologist and director of the Infant-Parent Program, University of California San Francisco

Most children have encounters with fear and opportunities to develop courage in their ordinary routine—in the doctor's office, the dentist's office, at school, and at summer camp. These ordinary situations give your child many small ways to practice being brave. This is how children learn courage best.

When your child is called upon to do something that makes her anxious, such as reciting a poem to her fifth-grade classmates, she has an opportunity to begin to experience courage. Although she may feel anxious—hands sweating and heart racing—she can choose to continue in spite of these feelings of fear and anxiety. Your teenager also will have to use courage to make strong decisions about whether to follow the crowd into a potentially dangerous and threatening situation or whether to speak up and say, "This is not for me." This is what courage feels like in its simplest form: continuing to do what is necessary or right, despite fear, anxiety, or pressure. Courage is practiced over and over again in tiny ways until it becomes a recognizable response for your child.

A Definition of Courage

All children need to understand what courage means before they can strive to achieve it. Parents have a very important role in talking with their young children about being "strong on the inside" and also "strong on the outside." Older children need to be reminded that courage is not necessarily contingent upon physical strength, but instead is a quality that starts on the inside and works its way out. Even little children can be strong and courageous. This distinction is important to reconfirm during childhood because kids are bombarded with many misconceptions about strength from cartoons and action heroes.

Children also need to know that courage is a trait of equal billing for girls and boys, for men and women. There are many examples of courage in the world around us that will help convey the message that courage is not determined by gender. There are real-life examples of girls and boys and men and women who are courageous in myriad circumstances. Use these stories as well as your personal experiences to teach your child the true meaning of courage.

The flip side to this point is that children need to know what courage is *not*. Bullying, for example, is not a sign of strength, but of weakness. Most bullies pick on only those people smaller in stature. Boasting and bragging about strength are also not what courage is about. Courage is

"The very best way to approach young children's fears is with compassion and reassurance. Very often because we want to protect our children, we have a tendency to dismiss fears. Dismissing them does not make them go away, and it doesn't give us the opportunity to address them....For instance, if a child is afraid of the dark, we don't say, 'Oh, that's silly.' Even if we may be tempted to do that, it doesn't help the child. Instead it's better to say, 'Of course, I understand that you could be afraid of the dark. Even grown-ups are afraid of the dark sometimes. But let's turn on the light in your room and look in all the closets and look under your bed and you'll see that your room is nice and safe and sound.'"

—Dr. Ava Siegler, psychologist and author of *What Should I Tell the Kids?: A Parent's Guide to Real Problems in the Real World*

a confident, quiet quality that doesn't need to be advertised.

All children (and adults) have fears of one kind or another. Many of these fears are fleeting. Others linger. It's helpful for your child to understand that courage does not mean the absence of fear; courage involves the mastery of fear. It is also helpful for your child to know that even the biggest football player on his favorite professional team is afraid of something—maybe it's the dentist, maybe it's delivering a speech—but there is something he fears, to be sure. This fear doesn't make him weak, it makes him human. He will work hard to overcome his fears just like everyone else, big and little.

There's another important aspect of courage that children must understand: courageous actions are preceded by good, clear thinking. Children and grown-ups alike must use thinking skills to assess their situation, to find solutions to problems, and to determine what actions are truly needed to stand up for what is right or what is necessary. This message takes years to learn, but can be taught in small ways throughout childhood. Look for stories to share with your child that show a child or grown-up who used good thinking in his effort to be strong or brave. Talk about friends and family members who were courageous good thinkers.

Courage can be found in many real-life situations: a single mother on a tight budget who succeeds each day in providing a loving and secure family in which her children can grow; a cancer patient who musters up every bit of his courage and determination to get well; or a young, talented musician who's alone, without family or savings, and works diligently to earn enough money to attend the music school she has dreamed of for so long. Courage is not reserved for the battlefield; it is present in ordinary lives. It's a human quality worthy of great celebration, and a childlike quality worthy of great support.

Everyday Opportunities to Practice Courage

Infant: Birth to Twelve Months

Courage is a foreign concept for infants. Babies are busy learning about the world and must have their needs cared for in every way during this precious, vulnerable stage of development.

They do, however, interpret or "pick up" on your feelings and your reactions. Practice being brave yourself when confronted with a necessary or important event that might make you uncomfortable; for example, when your baby is having a medical exam or receiving her immunizations, don't show any anxiety you may feel.

Toddler: Twelve Months to Two-and-a-Half Years

Toddlers are too young to learn much bravery. However, as they become more and more mobile and take minor spills on the ground, parents have some opportunities to encourage a hardiness in their child's personality. Don't rush to your toddler if his stumble seems minor. Hesitate a moment and wait to see his reaction. By responding this way to minor mishaps, you are helping your child find his own method for rebounding physically and emotionally from an upset. This is the beginning of your child's ability to tolerate mishaps and discomfort.

Preschool Child: Two-and-a-Half to Four Years

Preschool children are fascinated by stories and fantasy play. Because of their interest in action heroes and super beings, they are beginning to formulate an idea of what the concepts

> "If our daughters are going to proceed in the outside world as far as they possibly can, and if they don't have that ability to tolerate anxiety, they'll quit and they won't try. They won't become risk takers, and then they probably won't be able to realize their dreams....Courage, really, truly is the ability to feel the fear and act anyway. And that is the definition of anxiety tolerance."
>
> —Mindy Bingham, educator and coauthor (with Sandy Stryker) of *Things Will Be Different for My Daughter*

"strong" and "brave" mean. You need to provide information to round out their early impressions.

Daily Opportunities to Learn

- Select age-appropriate stories to read to your child that help her understand what courage really means.
- Encourage your child's resilience when small mishaps occur (don't overreact).
- Help your child act strong and brave during the ordinary childhood immunizations and dental checkups, and so on.
- Praise and reward your child's small acts of strength and courage.
- Be a good role model: find courage to face your problems with intelligence and determination.

School-Age Child: Five to Ten Years

School-age children have many opportunities to show inner strength and resolve when participating in new and potentially anxiety-producing situations such as reading to the class, performing in a play, or participating in church pageants. They are also old enough to understand the difference between courage and bravado.

Daily Opportunities to Learn

- Help your child learn that courage is dependent not upon physical strength but upon inner strength and good thinking.
- Editorialize to your child about bullies on the playground, boastful comments, or threats that indicate weakness rather than strength.
- Recognize and praise your child's small efforts to discover courage in her everyday life.
- Encourage your child to speak up about feelings and events that concern him.
- Show up for your child's school performances and be positive and calm about his participation.

Preteens/Early Teens: Eleven to Fourteen Years

Preteens are quite concerned with the actions and opinions of their peers. They do not want to embarrass themselves by acting like "babies," and yet they are not quite certain what being courageous means.

Daily Opportunities to Learn

- Teach your child that courage is of equal value to girls and boys. Help your child learn what "strong on the inside" means.
- Encourage your child to speak up about feelings.
- Encourage your child to use good thinking when making decisions about following the crowd and having the courage to say, "That's not for me," despite peer pressure.
- Have conversations with your child about real-life examples of individuals who have shown courage.
- Help your child learn to solve problems with peers without violence.
- Teach your child that sometimes the most courageous thing she can do when in trouble is ask for help.
- Be a good role model: face each challenge with courage and determination.

Teens: Fifteen to Nineteen Years

Teenagers must indeed exercise strength and courage to make good, sound decisions that are protective of their well-being. They are aware that they are well on their way toward becoming self-reliant, and this idea can be overwhelming.

Daily Opportunities to Learn

- Help your child understand that courage is of equal importance to girls and boys and men and women and is not based upon physical strength.
- Encourage your child to think for himself and act in a way consistent with his beliefs and well-being.

- Help your child learn to solve problems with peers without violence.
- Encourage your child to accept responsibility for his actions and admit his mistakes.
- Teach your child that sometimes the most courageous thing she can do when in trouble is ask for help.
- Have conversations with your child about real-life examples of individuals who have shown courage.
- Compliment your child's everyday efforts to incorporate courage and good thinking into her life.
- Help your child find practical, concrete ways to make unfamiliar situations manageable (summer camp, going away to college, and so on). Competence and confidence can pave the way for courage.

• • • • • • • • • • •

chapter twelve

Hope and Optimism

Rachel was a lively five-year-old girl with strawberry blond hair, freckles, and a sunny disposition. She was very excited on this day, because her best friend, Carly, was having a birthday party. Rachel had put on her "riding outfit"—cowboy boots, black jeans, a sweatshirt, and a cowboy hat—because she was going to ride a real pony at the party. At 11:30, a fierce thunderstorm rolled in. As Rachel was watching the rain through the front window, her mom approached to say the party had been "rained out." Rachel was quiet for a moment and then said, "I bet next Saturday will be the best horseback riding day ever, and I'll ask for an extra turn at riding."

Optimism is an essential ingredient in the development of your child's inner strength and character. At each twist and turn in her life, her attitude can help shape the opportunities that will come her way. Her outlook will help shape the outcome.

Optimism has many functions in your child's life. It can be a powerful feeling that motivates your child to action. It can be a quiet feeling that resides in your child's heart and is called upon to provide strength to get through difficult

> "Their way of explaining the world, of seeing the world...of interpreting it, needs to be optimistic. Now the way I tend to think about that is to think in every negative event, there is at least a positive thread....And in every positive event, there's probably a negative thread that runs through; we all have choices about which of those we focus on. I think the most important psychological principle (that) I probably tell people more than anything else is, 'You give power to what you focus on.' People have the choice to focus on the positive aspects of life or the negative aspects. And those who focus on the positive without denying the negative give their children the opportunity to grow up, not only seeing the positive but being positive about themselves."
>
> —Dr. Dale Olen, clinical psychologist and author of *Self-Esteem for Children: A Parent's Gift That Lasts Forever*

times. Hope and optimism are also the building blocks for your child's dreams.

Optimism is a characteristic found in great abundance in people who have hardy personalities. These individuals have a can-do attitude that helps them respond to the ups and downs of life in a positive way. They are resilient and resourceful. They have an internal belief system that says, "I know I can find a way; there must be a positive solution; something good *could* happen from this; tomorrow will bring new possibilities." These people don't just see the circumstances as they exist today, but look beyond to what they could be. They are not threatened by change; they respond to it as positively as possible. They are not idle dreamers; they are visionaries who act upon possibilities.

Optimism will help your child achieve a hardy, resilient personality. Although some kids may have more naturally upbeat personalities, optimism is an attitude that can be learned by children of all sorts of temperaments.

How Do Kids Develop an Optimistic Attitude?

Children start out with a spirit of optimism. Judging by their actions, babies and toddlers are some of the most optimistic people around. Babies and toddlers are can-do people. They appear excited about every possibility that presents itself—whether it's a key chain to grab and shake or big brother's basketball resting in the corner. Every day is a new opportunity. Babies and toddlers live in the present moment, under an optimistic belief system.

If you have seen a ten-month-old baby sitting up very straight in his high chair, using his thumb and fingers to carefully pick up and eat small

Parents' Role in Encouraging Optimism

Optimism is an attitude your child can learn. Your job is to be the guide, set the standard, and look for everyday opportunities to help your child develop an optimistic attitude.

Job Description for "Chief Optimist"

1. Show with your words and actions that you believe in your child's ability to meet the many challenges he faces as he grows.
2. Be a good role model for your child: live your life in a positive, can-do way.
3. Help your child feel comfortable with change, help her look for new opportunities as new circumstances occur.
4. Celebrate your child's progress and growth at each age of his life.
5. Encourage your child to dream about possibilities; talk about how those dreams might be achieved.
6. Share success stories with your child about people who overcame obstacles to follow their dreams.
7. Help your child develop a resilient personality.

pieces of Cheerios all by himself, you have seen an optimistic spirit in action. This is a glance at a baby who is driven by a belief that he can make good things happen. Early optimism is based in part upon your child's belief in himself. Your positive attitude about your baby's ability to meet new challenges reinforces his own natural belief in himself. Through your words and actions you can convey an important message to your child that promotes and maintains his early optimistic attitude: "You can do it!"

Children are influenced by optimistic parents. Your own positive approach to everyday life sets the standard for your child. Your child naturally imitates and emulates your behavior and attitudes.

As children grow and develop, they experience positive change in action. Children as young as three years old can marvel at all they have

> "I think good therapists are consultants. My favorite definition of therapist comes from a Canadian psychologist, Donald Meichenbaum, who defines therapists as 'purveyors of hope.' We motivate people to get to work to make their lives more intelligent, more consciously lived, more loving, and so on."
>
> —Dr. Mary Pipher, clinical psychologist, author of *Reviving Ophelia* and *The Shelter of Each Other: Rebuilding Our Families*

accomplished. When a mother says to her young child, "I'm so proud of you. Look at what you learned today," her child takes note of her own progress. Even a small child who sees how capable she has become can realize that more positive change is on the way. "You've learned to walk, to run, skip, and hop—soon you'll be ready to learn to ride a bicycle!" Much like the growth chart taped to the door frame marking off the inches your child has grown over the years, reflecting on progress can be an exercise in optimism for your child at each stage of her development.

Your fourteen-year-old daughter may be experiencing an awkward time at school, with weekly ups and downs involving friendship. Like other teens, she may be struggling to figure out "who she is." Unfortunately, in this probing process your child may compare herself to the cutest, most popular, or smartest girl at school to help establish her identity. These comparisons have little to do with who your child really is, inside or out. If instead your daughter took inventory of her own growth and accomplishments during this process of self-discovery, she might feel a surge of self-esteem and optimism about the future.

What if you said to your preteen or teen: "Here is a picture taken of you when you were only one day old. You've been a wonderful child right from the start—and you've grown so much over the years. It's been truly amazing to watch you grow! I'd like you to think about all the things you have learned to do since you were one day old and write them down in a list. You can include the big things like I learned to talk, I learned to walk, but include the little things, too—I learned how to make a barometer, I learned to multiply fractions. Then next week, on Friday, bring your list with you because you and I (and Dad/Mom) are going out to dinner to celebrate how much you've grown so far. We can also talk about the other things you would like to learn as you continue to grow." (Include plans for the summer, school year, next weekend, and so on.)

This assignment creates a tremendous list of big and little accomplishments that your child has mastered so far. It helps her see what her amazing growth looks like from a distance. It is a wonderful reminder of her ability to meet the challenges of today and tomorrow, and that's the spirit of optimism.

Everyday Opportunities for Optimism
Infant to Teens

Healthy children start off with an optimistic and enthusiastic outlook. Each day is a brand-new adventure with many possibilities for babies and toddlers. You can help keep this spirit of optimism alive in your child throughout all of childhood.

Daily Opportunities to Learn

- Imagine what the world looks like from your child's perspective at each stage of development. Celebrate the wonder of new discoveries with your child.
- Help your child adjust to change. Brainstorm about new possibilities that the new situation brings: starting school, a move to a new city, new neighbors next door, and so on.
- Read inspirational stories to your child—stories about individuals who overcame obstacles, about dreams fulfilled, and about good things that came from unexpected sources.
- Live the philosophy that tomorrow is a new day with new opportunities.
- Encourage your child to be a good thinker and problem solver.
- Give recognition to your child's competency and compliment his progress.

> "Protect your time with your children. Make that your top priority. Treasure those sweet, subtle, relaxed, emotional moments with all the relationships that we have."
>
> —Dr. Stanley Greenspan, clinical professor of psychiatry and pediatrics at George Washington University School of Medicine and author of *The Growth of the Mind, Building Healthy Minds, Playground Politics,* and *The Challenging Child*

- Help your child learn that sometimes the best bridge between discouragement and optimism is a good night's sleep.
- Help your child see that she has the power to direct the course of her own life with hard work and perseverance.

● ● ● ● ● ● ● ● ● ● ●

chapter thirteen

Integrity

Ashley was in second grade at Lehman Elementary School. Her teacher, Miss Williams, had baked Halloween cupcakes for the children in both of the second-grade classes. At 2:45, Miss Williams became ill and left one of the children in charge of passing out one cupcake to each child while she ran to the office to get the principal to take over her class. After she left the class, one boy immediately rushed forward and grabbed two cupcakes and said, "I don't care about the other second graders, I'm taking two cupcakes." Another six or eight students rushed forward and followed suit. Ashley was outraged. She jumped up on the top of her desk and shouted, "Stop! Half of those cupcakes are for the other class, so you need to put those extra cupcakes back right now."

Integrity is an internal road map that guides us to do what is fair and honest. It is a road map developed with many twists and turns, with mistakes made that sometimes require us to back up and take an alternate route. Integrity is the way that we translate our beliefs and values into action. While your child is young, you have many golden opportunities to help her develop the ability and skills to live a life that is a true reflection of her individual beliefs and values.

How Children Learn Honesty and Fairness

- They observe and imitate your behavior and actions.
- They acquire a clear, concrete understanding of right and wrong.
- They learn from your approval and disapproval.
- They learn to respect the needs and feelings of others.
- They learn to admit mistakes and take responsibility for their actions.
- They receive your encouragement and recognition for their efforts to be honest and fair.

Children Learn Honesty and Fairness Throughout Childhood

Integrity requires a combination of honesty, courage, fairness, and a sensitivity to the needs and feelings of others. These important values are learned very gradually by children, under the careful and consistent guidance of parents in the most ordinary of circumstances.

In order for children to be honest and fair, they must first learn the difference between right and wrong. They must learn from your words and actions which things are honorable and dishonorable, which are just and unjust, which are honest and dishonest. Some of these lessons are conveyed with clear-cut rules that even small children can understand— "stealing is wrong," for example. Other circumstances regarding fairness, for example, aren't easily conveyed in concise rules but instead require your child to develop a sophisticated, self-propelled understanding of fairness. These value judgments require your child to evaluate problems and circumstances with a sensitive heart and a keen mind.

"My father used to say, 'Character is how you behave when no one is looking.'"

—Dr. Robert Coles, child psychiatrist and Pulitzer prize–winning author of *Children of Crisis* and *The Moral Life of Children*

Family life is full of opportunities that teach these values. When your eight-year-old son comes home from school and mentions that his best friend stole a rare coin from the knapsack of another child, you have a real-life opportunity to talk about the consequences of stealing. When your thirteen-year-old daughter is caught cheating on an assignment at school, you have an important opportunity to establish firm consequences for her actions, show your disappointment, and help her find a way to learn from her poor judgment.

Every family with brothers, sisters, or cousins has repeated opportunities to help children work to find fair solutions and negotiate compromises with the other children in the family.

From the early years of life, your child is listening and watching you deal with conflict and respond to problems. Your child in fact is taking great notice of what you do each day of your life. Do you make up excuses or "white lies" when a friend calls and requests your participation on the neighborhood

> "When we're trying to communicate values to children, it's very important that we have some kind of appreciation for the limits of their understanding. Try to phrase things in ways that connect with their experience rather than with your experience."
>
> —Dr. William Damon, developmental psychologist and author of *The Moral Child*

Parents' Role in Teaching Honesty and Fairness

Your child will learn how to live with integrity by watching and listening to you. He also will be nudged on by your encouragement and editorializing about real-life events that represent examples of justice and injustice.

Job Description for "Honesty and Fairness Teacher"

- Express clear expectations to your child about telling the truth.
- Set expectations for fair play and justice.
- Be a good role model who tells the truth to your children and others in your day-to-day life.
- Be fair to your children and others you encounter.
- Teach your child effective ways to tell the truth without hurting feelings.
- Praise your child's efforts to play and act fairly with others.
- Recognize your child's efforts to speak up and stand up for what is right and fair.

> "They have no idea of what belongs to them and what doesn't. So gradually what parents do is try to put boundaries around children, not to contain them, but just to define them. If they don't get those boundaries set around them, as the children grow up, they don't have much sense about what is right and wrong and what to do and what not to do!"
>
> —Letitia Baldrige, author of *Letitia Baldrige's More Than Manners*

watch committee? Do you deceive family members routinely in an effort to avoid saying no or to avoid an unpopular decision? When you make a mistake or hurt someone's feelings, are you capable of admitting your mistake, making amends, and brainstorming for a way to rectify the damage? Your behavior is the measure of your own ability to translate your beliefs and values into action. *Your behavior is the best way to teach integrity to your child.*

Honesty

Very young children seem to be brutally honest about what they see and hear. They are surprised and intrigued by many of the new experiences they encounter. If someone is wearing a distinctive hat in the supermarket, your four-year-old child is likely to point and say, "Look at that silly hat on his head, Mommy!" Your three-year-old daughter might notice something she finds curious while standing in the checkout line at the hardware store and shout with great enthusiasm, "Look at that lady's purple hair, Mommy!" Or your five-year-old son might ask, "Daddy, why does that man have black stuff on his face?" as the tree trimmer comes inside for a glass of water. Young children express their thoughts and questions with little inhibition. This natural honesty is the starting point for your child's development of integrity. The honesty can be encouraged while the blunt remarks that are hurtful to others can be turned into thoughts in the mind rather than hurtful words.

> "I'm fairly convinced that the way kids develop values is by the strength of the connections that they have with their parents!"
>
> —Dr. Dale Olen, clinical psychologist and author of *Self-Esteem for Children: A Parent's Gift That Lasts Forever*

Teach Your Child Skills

As your child is learning to differentiate right from wrong, she also needs to learn skills that help her put her values into action. For example, she needs to learn what she can do whenever she makes a mistake. She must learn that rather than ignoring her mistakes (or actions that hurt the feelings of others), she has the power to try to improve the situation, to rectify the mistake. She will also learn that she can take her momentary feelings of failure, guilt, or shame and put them to work to improve her life and the lives of others. She must also realize that everyone makes mistakes. This is critical because a child who feels she must be perfect at all times is a child who will be reluctant to admit mistakes, tell the truth, and move on.

> "I think, as parents, we have to offer our children a safe and secure and sound environment and keep at a distance from them some of the dangers and threats of the world so that they can get their psychological and moral bearings and have a clear idea of what they believe is right or wrong and what they want to do to live up to those beliefs."
>
> —Dr. Robert Coles, child psychiatrist and Pulitzer prize–winning author of *Children of Crisis* and *The Moral Life of Children*

Teach your child a simple one-two approach to responding to mistakes once they are recognized: (1) own up to your mistake and make an apology to the appropriate person and (2) put time and effort into brainstorming to discover what you can do now, under the current circumstances, to make the situation better. (How can you fix the problem?) In some cases, the apology itself is all that is possible because the opportunity for rectification has passed. But the apology is an important response to mistakes. It's an admission that you do indeed understand the impact created by your carelessness or poor judgment.

Even for young children, this one-two response to mistakes is as simple as saying, "You made a mistake, so admit it, apologize, and let's think of a way to fix the problem." Your child will remember this simple theme throughout his life.

Your child must also have the skills and confidence to say no, rather than creating excuses that set the stage for using deception and white lies as the primary means for expressing one's personal preferences in life. Help your child find the confidence to say, "No, I'm sorry, I don't want to do that now."

Keep in mind that you want to be your child's teacher and guide in learning these values rather than

> "No. 1 is our ability as parents to live with integrity ourselves; I want my outside to match up with my inside."
>
> —Dr. Dale Olen, clinical psychologist and author of *Self-Esteem for Children: A Parent's Gift That Lasts Forever*

> "One of my favorite definitions of morality is 'acting in accordance with one's values.' So formulating values as a family is step one. The second part is acting in accordance with those values. If what is really important to the family is time together, for example, that may have implications for the work the parents do, where the family lives, the way the family spends money, and so on."
>
> —Dr. Mary Pipher, clinical psychologist, author of *Reviving Ophelia* and *The Shelter of Each Other: Rebuilding Our Families*

merely the external source of punishment when your child doesn't follow the rules. Yes, you need to establish consequences for behavior that is deceptive and unfair. But your job is to help your child establish an internal mechanism of integrity that is in effect whether you are looking over his shoulder or a thousand miles away.

Everyday Opportunities to Learn Honesty and Fairness

Infant to Teens

Children learn from your words and actions from the earliest years of childhood. You are the most influential teacher of values in your child's life.

Daily Opportunities to Learn

- Treat your child with fairness and respect. When you are overwhelmed and unable to be fair and even-tempered, take a short break to recharge your battery.
- Use clear (age-appropriate) language to teach right from wrong in your everyday life as opportunities present themselves. Be prepared to repeat these important lessons over and over again throughout childhood.
- Encourage and praise honesty; deal firmly with dishonesty.
- When conflicts arise with friends, family members, teachers, and others, ask your child to brainstorm about fair solutions to the problems.
- Talk with your child about real-life events that deal with justice and injustice, honesty and dishonesty. Encourage your child's thoughts and comments about these real-life events.
- Read and tell stories that help teach integrity.
- Teach your child what it means to be true to one's beliefs and values.

- Find stories in newspapers and magazines about real individuals who were guided by honesty and fairness.
- Be a good role model: live your own life in a way that puts your beliefs and values into action each day.

"Fairness does not mean, I win at any cost. It means, I follow the rules."

—Dr. William Damon, developmental psychologist and author of *The Moral Child*

· · · · · · · · · · ·

chapter fourteen

Faith

Jessie was a rambunctious five-year-old girl who was delighted to play outdoors. Her mother took her to a city park over Easter weekend to see the azaleas and daffodils, which created a spectacular display of color. Jessie skipped over to the flowers along the edge of the pond and stooped down to sniff to see if they had a sweet smell. She turned to her mother in dismay and said, "Mama, God forgot to put perfume in this flower, but it still looks pretty."

Young children possess a wonder about the smallest details of the world, and grown-ups are often amazed by the special brand of wisdom that emerges from their innocence. They have a simple way of looking at the world that transforms the ordinary into the profound.

The billions of people that live in this big world participate in a diverse array of religions. Each form of religion has its defining principles and practices. As individuals, we each have important choices to make in pursuit and expression of our innermost thoughts, feelings, and beliefs. In the United States, we have the freedom to practice our own form of religion as well as the freedom to dismiss religious ideology. We also have the privilege of sharing our beliefs and values with our children.

Most parenting books avoid the subject of faith. A family's faith and beliefs are highly individualized and therefore not easy to discuss. Freedom of religious choice is a basic tenet of American society, and we are very fortunate to claim this freedom.

Parents' Role in Faith and Spirituality

While your children are taking notice of all the many sights, sounds, and people they encounter, they are greatly influenced by what you do. Here are just a few of the ways that children may begin to formulate their beliefs.

Job Description for "Advocate of Faith"

- Enjoy the beauty and wonder of the world with your child at each age of childhood; expand the scope of this world as your child grows.

- Read and tell age-appropriate stories that reflect the beliefs that you hold dear.

- Answer your child's questions about the mysteries of life honestly, to the best of your ability.

- Ask your child what *she* thinks as she asks you what you believe, so that you can understand her perspective.

- If attending church or synagogue is a part of your family routine, encourage your child's participation according to her maturity and attention span.

- Look for opportunities for your child to make small contributions to his world. Teach him to brainstorm about what he might be capable of doing to help another or nurture a living thing.

- If prayer is important to you, teach your child how to pray as a part of her regular routine.

- Expect your child to make mistakes and behave selfishly from time to time; help her find an opportunity to try again.

- Encourage your child to respect the diverse religious beliefs of others; be a good role model in this regard.

With this diversity and freedom recognized, however, I have included this chapter on faith because the kind of faith I'm referring to is one that occurs naturally in children, regardless of their family's religious affiliation. It is a faith that springs from the child's natural tendency to believe in and emulate goodness. This childlike belief reflects a part of the human spirit that is worthy of recognition and encouragement.

A Definition of Faith for the Children of the World

Faith at its most basic is the belief in goodness. Spiritual development allows us to appreciate and emulate goodness. Our deepest beliefs and values are put into practice in our day-to-day lives. These basic principles of spiritual development are important to children. This simple definition of faith also fits neatly with your child's natural inclination to trust and believe in the goodness of the world and to marvel at its beauty.

When you take your six-month-old baby for a ride through the neighborhood in her stroller, she is likely to be delighted with each new person she meets and greet each new face with a smile. Your four-year-old child might be thrilled to watch a beautiful butterfly that floats through your backyard. Your ten-year-old son might be moved when he witnesses an elderly neighbor rush to the street to grab the hand of a wandering toddler. Your fourteen-year-old daughter might be awestruck when reaching the top of the foothills on your Great Smoky Mountains hike. These reactions are in part based upon a childlike appreciation and belief in wonder and goodness.

Children seem instinctively to believe in and marvel at the goodness and beauty of the world at an early age. They also trust that the people in their world will do good. This precious faith in humanity is worth protecting and encouraging. The innocence and trust generated by children creates a natural order for their world, in which the big people (grown-ups) are supposed to care for and do good for the little people (children), which is what makes it so tragic when children are hurt, neglected, or victimized by

> "The hardest thing in the world, and yet the most important thing in the world for all of us, is to live out what we believe!"
>
> —Dr. Robert Coles, child psychiatrist and Pulitzer prize–winning author of *Children of Crisis* and *The Moral Life of Children*

the grown-ups who hold their trust. These tragedies of trust create a deep hurt and undermine a child's sense of self as well as their expectations of and faith in grown-ups. In reality, the world is not always a good place, nor can all people be trusted. Parents must strike a balance between encouraging a child's faith and protecting them from the real dangers of the world by teaching them how to protect themselves.

In addition, if you draw great strength and guidance from your own religious beliefs, you can share your convictions with your child in countless ways throughout your lives together.

The Value of Faith

First, faith and spiritual development can enhance your child's life by encouraging an appreciation of all that is good in the world and its people. Second, faith gives you a context in which to encourage your child to contribute to the world in which he lives. Third, your child's inner sense of faith may offer great perspective and/or comfort to him through good times and bad. Faith may also help your child develop a sense of belonging and a discovery of his connection to the grander picture of the world. And last, faith establishes a philosophy for living that values moving forward and growing through challenge and experience.

Faith and Spirituality Put into Action

The best measure of a person's spiritual beliefs is her words and actions. A bumper sticker on your car might announce your affiliation with a church or religious ideology, but it does nothing to put that belief into action in the world. It is simply an advertisement. It is through your daily actions that you give expression to the beliefs that you hold dear, and your example is what your child will absorb.

These lofty goals are accomplished in the ordinariness of life, through stories and conversations about beliefs and values, through the practice of familiar and comforting family celebrations and customs, through the appreciation of the beauty of the physical world all around us. Parents can create a bridge for their child—a bridge of faith.

Everyday Opportunities to Develop Faith

<u>Infant and Toddler</u>: Birth to Two-and-a-Half Years

- Honor the innate trust that your baby has in your goodness; care for her lovingly and be worthy of her trust and expectation.
- Be a good role model for your child; use words and actions that illustrate your innermost beliefs and values.
- Take a break when your weariness interferes with your ability to live your beliefs in the routine of life. Remember, your actions are the best expression of your own spiritual beliefs.

<u>Preschool Child</u>: Two-and-a-Half to Four Years

Your preschool child is highly aware of the subtleties of your words and actions and loves to imitate.

Daily Opportunities to Learn

- Care for your child in a loving and positive way that is consistent with your values. (When you are fatigued and overwhelmed, take a break and get someone to help.)
- Be a good role model for your child through the words and actions you use in everyday life to put your innermost beliefs into action.
- Read simple, lively, age-appropriate stories to your child that teach the values you believe in and expose your child positively to the celebrations and holidays of your faith.
- Help your child see that she has the free will to contribute positively to her family and friends in the routine of her life.
- Answer with sensitivity your child's questions about the mysteries of life and the workings of the world; listen to his ideas and confusion.
- If your family attends church or temple, begin to include your child in preschool Sunday school.

> "We are not there to legislate theology, we are there to share our religious resources with them to say, 'These are thoughts that give me meaning and purpose.'"
>
> —Dr. Earl Grollman, rabbi and author of *Talking about Death* and *Talking about Divorce and Separation*

School-Age Child: Five to Ten Years

Your school-age child will begin to be aware of the religious beliefs and customs of other children and families. He may also have many questions for you related to values, traditions, and holidays.

Daily Opportunities to Learn

- Care for your child in a loving and positive way; when you are fatigued and overwhelmed, take a break and get someone to help.
- Look for the positive real-life experiences that reflect your beliefs and regularly share them with your child.
- Make yourself available to chat; answer questions about your beliefs and the many mysteries of life. Answer questions honestly and sensitively.
- Help your child discover ways to use her talents and interests to contribute to your family, neighborhood, and community.
- Let your child's age and maturity level be your guide in determining how he might participate in your church or synagogue.
- Be open to learning about the customs of other cultures and religions of the world with your child.
- Be a good role model; let your innermost beliefs be expressed by your words and actions in your daily life.
- If your family attends church or synagogue, encourage your child to attend Sunday school or church service.

Preteens/Early Teens: Eleven to Fourteen Years

Preteens often ponder the order of the world. They also hear confusing and conflicting comments about religious beliefs in the course of their play and school routine. This is an age that naturally calls for family discussions to answer your child's questions and listen to her comments.

Daily Opportunities to Learn

- Let your own values guide the way in which you parent your child each day; when you are overwhelmed, take a break.

- Help your child discover what inspires him or creates a peaceful time for reflection (perhaps music, creative projects, volunteering for a worthy cause, poetry, hiking, canoeing, or bicycling).
- Enjoy the goodness and beauty of the world with your child.
- Help your child put her talents and interests to work to make contributions that enhance your family, neighborhood, or community. (Praise these efforts when you see them in action.)
- If your family attends church or synagogue, encourage your child to attend Sunday school or church service.
- Encourage discussions about values and goodness. Listen to your child's point of view.

Teens: Fifteen to Nineteen Years

As teens try to clarify their own independent identities, they sometimes struggle with confusion about the larger picture.

Daily Opportunities to Learn

- Make a weekly schedule of time spent together pursuing a worthwhile cause that is enjoyable to you and your teen.
- Encourage sophisticated discussions of values, of good and evil, of truth and justice. Respect your child's opinion.
- Help your child discover what inspires him or creates a peaceful time for reflection (perhaps music, creative projects, volunteering for a worthy cause, poetry, hiking, canoeing, or bicycling).
- Help your child put her talents and interests to work to contribute to your family, neighborhood, or community. (Praise these efforts when you see them in action.)
- Become familiar with any church or religious organization with which your child might choose to align herself.
- Be a good role model for your teen: live your day-to-day life in a way that reflects your beliefs and values.

making their way in the world

• • • • • • • • • • •

chapter fifteen

Learning to Communicate

It was a Mother's Day to remember always. The baby was nearly six weeks old. On this Mother's Day morning, Lynn had fed her baby, burped him, and laid him on the bed to change his clothes. As she dressed him, she chatted with her baby about what was planned for the day. He in turn gave his mother a response she would never forget—a broad beaming smile—his first smile ever. Her heart swelled with pride at the sight of that first toothless grin from her baby boy.

Babies communicate their needs and desires from the very first moments of life. Their cries let you know they are hungry, tired, frightened, sick, wet, or uncomfortable. Then sometime at around six to eight weeks of age, your baby's repertoire of communication takes a profound leap forward with that wonderful first smile. It is a gratifying moment that signals a happy new way to communicate.

Over the months and years of childhood, your child will expand her repertoire of communication. She will talk, ask questions, tell jokes, write stories and poems, express her opinion, sing, and argue.

While much of this communication unfolds naturally, you are your child's mentor for the rich tapestry of ways to express her wants, needs, feelings,

Parents' Role in Communication

Your job is to help your child learn how to talk and communicate effectively in all sorts of real-life situations. You are your child's "Director of Communication." Job Description for "Director of Communication"

1. Include your child in conversations right from the start. Help her join in.
2. Teach your child to use words to express feelings.
3. Encourage your child to speak up—to ask questions, gather information, express ideas, ask for help, and contribute to the conversation.
4. Show your child how to communicate in a way that is respectful of others.
5. Help your child learn to communicate in all sorts of real-life situations—on the phone, in class, talking with smaller children and with the elderly, writing letters and poems, and so forth.
6. Expect communications mistakes along the way and provide an opportunity to try again.
7. Be a good communications role model, one who uses words to express feelings and solve problems.

ideas, and opinions in all sorts of situations; at home, at school, with friends and adversaries—you are your child's most important communications teacher.

How Children Learn to Communicate

Long before your baby utters his first words, *Mama* or *Dada*, he is learning to talk. He begins by listening attentively to your voice and to your words. He was born with a natural talent for listening; day in and day out, your baby studies language by listening to you. If you watch your three- or four-month-old baby as he moves his head from side to side to follow your soft voice around the room, you can see this early listening in action. He doesn't understand the exact meaning of the words you speak in the beginning, but as time goes by, he can interpret a mood of general meaning from your tone of voice—soft and loving or impatient and harsh.

When you become a parent, you have a whole new range of experiences and learn many new lessons about life. You also have a chance to relearn prior lessons that have faded with age. One of these lessons is listening. When you were a baby, you started out with a natural talent for listening keenly to the people around you. Your survival required you to be attentive, to listen carefully, and to study the language of your parents in order to learn to communicate your needs and desires in a way that would be understood. We all start out with a keen talent for listening.

> "Probably the most important thing for a child is to be heard and to be understood. It's probably the most important thing for any of us. We don't always have the expectation that things are going to be fixed, but boy, do we ever want somebody to understand how we feel."
>
> —Dr. Jeree Pawl, clinical psychologist and director of the Infant-Parent Program, University of California San Francisco

Now that you are a parent, your child needs you to rediscover your talent for keen listening all over again. She needs you to listen attentively to what she is trying to communicate throughout all of childhood. This is as true when she is six weeks old as it is when she is seventeen years old. Because your child is just learning to communicate, sometimes she is unable to express her fears, needs, and desires clearly. If you devote time to your child for quiet moments of chatting throughout all of childhood, and if you become a keen observer, often reading between the lines, you will be in touch with just what your child is thinking and feeling. This aspect of parenting is always important, but it becomes even more critical when your child is experiencing a change (a move, a divorce, or an illness or trauma), and of course when your child becomes an adolescent. Communication between you and your child is the conduit through which you are best able to understand your child's perspective and offer appropriate support and guidance.

You are your child's most important communications teacher, and a communications teacher must first know how to listen.

Throughout childhood, your child will often be on the receiving end of communication—hearing the thoughts, feelings, ideas, questions, opinions, and demands of others. He must learn to listen carefully, not only with his ears, but also by using his other senses to interpret the messages he receives. He will learn to use his thinking skills, prior experiences, and past information to develop a sense of intuition about what he sees, hears, and perceives. This is a sophisticated aspect of communication that develops very slowly over time, in humble steps, layer upon layer, during life's ordinary activities. It's up to you to help provide the daily opportunities for your child to learn to communicate—to send and receive messages.

Learning to Talk

At around two months of age, your baby begins to experiment with her voice—cooing, gooing, and babbling. When you coo and goo back at her, she responds with more babble and chatter, and voilà, conversation is born! Many months later, she tries to imitate actual words she has heard you say: "Mama...Dada...ball...juice...doggy!" She comes close enough to replicating these words so that you understand her meaning. You exclaim, "She's asking for a cup of juice!" (Miraculous!) Then later, she strings two words together to express her wishes to you more clearly: "Do dat!" as she points her finger at the backyard swing set, which you understand to mean, "I want to do that!"

By the age of four, most children have mastered the basics of language and speak in complete sentences with an extensive vocabulary. They expand and apply their early language skills so that they can express more complex thoughts, feelings, and ideas. "I don't want to go to the doctor for my shot. I want an ice cream cone now."

As your child's thinking ability expands (adding logic, reason, and abstract thinking), his need to communicate grows right along with his expanding mind. As your child's ability to think abstractly and critically unfolds, so too does his ability to express these thoughts, questions, and opinions. "Mommy, does Grandpa see the stars shining when he is up in heaven?" Communication is the glue that holds humanity together. It is the superglue that holds a family together, giving each family member a way to express ideas, feelings, fears, hopes, dreams, and opinions. For your baby, all of this develops from the humble beginnings of listening to your voice each day as you chat with him.

Using Language Effectively

It is important for your child to recognize the great power of words, particularly when combined with good thinking. Knowing how to speak is only a part of learning how to communicate effectively. Encourage your child to use words to express her thoughts, questions, feelings, and opinions so that she is comfortable speaking to one and all. Language will be key to solving problems that occur in her life.

Using Language to Express Feelings

Young children have a tendency to "act out" their feelings of anger and frustration rather than using their words to express themselves. Your six-year-old is not likely to come home from an unhappy day at school and say, "I'm really angry with that Jonathan. He's so insecure with himself that he bullies me on the playground every day at lunchtime. I'm getting fed up with it

Priscilla Vail: "If I could tell you a little story…when our youngest child was three and a half, I took him to a doctor's appointment. We got there early and sat in the waiting room downstairs. He's a country child. This was a city doctor's appointment. We sat there down in the lobby of the hospital where the doctor's office was, and we were across from the elevator. He kept watching people go in and out of the elevator. Finally, it was time for us to go up to see the doctor. So I said, 'Let's go now.' And he said no! I said, 'Well, come on. Let's go. This is what we came here for.' And he said no. I looked in his face and saw that there was absolute terror and insistence. He was not getting in that elevator, and he's usually a cooperative fellow. So I said, 'You won't go in the elevator?' 'No!' And I said, 'Why?' He pointed to the door and looked at me as though I were feebleminded and said, 'Don't you see, Mom? Everybody that goes in there comes out different.' "

Bobbi Conner: "That's some doctor!"

Priscilla: "He had seen the elevator doors open, in go the people. Elevator doors closed, elevator doors open. Bingo…out come different people."

Bobbi: "But the idea is that by his ability to use language, he could express to you, the caregiver, what the problem was that was floating around in his mind."

Priscilla: "Right."

—Priscilla Vail, learning specialist and author of *Emotion: The On/Off Switch for Learning* and *Words Fail Me*

Tips for Communicating with Young Children

Many working parents ask their children, "What did you do today at pre-school (or school)?" as soon as they greet their child at the end of a busy day. Most children respond superficially with, "Nothing," or "Played all day"; an older child might say, "Just the usual." All of these answers leave parents feeling dissatisfied that their child is not sharing details of the day. Parents can very often change this scenario with two important techniques: (1) pick a quiet time to chat about the day after your child has settled at home (made a transition to home), and (2) ask the right questions to stimulate a conversation with your child.

Here are some sample questions you might ask your child at dinnertime, bedtime, or in between to hear the details of your child's day at school or day care:

"Did anything funny or silly happen today that made you laugh?"

"What one thing did you learn today?"

"Who was your best friend today? What did you do with your friend?"

> "Human beings are uniquely wired for language. We have a predisposition to words. As children learn words and learn what things are called, they are able, through the use of language and labels, to sort their own experiences and thus to become, if you will, the curators of their own existence."
>
> —Priscilla Vail, learning specialist and author of *Emotion: The On/Off Switch for Learning* and *Words Fail Me*

so I'm going to speak up tomorrow when he approaches me." Instead, you might receive a note from your son's teacher saying, "Todd was in the principal's office all afternoon because he punched Jonathan and made his nose bleed. Please call me tomorrow to arrange a meeting to discuss these behavior problems."

Although the inclination to act out feelings such as anger, frustration, and sadness may persist throughout childhood, parents can begin to help children find a voice for their feelings early on.

Four-year-old Danielle was angry at her playmate Elizabeth for grabbing the kitchen set from her hands. Danielle tightened her two small fists and appeared ready to hit when her teacher appeared and said, "Danielle, use your words." This reminder triggered Danielle to say to

Elizabeth, "I was playing with that kitchen set. You give it back to me and wait your turn!" Her teacher gently took the toy out of Elizabeth's hand and transferred it to Danielle's. The teacher then took Elizabeth by the hand, walked to the playhouse, and said, "It's Danielle's turn with the kitchen set now. Let's see if the teakettle and cups are still inside the playhouse." This day care incident provided an opportunity to teach these small children the power of words to express anger and find solutions to problems.

> "In the little preverbal child, you'll hear them babbling and it sounds just as though they are really, really talking because they have inflections and pauses. Then you listen. They aren't using real words at all, but they're mimicking the music of the language that they hear around them."
>
> —Priscilla Vail, learning specialist and author of *Emotion: The On/Off Switch for Learning* and *Words Fail Me*

This theme, "use your words" to express anger, is a lesson that is worth repeating many, many times throughout the months and years of childhood. It is a critical lesson to incorporate into the fabric of your family life too. You and your spouse must be good role models in the family, using your words to express anger and frustration constructively and to find, and articulate, solutions when tempers flare. This will help your child create an automatic response for dealing with anger, frustration, and hostility at home, at school, at work, and with his future family when he grows up.

Children who are raised in a family in which anger and frustration are expressed with words rather than actions have a much better chance of carrying these principles into their workplace, their adult relationships, friendships, and parenting later in life. A teenager who has been encouraged throughout childhood to "use words" to express intense feelings will have a familiar, automatic way in which to express conflicting feelings, pressures, and stress.

In addition to using words to express anger, words can also be used to express tenderness. Most small children, boys and girls alike, spontaneously say the most tender things to their friends, families, baby-sitters, teachers, and pets in the normal course of their day. But for some children, these expressions of tenderness are replaced with reservations as they grow older. Some older kids, preteens and teens, mistakenly equate

> "Listening from your heart is a totally different way of listening. A lot of parents, unfortunately, don't do it. What I mean by that is listening...with a sense of wonder...to find out what life is like from your child's experience."
>
> —Judy Ford, family therapist and author of *Wonderful Ways to Love a Child* and *Wonderful Ways to Love a Teen*

verbal expressions of love, appreciation, and recognition with weakness. Let your children see you, as moms and dads, expressing appreciation, love, and tenderness with both words and deeds as a normal part of your routine. As time goes by, they will begin to understand which circumstances call for strength and courage and which call for quiet expressions of appreciation and recognition.

Learning to Speak Up

All kids must learn to speak up about what's on their minds and in their hearts. Children must know that they have the right to express concerns, ask questions when curious or confused, ask for help, and express their own thoughts and ideas.

Speaking up means feeling perfectly comfortable raising your hand in class to ask a question about something you don't understand. It is using language to gather information that helps your mind expand. Speaking up also means expressing your preferences and tastes to show your individuality. Speaking up means contributing your ideas and thoughts to the discussion at the dinner table, in the school cafeteria, and in the locker room. Speaking up means letting someone know when something is hurtful to you. These are some of the positive objectives that are achieved when your child knows she is allowed to voice her thoughts and feelings.

Children, however, are quite inexperienced and clumsy at understanding the general rules of civility. When your five-year-old announces spontaneously and rather loudly in a restaurant, "Daddy, that man is polluting the air with his smoking. His lungs are turning black from the smoke and he's gonna get sick," you realize the fine-tuning required when encouraging your child to join in family conversations in his tender years. When your teenager, whom you have encouraged all these years to speak up and express herself, suddenly debates every comment you make at the dinner table, you again may momentarily wish you had espoused the rule that children should be seen and not heard.

What these mishaps indicate, however, is that your child must learn the rules of respecting others' opinions and freedoms. He must learn what is appropriate and what is not, what is fair discussion and what is hurtful. You are his teacher in all of these matters of communication. You will have countless opportunities to teach these lessons over and over again in the routine of your lives together.

> "Kids love to hear their parents talk about when they were little and tell the stories of their lives. My observation is that fewer and fewer parents are doing this. Ever since we walked upright, we've been sitting around campfires telling stories. Now we're sitting around TVs watching them."
>
> —Ina Hughes, newspaper columnist for the *Knoxville News-Sentinel* and author of *A Prayer for Children*

Keeping the Lines of Communication Open

Communicating with children takes both instinct and openness. We all know adults who have a special relaxed way of communicating with children of all ages. These people naturally engage a three-year-old in a lively, spontaneous conversation about a caterpillar crawling along the sidewalk, and successfully chat with a shy sixteen-year-old nephew about canoeing. These adults are usually good listeners and keen observers. They shift gears naturally into using words and discussing interests appropriate to their audience. They listen for answers from the child without giving lectures or directions. Most important, they appear to have all the time in the world when chatting with a child, even if in fact they will be leaving in thirty minutes. For the brief time spent chatting, these adults are themselves truly interested and engaged in their conversation.

Children are extremely perceptive about adult communication. From the time they are very young, they can tell when adults are preoccupied, distracted, or perhaps ready to give a predetermined, parental lecture. Kids, like adults, close off when they don't like the tone, direction, or lack of listening in a conversation. Also, if they see and hear that their part of the conversation is being ignored or discounted, they become angry or disinterested.

Here are some tips to keep open the door of communication with your teenager.

- Try to have conversations daily or weekly in which everything else is put on hold and your teen has your undivided attention.
- When your child speaks, truly listen to all that she is saying and preserve your thoughts for later in the conversation.
- When having discussions about difficult topics, such as curfew, house rules, and so on, keep yourself calm. Listen to your child's viewpoint, offer to negotiate or bend slightly over minor issues, and stick firmly to the rules that matter most—but do so in a matter-of-fact, respectful way.
- When your child is blatantly hostile or disrespectful to you, calmly end your participation in the conversation until a later time when your child can regain her self-control.
- Find mutually enjoyable activities that are conducive to chatting to ensure you have some noncontroversial, lighthearted conversation each week. (These ordinary chats will help offset the more serious, but important, discussions you have with your teen.)

When you are communicating with your child, remember that what you want is to help and support your child throughout childhood. To do this, you need to maintain open lines of communication so that she always feels that she can talk with you with excitement to share or problems to solve.

> "Many problems are really a direct result of miscommunication or of children feeling that they're not validated because nobody listened to them."
>
> —Dr. Marilyn Gootman, professor of early childhood education at the University of Georgia and author of *The Loving Parents' Guide to Discipline*

One final word about communication. Responsibility falls to you to speak up on behalf of your child when he is threatened or harmed in any significant way. Children develop the strength and confidence to speak up on their own in all sorts of situations through years of practice, but throughout childhood you remain your child's most important advocate.

Everyday Opportunities to Communicate

<u>Infant</u>: Birth to Twelve Months

Your newborn baby is studying language by listening to the voices around her. As she listens over the months, she will imitate the sounds she hears and eventually speak recognizable words.

Daily Opportunities to Learn

- Respond to your baby in a positive way when she cries; this is her only way of communicating in the beginning.
- Talk to your baby throughout your day together.
- Show your pride and joy at your baby's smiles and giggles; your reaction will encourage these important ways of communicating.
- Express the love, appreciation, and delight you feel toward your baby in words each day; he will understand your meaning.
- Read stories to your baby and sing songs so she experiences the rich variety of the ways that you communicate.
- When your baby babbles, chatter right back to him so he can begin to understand that communication is back-and-forth language.
- Play peek-a-boo with your baby; she'll experience the pure joy of communicating, the element of surprise, and she'll learn to "take turns" in conversation.
- Play quiet and soothing music when your baby is awake; he'll learn that music expresses feelings and moods.
- Include your baby in occasional outings (lunch dates, for example) with your adult friends; she will observe how you talk and laugh with others.

"Listen with interest; that means with eye contact and undivided attention instead of running around the house doing fifteen different things while you're supposedly listening."

—Dr. Marilyn Gootman, professor of early childhood education at the University of Georgia and author of *The Loving Parents' Guide to Discipline*

<u>Toddler</u>: Twelve Months to Two-and-a-Half Years

Most young toddlers can use simple words and point to express their immediate needs and wishes. During this eighteen-month period your child will make an amazing leap into communicating with short sentences. (He will also understand a great deal more conversation than he can actually imitate.)

Daily Opportunities to Learn

- Talk to your toddler throughout your day together. Include your toddler in family conversations (be patient with his slower pace of speaking).
- Read books to your toddler, sing songs, tell stories, and recite poems and nursery rhymes.
- Encourage your toddler to ask questions and ask for help when she needs it.
- Have fun with language; play silly word games.
- Use short, understandable words to make a request or set limits with your toddler: "No hitting, it hurts Annie."
- Provide toddler-safe crayons and paper for scribbling and drawing. (Drawing and writing will eventually become important ways of communicating.)
- Provide a toy telephone for practice at talking on the phone.
- Relax about toddler mispronunciations; they are still learning by listening and will eventually be able to enunciate words properly.
- Ask your toddler questions and be patient while waiting for a response; it takes time for a toddler to think and then express his idea in words.
- Encourage your toddler to "use words to tell me what you want" when she is frustrated.
- Be a good role model: use words to express feelings and solve problems.

Preschool Child: Two-and-a-Half to Four Years

During the preschool stage of development, your child will learn to express herself in complete sentences and will add an extensive list of words to her vocabulary. Preschoolers are enthralled with language and begin to appreciate the silliness that words and rhymes can create.

Daily Opportunities to Learn

- Take time to talk to your child each day; listen carefully as he expresses his feelings and thoughts.
- Include your child in family conversations at the dinner table, and encourage older siblings to respect his contributions to the chats.
- Have fun with language—play word games, read stories, invent stories, tell age-appropriate jokes, sing songs, invent songs together, read poems, and invent poems together.
- Provide child-safe markers, crayons, pencils, and paints, and encourage your child to express herself on paper and practice at scribbling and "writing."
- Encourage your child to use words to ask for help, express his feelings, and share his ideas.
- Find the patience to answer your child's many questions and offer explanations; this is one way of learning.
- Encourage your child to use words to solve problems when she is angry.
- Begin to teach your child how to communicate in all sorts of settings—at home, at restaurants, at church, at a concert or play, at a birthday party, and so on.
- Be a good communications role model for your child: Use language to find answers to questions, solve problems, and deal with anger and hostility in the family without hitting or hurting.

> "The baby is an excellent nonverbal communicator by eight to ten months. And, in fact, the adult's ability to read nonverbal cues has its foundation in this stage of infancy."
>
> —Dr. Stanley Greenspan, clinical professor of psychiatry and pediatrics at George Washington University School of Medicine and author of *The Growth of the Mind*, *Building Healthy Minds*, *Playground Politics*, and *The Challenging Child*

> "Of particular interest is to talk to your baby about things that the baby is interested in. If your baby goes 'oh-oh' and points up at the sky at a thing going by you'd be crazy not to say, 'There goes an airplane!' Tune into what's of interest to babies, help them name and understand their world through language."
>
> —Dr. Jean Berko Gleason, professor of psychology at Boston University and author of the college textbook *The Development of Language*

> "There is no baby too young to talk to! They are so much better at understanding language than they are at expressing it."
>
> —Dr. Jeree Pawl, clinical psychologist and director of the Infant-Parent Program, University of California San Francisco

School-Age Child: Five to Ten Years

Because school-age children are out in the world, at school, and on the playground, they will be learning how other adults and children outside your immediate family communicate.

Daily Opportunities to Learn

- Spend some time each day in a relaxed conversation with your child.
- Encourage lively, noncontroversial conversations at the dinner table, in the car, and so forth, and invite everyone's participation.
- Help your child learn to speak up about what's on his mind and in his heart in a way that is respectful to others.
- Encourage your child to use words to solve problems and express anger.
- Encourage your child to ask questions and ask for help when it is needed.
- Help your child learn how to communicate in all sorts of real-life settings—in the classroom, on the phone, at restaurants, with the elderly, or with small children.
- Read to your child or tell stories. Encourage your child to read to you.
- Provide paper, pens, markers, paints, and brushes for creative and expressive projects.
- Encourage your child to write poems, stories, and letters to friends and family.
- Expose your child to a variety of expressive music and concerts. Have conversations about what you hear and how it makes you feel.
- Be a good role model for your child: use language to find answers to questions, solve problems, and deal with anger and hostility in the family without hitting or hurting.

Preteens/Early Teens: Eleven to Fourteen Years

Preteens have a wonderful command of language. Logic and abstract thinking become parts of their communication. Debate and argument become a part of the preteen's style of communicating.

Daily Opportunities to Learn

- Be available to chat with your child each and every day.
- Initiate friendly conversations with your child; show respect for her contributions to the discussion.
- Encourage your child to express feelings (including anger and frustration) in words, not hurtful actions.
- Encourage your child to use words to solve problems, seek information, and ask questions.
- Provide your child with a dictionary, a thesaurus, and an encyclopedia, and teach him how to use these resources.
- Provide opportunities to listen to music, attend dance recitals, and experience other expressive and creative ways of communication.
- Encourage your child to write poems, stories, journals, and letters to friends and family.
- Help your child learn how to communicate in all sorts of real-life settings—in the classroom, on the phone, at restaurants, with the elderly, or with small children.
- Set limits surrounding respect when engaging in debates and discussions. Help your child learn the difference between expressing a difference of opinion and making hurtful comments.
- Encourage your child to read for pleasure; let her select magazines and books of interest.

> "More and more we have research that shows us that the development of language has implications for every aspect of our lives. Already by the age of three we can see behavioral differences in children who have been brought up in a rich language environment versus those children who have been brought up in an impoverished language environment."
>
> —Dr. Claire B. Kopp, developmental psychologist and author of *Baby Steps: The Whys of Your Child's Behavior in the First Two Years*

> "It turns out that the things parents can do to encourage language development are just so easy, low cost, and normal; narrate the world to your child, talk to him about what's happening. The child is looking back and forth and listening. That is the premier learning situation."
>
> —Dr. Elizabeth Bates, professor of psychology, professor of cognitive science, and director of the Center for Research in Language at the University of California San Diego

- Be a good role model for your child: use language to find answers to questions, solve problems, and deal with anger and hostility in the family without hitting or hurting.

Teens: Fifteen to Nineteen Years

Teenagers are still learning the rules of good communication. Because they are so interested in the acceptance of their peers, they may need to be reminded of earlier lessons of communication—using words to express feelings of anger and tenderness, and so on.

Daily Opportunities to Learn

- Spend relaxed, calm time in one-on-one conversations that value your child's thoughts, ideas, and experiences.
- Help your child learn to communicate in many of the new situations that arise: job interviews, when solving problems with teachers and friends, or at work, when dealing with customers.
- Recognize and praise your child's efforts to talk through problems rather than resorting to violence for solutions.
- Help your child gain confidence for public speaking in the classroom; be available to listen as he rehearses. (Also share your nervous moments with public speaking in which you persevered.)
- Encourage your child to find creative outlets for expression: visual arts, music, theater, debate team, writing for the school yearbook, magazine, or creative writing for personal pleasure.
- Encourage your child to read for pleasure, whether it is books, magazines, or poems that interest him.
- Set limits about showing respect when engaging in debates and discussions. Help your child learn the difference between expressing a difference of opinion and making hurtful comments.

- Help your child understand the need for words of kindness and appreciation to others.
- Be a good role model for your child: use language to find answers to questions, solve problems, and deal with anger and hostility in the family without hitting or hurting.

"I think we can do a lot to expose children to literacy by reading to them and talking with them and having lots of wonderful conversations without pressuring children to actually learn to read at very young ages."

—Toni Bickart, coauthor of *Preschool for Parents* and *What Every Parent Needs to Know about 1st, 2nd and 3rd Grades*

• • • • • • • • • • •

chapter sixteen

Independence

The little toddler with wispy red hair tugged on her sweater and resisted as her mother tried unsuccessfully to get her tiny arm inside the sleeve. The little girl's face became crimson, her small fists tightened, and she let out a shriek that surely the downstairs neighbors could hear. This was followed by the defiant words that are branded into every seasoned parent's memory: "No! Me do!"

These defiant words are not the first signs of independence, but perhaps have the distinction of being the first show of independence articulated in words that every grown-up understands. This sometimes rocky, sometimes prideful desire of children to learn to do for themselves continues throughout all the years of childhood and adolescence. While the individual moments and efforts might ruffle a parent's patience, they mark the beginning of a wonderful process of growth.

From an early age, a child's search for independence is fueled by several powerful motivators:

1. A desire to make things happen in their world
2. A longing to feel competent and capable
3. A need for individual expression and choice

Parents' Role in Child's Independence

Think of yourself as the "supervisor of independence" for your growing child. Your tools of the trade are endless doses of love and support, encouraging exploration and curiosity, teaching skills, allowing kids to make age-appropriate choices, and sometimes standing by with a safety net to catch your child as she falters. Over the span of your child's growing years, this job requires the same basic job description for you with a different delivery contingent upon your child's age.

Job Description for "Supervisor of Independence"

1. Provide age-appropriate opportunities for your child to try to do for himself. (Learn the basics of the stages of child development so that you know what is age appropriate for your individual child.)

2. Allow your child to experience small doses of frustration as she tries to do for herself; step in to prevent overwhelming frustration.

3. Encourage your child to explore and be curious.

4. Teach your child life skills (major and minor) along the way so he understands how to accomplish tasks on his own.

5. Recognize your child's efforts and successes along the way and encourage your child to recognize her own efforts and take pride in her progress.

6. Expect mistakes along the way and provide an emotional safety net for your child.

Make Things Happen

The desire to make things happen is a wonderful motivator for children of all ages. This noble desire makes itself known even in the earliest months of life.

When an eight-week-old baby grabs a rattle and shakes it, she may not realize that sound was caused by her own effort. But it won't take long for her to make this connection and purposefully move to make these rhythmic sounds. The absolute determination and delight expressed in the face of this baby speaks volumes to an observant parent about children's inherent drive to make things happen.

> "As early as children can begin to talk, parents can start to encourage independent decision making, and do this in a slow, careful process."
>
> —Dr. John Clabby, psychologist and coauthor (with Maurice J. Elias) of *Teach Your Child Decision Making*

Sometimes this desire to "make things happen" takes babies, children, and teens down a rocky road that requires parents to set clear limits. When a nine-month-old finishes her food, takes the bowl of pureed squash, and hurls it across the floor, many fascinating things happen. First, that bowl makes a loud and impressive bang on the floor. Next, Mom rushes over and engages in animated conversation intended just for the baby. (This may appear to an observer to be rather angry attention, but from the baby's perspective, Mom came running!) And if baby is really lucky, the furry family dog might race to the point of intersection and dance around the bowl, tail wagging, lapping up the spilled contents. All this makes for a wild assortment of sights, sounds, and activity. This is an impressive list of reactions from one simple effort on the part of the baby. You can see how intoxicating it is for a child to begin to make things happen. As parents, we are called upon time and time again to channel this desire into constructive and positive examples of independence and to set clear limits surrounding misbehavior.

Feelings of Competence

All children want to feel capable and competent. Your child formulates his opinion about his competence to a large extent based upon your response to him (and that of other significant care providers). When your three-year-old is building with his wooden blocks or coloring on paper and he repeatedly

> "If you want your child to be the kind of person who's going to stand up for what she believes in and not be pushed around by other people, you're going to have to expect that a little bit of that is going to be exercised at home! You can't have it both ways. You can't raise a child who's going to be independent and open-minded outside the house, but obedient and conforming inside the house. It's just not going to work that way!"
>
> —Dr. Laurence Steinberg, professor of psychology at Temple University and coauthor (with Ann Levine) of *You and Your Adolescent*

"I Can Do It Myself, Thank You!"

Self-Care Tasks Your Child Can Accomplish (to Encourage Independence)

Self-Reliance Skill	Typical Age of Mastery
Drinking from a cup	8 to 12 months
Feeding self	8 to 14 months
Putting on jackets or sweaters	2 to 3 years
Putting on socks and slip-on shoes	2 to 3 years
Putting on socks and tying shoes	4 to 6 years
Brushing teeth	2 to 3 years
Washing hands	2 to 3 years
Brushing or combing hair	4 to 6 years
Putting away clothes	5 to 7 years
Selecting clothes for next day	6 to 8 years
Dressing oneself from head to toe	5 to 6 years
Showering or bathing	6 to 7 years
Washing hair	7 to 8 years
Drying hair	12 to 14 years
Clothes shopping	10 to 14 years
Family chores	4 to 6 years
Setting the table	5 years
Folding clean laundry	5 to 7 years
Polishing furniture	8 to 10 years
Washing and drying laundry	11 to 13 years
Watering plants	7 to 10 years
Sweeping with vacuum cleaner	8 to 12 years
Mopping the floor	12 to 14 years
Putting away groceries	10 to 13 years
Washing the car	12 to 14 years
Using the microwave for heating foods	11 to 14 years

continued

"I Can Do It Myself, Thank You!" (continued)

Cooking with stove top and oven	12 to 14 years
Raking leaves	8 to 10 years
Weeding flower beds and garden	7 to 9 years
Mowing the lawn	12 to 14 years
Grocery shopping alone	15 to 17 years

exclaims, "Look, Mommy!" or, "Look at what I made, Daddy!" he is looking for your recognition and approval of his creation. This interchange of his accomplishment and your recognition plays itself out in small moments of your daily routine throughout all of childhood. You are a mirror that reflects back to your child an image of competence and capability.

One of the tricky things for parents to remember is that as children mature, they drastically change their ways of communicating but still have many of the same emotional needs. Preteens and teenagers, for example, will no longer run into the living room where you are reading the newspaper and clamor, "Look what I made!" Yet these older kids still have a great need for your attention and recognition. The burden to remember this need for recognition and its tie to your child's feelings of competency falls almost exclusively to you when your child becomes a preteen or teen. The responsibility also falls to you to continue to provide everyday opportunities for your child to fulfill these needs.

Children pick up on your attitudes and often adopt them. Your enthusiasm for your child's exploration, curiosity, and learning sends an important message that these activities are valued by you. These are the ways a child first experiments with independence.

Independence not only requires the will to do for oneself, but the ability. How do I make myself a grilled cheese sandwich when Dad isn't here? How do I use the microwave, the sweeper, the dishwasher? How do I wash my favorite jeans to wear to the dance this Friday? If you pay

> "Children will always want to come back to you if you have let them freely go. If you hang on, they will become resentful and hostile, and you will be left alone at the end with empty hands....Good parenting is biodegradable; you work yourself out of a job!"
>
> —Fredelle Maynard, author of *Raisins and Almonds*

close attention to your child, you will know when she is capable of trying a new task at home. Young children absorb and observe parts of these practical tasks by watching you. They can also help you while you work. They can fold laundry, wash the lettuce while you cut vegetables, help load the dishwasher, and find the sewing kit or button box. These are preliminary steps in acquiring the skills necessary to doing more for oneself.

Every teen, for example, must have opportunities to learn to cook, wash dishes, iron clothes, sew a missing button on a shirt, back the car out of the driveway, and manage money. Many of these tasks require practice with tools, machinery, and equipment. You can also count on some minor mishaps along the way: white boxer shorts turned purple by the red and blue clothes thrown in the washer, or a kitchen consumed by soap suds on the floor when the wrong dish detergent was generously squirted in the automatic dishwasher.

Expression of Individual Choice

> "Children do need to have a sense of where the boundaries for behavior are, but within those boundaries they need to be given as much freedom and autonomy as possible, and along with that respect as individuals."
>
> —Teresa Amabile, professor of business administration at Harvard University and author of *Growing up Creative*

A child's need for independence also grows out of the desire for individual choice and expression. Teenagers give parents a classic glimpse into this process with their choices about the way they dress and the music they listen to. These are broad efforts on the part of teens to set themselves apart from their parents. But long before your teenager chooses to wear tattered blue jeans as a personal statement, he is capable of many small choices that help develop his independence.

Respect your two-year-old's individual preferences by giving her the choice between wearing the red sweater or the yellow one before going outside on a brisk day. Let your school-age child decide which days she would like to do her household chores—Monday and Wednesday or Tuesday and Thursday. Every child over the age of two not only needs to feel in control of small aspects of her life, but actually learns a great deal through the trial and error of making these small choices. These are all steps toward independence and self-expression.

> "It's critical to give them choices. It's the way we help them recognize that they do have some control over their world."
>
> —Dr. Dorothy June Sciarra, professor emerita of early childhood education at the University of Cincinnati

Everyday Opportunities for Independence
Infant: Birth to Twelve Months

The little steps toward independence that take place in the first twelve months of life happen quite naturally. During this stage in your baby's life, she will learn to lift up her head, roll over, sit up, scoot, crawl, and later learn to walk. All of these efforts on the part of your baby will happen on her own time frame. They are all significant milestones as she moves toward independence. Your baby needs your love, affection, and nurturing in order to feel secure and confident to attempt these important developmental milestones that launch her on her way toward independence.

Daily Opportunities to Learn

- Provide safe, age-appropriate toys that allow your baby a chance to make things happen—safe rattles, bells, busy box, toys that roll, squeak, and scoot.
- Set the stage from the beginning with an attitude that values exploration, curiosity, and play.
- Respond with genuine enthusiasm to your baby's efforts to learn and do for herself, such as grabbing a toy, rolling over, sitting up alone, crawling, and walking. These are wonderful accomplishments that deserve recognition.
- During the second half of this year, when you see that your baby is capable of feeding herself, let her occasionally enjoy the excitement and freedom of

> "The best parent is the one who prepares a child to operate successfully without the parent."
>
> —Richard Eyre, coauthor (with Linda Eyre) of *Teaching Your Children Values* and *Three Steps to a Strong Family*

feeding herself with baby-safe foods and utensils. Put a vinyl tablecloth under her high-chair for easy cleanup, and stay close at hand to assist as needed.

- Provide a secure, baby-proof environment that allows your child's exploration.

Toddler: Twelve Months to Two-and-a-Half Years

Toddlers are curious and daring, and they alternate between clinging to you and demanding independence. They also have little or no judgment concerning their safety, so you must provide a safe environment in which your toddler can explore and experiment under close supervision.

Daily Opportunities to Learn

- Provide safe, toddler-tested toys that allow your child to make things happen—toys that roll, scoot, push and pop; safe pots and pans and plastic cups. Let your child direct her own playing.
- Project an enthusiastic attitude that values learning and doing.
- Encourage your toddler to do for himself each day, selecting tasks that are appropriate to his age and coordination, such as putting on socks, shoes, and hats, and feeding himself. (Designate a low kitchen cupboard with toddler access for containing plastic bowl, cups, and utensils just for your toddler's use to encourage his independence.)
- Encourage your older toddler to do for others by helping with small daily chores: placing napkins at the dinner table and placing wooden or plastic salad bowls and plastic cups at each place setting.
- Give your child small choices each day as a way to exercise a small measure of control over her daily life. These choices might include which healthy snack to eat (apples or bananas), which jacket to wear (blue or white), which story to read, song to sing, cassette tape to play, and so on. At the same time, set

clear and firm rules surrounding all issues of safety and acceptable behavior.

- Take time to recognize each small effort and any progress made.

Preschool Child: Two-and-Half to Four Years

Preschool children are curious and active and have developed a sophisticated command of language. Your child is now capable of expressing many thoughts, feelings, and desires with her words and is ready to take some bigger steps toward independence. (Close adult supervision is still required!)

> "The stress between encouraging them to become attached to us and encouraging them to become really independent, right from the beginning, is a terrible dilemma."
>
> —Dr. Sophie Freud, professor emerita at Simmons College, Boston, and author of *My Three Mothers and Other Passions*

Daily Opportunities to Learn

- Encourage your child to "make things happen" through creative play and exploration. Have an assortment of materials on hand for your child's creative experimentation: nontoxic paints, paper, markers, fabric, Play-Doh, and safe musical instruments; let him direct his own playing.
- Encourage your preschool child to do for herself on a daily basis. Self-care tasks might include washing up at the sink, brushing her teeth, dressing herself, combing her hair, folding and putting clothes away, and putting toys away. (Set up your home in a way that makes doing these tasks possible for a small child.)
- Establish family chores that are appropriate for your preschooler so that he continues to do for others: setting the table, washing fruits and vegetables, filling the bread basket, folding towels, putting away toys and clothes and tidying his room, or using child-size rakes to assist with outdoor cleanup.
- Provide your child with choices each and every day: which healthy cereals to buy at the grocery store, which favorite animals to see first at the zoo, which games to play, books to read, and music to play.

- Engage your preschooler in playful conversations that allow her to fine-tune her thinking and decision-making skills.
- Show your genuine enthusiasm and recognition of the many small accomplishments your child makes each week.

<u>School-Age Child</u>: Five to Ten Years

Once your child goes off to school, he has taken a bold step forward toward more independence. During these early school years, he will make choices and decisions about his daily life regarding friends and play, school projects, and sports. This stage offers many opportunities to learn practical skills that facilitate more independence.

Daily Opportunities to Learn

- Encourage your child to do more for himself: showering, shampooing, brushing teeth, combing hair, getting his own cereal, packing a lunch, and picking up after himself each day. Use gentle reminders to help keep him on track with these many daily tasks.
- Provide your child with a weekly allowance to begin experimenting with spending and saving. Allow your child discretion for spending all or part of this money as a way to learn financial decision-making skills. (Also establish a savings account for your child to build upon.)
- Expand the list of family chores for your child: clean room and change sheets each week; assist with meal preparation, make tossed salads, fruit salad, sandwiches, learn beginning microwave cooking skills; wash the car; clean the basement; water plants.
- Honor your child's choices whenever possible, yet continue to establish and maintain firm rules and set limits about important issues.

- Allow your child to select one "late night" each week in which his bedtime is delayed by thirty minutes. (This thirty minutes won't significantly deprive your child of sleep, but will give a sense of personal choice.)
- Encourage your child to do her own homework; your role is that of "educational consultant."

Preteens/Early Teens: Eleven to Fourteen Years

Your preteen is capable of abstract thinking, questioning, and problem solving. She is also skilled in many matters of daily living and keenly interested in or quite observant of peers. This is a wonderful age to engage in thought-provoking conversations and allow for opportunities to fine-tune decision-making skills.

Daily Opportunities to Learn

- School and peer relationships provide tremendous daily challenges leading toward independence. Honor your child's choices about when to do homework—after school or after dinner; her preference in clothing, and weekend activities; and how she spends her allowance. Continue to set firm rules about all matters related to your child's safety and health.
- Encourage your child's interest in summertime jobs such as babysitting, yard work, or pet care as opportunities to gain skills and responsibility (you must provide general supervision).
- Teach your daughters and sons practical life skills: simple sewing, basic cooking, doing the laundry, washing dishes, or ironing.
- Encourage your child to do her own homework. You serve as "educational consultant"—assist by suggesting organizational skills and planning systems (all children this age need a daily planning book to remember homework, meetings, etc.).
- Help your child learn to reduce complex projects into smaller, more manageable steps.
- Recognize your child's many accomplishments and efforts.

<u>Teens</u>: Fifteen to Nineteen Years

These are the years that parents sometimes associate with independence. In fact, your child has been training for independence since early childhood. This stage of development is critical for fine-tuning decision-making skills, being responsible, and practicing necessary living skills.

Daily Opportunities to Learn

- Encourage your teen to spend time alone, with pen and paper in hand, before making a significant decision. Ask him to write down the pros and cons of the anticipated decision so that he can see the possible repercussions from making it.
- Allow your teen choices about hairstyle, dress, friends, sports, and music within reason. Continue to set and enforce rules surrounding important health, safety, and well-being issues.
- Encourage your teen to help with family chores that allow for more practice at life skills: compiling a grocery list and doing the grocery shopping, doing laundry, cooking (especially teen-friendly meals: tacos, homemade healthy pizza, or pasta).
- Encourage your child to find a summertime job in her area of interest: sports or music camp counselor, landscaping, child care, veterinary assistance, cooking, retail, or fashion.
- Encourage your teen to establish and use his own checking account.
- Stay involved in your child's life. Spend time alone with your teen and provide the confidence, support, and love she needs for spreading her wings.

● ● ● ● ● ● ● ● ● ● ●

chapter seventeen

Responsibility

Fourteen-year-old David dearly wanted to get a puppy, but he knew his divorced mother had little time to care for puppies. For three months, he rode his bicycle past the animal shelter in his neighborhood to look at the dogs. For three months, he begged his mother to let him get a puppy. He promised that he would "care for and feed the dog each day—from now until forever." He borrowed a book on puppy care and training from the library and read the book from cover to cover. He made a chart of all the chores required in caring for the puppy during the first year, and put his initial after each chore to show that he would be responsible. His mother came to believe he would be responsible for the dog, and just last Saturday, they went to pick out their new puppy.

Responsibility is a grown-up concept that blends reliability and accountability. Responsibility is an essential ingredient in independence. True responsibility also requires commitment and good judgment. Children develop these skills very gradually over the course of childhood.

When your child becomes an adult, she must be responsible for herself and accountable for her actions. She must be responsible for her work, to her

Parents' Role in Teaching Responsibility

You are your child's "partner in responsibility." You must help guide your child through the daily opportunities that encourage responsibilities throughout the many years of childhood.

Job Description for "Partner in Responsibility"

1. Be a good role model. Tackle your family and work responsibilities with a positive attitude; take time to rest and relax so you are recharged to do your job each day.

2. Assign your child age-appropriate tasks that involve caring for herself and helping with family chores.

3. Help your child understand the connection between responsibility and privilege; give appropriate additional privileges as your child acquires and maintains additional responsibilities. When he is blatantly irresponsible, withhold corresponding privileges.

4. Expect mistakes along the way. Help your child dust herself off and try again.

5. Give your child recognition for jobs well done and responsibilities maintained.

> "I think that if there's one place that modern living has fallen short in the family, it's that we really don't put a high enough priority on having our children develop a sense of responsibility."
>
> —Dr. William Damon, developmental psychologist and author of *The Moral Child*

friends, to her community, and to her family. She must learn to understand that how she behaves and what she does has an impact on each of these groups and individuals; sometimes in small ways, sometimes in larger ways. Your goal is to raise a child who, as a young adult, is capable of being responsible, with spirit, honor, and commitment. Put in this way, this task seems huge, but like so many other essential lessons of childhood, it is learned in such small steps along the way that its development is hardly perceptible.

How Do Children Learn to Be Responsible?

Children learn to be responsible by

1. Observing responsible adults
2. Having specific tasks assigned to them
3. Doing, with trial and error being their greatest teacher

Your child's willingness to become responsible will be shaped in part by your expectations and in part by his good intentions.

One of the fundamental principles of responsibility is this: each of us is ultimately responsible for our actions and our behavior. Of course, circumstances and the actions of others help create some of the options we each have in life, but we choose how to behave, how to act, and how to react with free will. Responsible adults realize that there are consequences for their actions—sometimes good, other times difficult. Learning this cause-and-effect relationship goes a long way toward helping your child understand personal responsibility.

> "In general, if our kids seem to be heading on the road toward responsible behavior, to self-control—not doing things because they're afraid they'll get caught, they're doing things because they know it's the right thing to do—I think then we can feel like we've set them right on the path to success in life."
>
> —Dr. Marilyn Gootman, professor of early childhood education at the University of Georgia and author of *The Loving Parents' Guide to Discipline*

Babies and toddlers are so busy learning to use their bodies, learning to talk, and learning how things work in the world that they don't have the capacity to learn responsibility. They are in fact dependent upon you to care for their needs. But they are watching and listening to you intently. They see how you behave and what you do for yourself and for others. They take notice of the way you can make things happen. They see that you are busy doing for yourself and doing for others every day of your life. A seed is planted in their minds by these early observations.

Preschoolers are enthralled with the world. They can interact through language and do a great deal for themselves. They live an exciting and active life. They also take notice of what you do each day of your life, and they imitate your actions. As you mix up the pancake batter for the Sunday-morning pancakes, they pretend to make pancakes nearby. As you gather up your briefcase to go off to work in the morning, they pack their "work" in the old tattered suitcase and pretend to go

> "Everybody needs to go to bed at night knowing that the family and the world functioned better that day because they were in it. They need to be needed."
>
> —Marguerite Kelly, syndicated columnist and author of *Mother's Almanac* and *Marguerite Kelly's Family Almanac*

off to the office. In broad strokes, they imitate the actions you take and responsibilities you assume to care for your family.

School-age children begin to do more for themselves: they brush their teeth, bathe or shower, comb their hair, and pick out their clothes. They begin to help others too: they feed the cat, help their younger brother put his sweater on, and set the table at dinnertime. They also begin to take responsibility for their schoolwork and homework and try to follow the rules on the playground.

Preteens juggle their schoolwork, family chores, and sports activities. They set their alarm clocks each evening and wake themselves up in the morning, shower, and get off to school on time. They mow the lawn each week in the summer. They baby-sit, sell Girl Scout cookies, gather signatures to change school policy, and raise money for the American Heart Association.

Teenagers baby-sit, manage schoolwork and homework, help younger brothers with math problems, help with family chores, participate in the spring cleanup in the neighborhood, and raise money for a needed medical procedure for an ailing teacher.

All of these efforts to take responsibility are important to your child. She is learning that she can contribute and also that there are consequences to her actions. As she makes contributions for her own care and that of others, she feels a budding sense of competence. She begins to see that her community and the world function through shared effort and responsibility.

Some children learn these lessons more easily than others. Some personalities take naturally to helping others, for example. Some kids need more prompting to be generous with their time. Some children understand the concept of personal accountability; others want to find external blame for every mishap. All children, however, can learn to be responsible with the gentle guiding hand of their parents.

The Relationship between Responsibility and Privilege

There is an important connection between responsibility and privilege that most kids understand. Articulating this connection to your child is beneficial in your efforts to encourage your child to be responsible. The overall concept is this: you earn privileges in life by living up to responsibilities. If you say to your fifteen-year-old daughter, "When you start driving the car next year, you will have to buy your own gas and wash the car once each week in exchange for the privilege of sharing the family car with me," she will understand the connection between earning a new privilege and acquiring a new responsibility. Your eight-year-old son will understand that if he wants to have his three friends spend the night on Friday, he will have to straighten up his room to make a place for four sleeping bags on the floor.

In both of these examples, your child is personally reaping a benefit or privilege so it's easy for him to see the connection between privilege and responsibility. Other responsibilities such as setting the table at dinnertime, washing and folding the laundry, or doing the dishes, don't reap an instant privilege but instead contribute to the overall good of the family. These are responsibilities that go along with being a member of the family, and all family members must pitch in to make the family work.

Most children also grasp this rule: the older you are, the more privileges you get (like staying up later at night) and the more responsibilities you have (because you are more capable). These rules are quite simple, but they work. While every child and every family is unique, it's comforting to have some general operating principles. These rules about responsibility provide a simple, easy way to establish a framework on how the family system works.

The Balance of Responsibility

Children are capable of only so much responsibility during each stage of development. If you ask your child to take on a responsibility long before she is capable,

> "One family gave their child a nickel every time he took the trash out. When he took it out without being reminded, then he was given ten cents!"
>
> —Elizabeth Crary, parent educator and author of *Kids Can Cooperate*

the results will be discouraging to you and your child. Parents must have a sense of what their child is capable of as she grows. These capabilities depend in part upon the individual child's personality and maturity. You may have one son who was competent and reliable enough to baby-sit a preschool child by the time he was twelve years old. Your other son may not be mature enough for baby-sitting responsibilities until he is fifteen years old. You must take your cues from your child.

Older children run the danger of taking on too many responsibilities. We all know as adults that our lives feel most balanced when we have a mix of responsibility and relaxation. But adolescents and teens may overload themselves with part-time jobs, a full social life, and school and homework demands. Or perhaps they cut corners on their schedules by getting only six hours of sleep and end up cranky much of the day. Help your older child keep the right balance between responsibility and rest.

Everyday Opportunities to Learn Responsibility

Infant and Toddler: Birth to Two-and-a-Half Years

Infants and toddlers are learning so many important things: how to roll over, grasp objects, sit up, crawl, walk, and talk, to name just a few. They are busy learning to master use of their bodies, how the world works, and how to communicate their needs.

Although toddlers do take notice of their parents' routine and may begin to imitate what their parents do at home, they are not ready to notice the signs of parental responsibility.

There will be plenty of time in later years for your child to practice becoming responsible gradually. For now, provide your baby and toddler with a safe, nurturing world, care for his needs, and provide him with opportunities to learn and grow.

Preschool Child: Two-and-a-Half to Four Years

Your preschool child is very interested in watching and imitating what you do each day. She will observe you in action carrying out your responsibilities, but she is just beginning to be capable of practicing tiny steps toward responsibility, primarily through learning to do for herself in small ways.

Daily Opportunities to Learn

- Encourage your child to do small tasks for himself—put on his shoes and coat, put away toys, clean up art materials, and so on.
- Give your child small daily chores to help the family—placing napkins at the dinner table or retrieving plastic cups from a low-lying kitchen cupboard to set the table, for example.
- Talk to your child in short, simple sentences about how a family works, with everyone helping out in some way.
- Begin to talk simply and briefly about friendships and the responsibility of caring for and about friends.
- Encourage your child to help with the family pet in small ways—brushing the dog once a week, for example.
- Give your child pats on the back for his efforts to help with his daily care and to contribute help to the family.

School-Age Child: Five to Ten Years

This stage of childhood offers a window of opportunity for teaching your child lessons about responsibility to oneself and others in small everyday experiences. School-age children are still very interested in their parents' thoughts, comments, and acceptance, and they have become competent at many skills and tasks.

Daily Opportunities to Learn

- Establish a manageable list of family chores that your child is responsible for each week.
- Encourage your child to do for herself as part of her daily routine—shower, sort and select school clothes, pack school lunches, and so forth.
- Help your child develop organizational skills: make sure he uses his daily calendar for homework assignments, and puts

finished homework in a homework folder that is always in its proper place. These organizational skills will help your child meet his daily school responsibilities.

- Encourage your child to be responsible with money; give her a small allowance and the freedom to manage it.
- As everyday situations arise; help your child see the relationship between actions and consequences, both positive and negative.
- Encourage your child to participate in annual projects that help the neighborhood or community.
- Firmly establish the rule that your child has a responsibility to notify you of his whereabouts when visiting friends, staying after school, playing in the neighborhood, and so on.
- Read stories and articles to your child that focus on individuals in the sports world or community who contribute time and effort to help others. Explore the environment and talk about our joint responsibility to protect it.
- Expect mistakes along the way; provide ways to try again.

Preteens/Early Teens: Eleven to Fourteen Years

While preteens are interested in exercising more independence and individual choice, they understand the concept that extra privileges mean extra responsibility.

Daily Opportunities to Learn

- Establish a list of family chores that your child is responsible for; for variety, rotate the chores among family members.
- Expect your child to do for himself as part of his daily routine: shower, sort and select school clothes, pack school lunches, and so on.
- Help your child make a realistic assessment of how many sports and extracurricular activities her schedule will manage.
- Encourage your child to manage his homework assignments effectively; tie privileges to completion of his responsibilities.

- Set firm rules concerning curfew; insist that your child notify you of her whereabouts at all times. Let your child know that this is an ongoing and important responsibility.
- If your child shows interest and maturity, help him establish summertime work projects: providing baby-sitting or pet care for neighbors, mowing grass, and cleaning flower beds.
- Encourage your child to participate in events that show neighborhood or environmental pride and community responsibility.
- Provide your child with a small allowance and the freedom to manage this money.
- Give your child recognition for each effort to be responsible.
- Be a good role model: fulfill your responsibilities to your family and work—and take good care of yourself!

<u>Teens</u>: Fifteen to Nineteen Years

Teenagers are still children in the process of learning to be responsible. They especially learn through trial and error. Look for opportunities for your child to learn from her mistakes rather than simply suffer punishment.

Daily Opportunities to Learn

- Expect your child to contribute time and energy to family chores.
- Put a high priority on the responsibility to obey family curfews and rules regarding parties and insist that your child let you know his whereabouts at all times.
- Help your child get organized to tackle large responsibilities—part-time jobs, comprehensive school projects, college admission tests, and so forth.
- Combine every new privilege with a corresponding new responsibility.
- Encourage your child to participate in projects that protect the environment and help children, the elderly, and disadvantaged families.

- Be available to listen and talk with your child every day; help your child think through possible consequences for decisions and actions he is considering.
- Give your child praise and recognition for all his progress in learning to be responsible.
- Encourage your child to manage a portion of her finances, and include a long-range plan for saving.
- Encourage your child to participate in career mentor programs for a bird's-eye view of the responsibilities for various professions.
- Be a good role model: meet your family and work responsibilities—and take good care of yourself!

• • • • • • • • • • •

chapter eighteen

Competition

Five-year-olds Matt and Steven had a laundry basket filled with wooden blocks. Each boy began to build a tower with the blocks. Steven glanced at Matt's tower and said, "My tower is taller than yours." Matt quickly began to add to his tower. "Now mine is taller than yours!" he said. Steven grabbed three blocks and stacked them hurriedly, one on top of the next. The tower suddenly swayed and fell apart with a great clatter, in reaction to which Steven proclaimed, "Well, my tower is the loudest tower ever!"

Children have a natural tendency to compete. They compete with their brothers, sisters, and peers. The first outward signs of competition may begin to creep into your child's behavior between ages three and five. These early episodes of competition, of "me, me, me" and "mine is better, taller, bigger, louder than yours," can be disconcerting. But that competitive instinct is entirely normal, and in time it can be tempered by compassion, cooperation, and empathy.

For very young (preschool) children, competition may first show itself during "pretend" play. Your child may spend considerable time pretending to be a hero or heroine who is competing against (and overpowering) other superheroes. For a school-age child or teen, competition may play itself out in sporting events or academic or musical contests.

Sibling Rivalry

For siblings of all ages, all around the world, competition and jealousy are a fact of family life. This competition between siblings is a natural and, in some cases, a lifelong yearning to be the best loved and most praised and to win the most attention. Sibling rivalry can indeed get out of hand, but if understood by parents it can be appropriately managed and minimized.

A good place to start is to try to understand the feelings and needs behind rivalry. Each child in your family needs to feel your love, commitment, and appreciation. The intense emotional bond between par-

Parents' Role in Shaping Competition

You are your child's "coach of competition." Your first task is to take a quiet moment and think about your attitudes toward winning and losing. You may discover attitudes that need fine-tuning.

Job Description for "Coach of Competition"

1. Help your child develop an attitude of fair play.
2. Encourage your child to "compete against herself" for personal improvements.
3. Attend as many of your child's competitive events as possible and adopt an encouraging, positive attitude.
4. Shop carefully to find good coaches and mentors who teach attitudes of personal best, fair play, and learning skills.
5. Listen attentively when your child is disappointed about losing, then later encourage your child to dust himself off and try again.
6. Value your child for the total of who she is on a daily basis; let her know her self-worth is not contingent upon winning or losing a competition.

ent and child creates the emotional foundation of security and acceptance necessary for your child to thrive. When there are several children in your family, they can find it difficult to accept that they must share your love and devotion with the other children. They are too young to understand their own uneasy feelings and would be unable to articulate them—for example, "Gee, Mom, I'm having a hard time with this feeling that you might love my brother Teddy more than you love me. Can we talk about it?" Even grown-up brothers and sisters who are emotionally mature might have a hard time putting these feelings into words. More likely, your child will act out these feelings of insecurity and competition.

> "Part of our desire to improve the world, to cure illnesses and build big houses, to build new roads and develop new inventions is fueled by that assertive, competitive mastery side of ourselves of which aggression is a component."
>
> —Dr. Stanley Greenspan, clinical professor of psychiatry and pediatrics at George Washington University School of Medicine and author of *The Growth of the Mind, Building Healthy Minds, Playground Politics,* and *The Challenging Child*

For instance, your three-year-old may kick his five-year-old sister and feel a certain satisfaction when you come running. Perhaps your eight-year-old daughter sneaks into her little brother's room and scribbles all over the drawing that generated so much praise and excitement from Mom and Dad moments before. These are both examples of clumsy attempts to gain much-needed reassurance and attention from the most important people in the life of your child—you, the parents.

Your teenager will compete for attention in the family in a more sophisticated way. Your fifteen-year-old daughter may delight in "ratting" on her brother, who had detention after school today. She'll take special delight in seeing your reaction to this news and the loss of privileges that were imposed upon your son at home. And most likely, your son will be looking for an opportunity to pay back his sister by tattling the next time she uses poor judgment at school or at home. Recognizing what's really going on will not make sibling rivalry magically go away, but it will help you develop a plan of action to manage it.

The first rule is to spend one-on-one time regularly with each child. This might mean reading a twenty-minute bedtime story to a younger child or taking out an older child every week for ice cream, lunch,

> "Once the rules are established between you and your child in a game, it's important to stick to them because that is part of setting limits. Even if it means that the kid is going to be disappointed because he comes out on the short end of the stick. The child has to learn to lose well as well as how to win."
>
> —Dr. William Damon, developmental psychologist and author of *The Moral Child*

dinner, a movie, or a baseball game. This investment of individual time is deeply reassuring to your child.

You must try never to compare one child to another in your family. You may think you are encouraging your child to shape up or try harder when you say things such as, "I wish you could be more like your sister; she's the responsible one in the family," or, "Your brother gets all *As* each term at school, and you barely squeak by with Cs. Why can't you be more like him?" but your words will have the opposite effect.

Recognize that siblings learn to negotiate and work out differences through trial and error. Make firm rules that no one in the family may

Making Sports a Positive Learning Experience for Young Children

Sports offer a great context in which school-age children can learn positive lessons about competition, good sportsmanship, team effort, setting goals, making improvements, and winning and losing. Here are some basic guidelines to follow when young children are involved in organized sports:

- Each child should be given equal time of play; the best way to improve is through playing time and practical experience.
- Children should play various positions to gain the most experience and develop a variety of skills.
- Make certain the coaches and parents promote and model skills and improvement rather than beating the opponent.
- Parents must remain involved and supportive, attend their child's weekly games, and be available to listen.
- Select a coach that lives by these same rules for young children to make sports experiences a boost to self-esteem.

Competition Can Be a Positive Force in Your Child's Life

Competition can:

- Help shape your child's personal aspirations
- Help your child set goals and work toward them
- Provide a context in which your child learns important lessons about winning and losing and perseverance
- Provide an opportunity to see realistically that others may be better at certain tasks, without undermining your child's sense of self-worth

hurt or hit another family member (including siblings). Set clear limits to enforce this rule. When children break the rule, separate them, giving each child a time-out to cool off. If necessary, when the time-out is over, send the children off to play alone to ensure a longer cooling-off time. Try not to play judge for each minor episode of sibling squabbling by asking, "Who started the fight?" This is an open invitation to intensify the squabbling, with each child telling on the other in an effort to win the fight.

Also, be sure to take note quietly of your children cooperating and getting along. Let them know that you appreciate their efforts to play well together and to help each other out.

The Positive Value of Competition

Recognize that through competition, children learn about themselves in relation to others around them: what can I achieve? What can you achieve? How do I compare? From these humble beginnings, parents can help expand these questions to include: how can I improve? What goals can I set for myself? What little steps can I take to achieve my big goals

"I go down to soccer fields sometimes when I'm in a school area, and I see the kids playing soccer. And the parents seem to be much more involved on the outskirts of the field, playing through the kids, and it's rather disturbing to me."

—Dr. Thomas Armstrong, learning specialist, psychologist, and author of *The Myth of the A.D.D. Child* and *In Their Own Way: Encouraging Your Child's Personal Learning Style*

> "I've developed a technique that I call positive charting. If I'm coaching a baseball game or basketball game, I have a clipboard with a blank piece of paper, and on it I put each of the names of the kids with some space by each name. Whenever one of my players does something positive, something correct, something that helps the team in the game, I make a note of it. I write just enough so I will remember what it was they did. So at the end of the game, I've got this list of three or four things that each kid has done positively with regard to what their capabilities are. At the next practice, we have a team meeting, and I go over person by person...this is what Billy did, this is what Sara did...and you can imagine the emotional energy level of that team when we are ready to practice."
>
> —Jim Thompson, author of *Positive Coaching: Building Character and Self-Esteem through Sports*

and dreams? With a little planning and a lot of careful guidance, you can help your child use competition as a springboard for personal growth and development.

Personal Surge of Energy

Competitive events can also be where your child first experiences that sensation of her physical and mental capabilities kicking into high gear. When your eleven-year-old participates in the annual school relay races, her excitement builds as she awaits her turn to race. Once she takes off across the starting line, she will experience that surge of physical and mental energy and determination that is deep within us all. This untapped energy is something that she will be able to call upon time and time again. When your sixteen-year-old son competes in the regional Latin competition, that same burst of energy allows him to excel under pressure. Becoming comfortable with this powerful mixture of anxiety, excitement, and adrenaline will serve your child well throughout her life.

Competition as a Backdrop for Personal Excellence

The idea of "competing against oneself" is important to keep in mind as you guide your child through competitive events and activities. Although he may be competing against others, his focus can still be on his own improvement and growth.

When your seven-year-old daughter joins the soccer team, she has a context in which to run, kick, and play with her teammates. You can help shape this scenario into an opportunity for your child's personal

Give Your Child a "Progress Report Card" for Sports

In an effort to help your child stay focused on personal improvement and personal best, issue a "Progress Report Card" for your child during each sports season. Remember to accentuate the positive and help your child see the progress he has made along the way. Here are some of the many skills that you might wish to evaluate in your child's "Progress Report Card for Sports":

Livy's Progress in Soccer

Team: Panthers   Player: Livy   Age: 12

Enthusiasm

Effort

Good sportsmanship

Fair play

Teamwork

Individual Skills:

    Passing

    Running

    Attempts on goal

    Maintaining position

    Endurance

    Confidence

Greatest improvements this season

For Livy to complete:

Player comments about this season:

What did you learn or improve on this season?

What would you like to work on next season?

> "I typically say a winner is not the person who has the most points at the end of the game. A winner is somebody who gets back up after they've been knocked down."
>
> —Jim Thompson, author of *Positive Coaching: Building Character and Self-Esteem through Sports*

improvement. Perhaps she will learn to get along better with other children. Perhaps she will increase her physical or mental stamina, learn new skills, develop self-confidence, or enjoy exercise. When your ten-year-old daughter competes in the spelling bee at school, it's an opportunity to improve her spelling skills, and also to keep trying if she loses.

Learning to Set Goals

Competitive activities can also create an arena for children to learn to set goals for themselves. All children need to learn how to take a big goal, such as performing in the state music competition, and break it down into smaller steps. Your job is to help your child identify the many small steps he needs to work on to achieve his bigger goal or dream.

Along the way, parents also have an important opportunity to encourage their child's "self-recognition." Part one of this task is for parents to show their pride in their child's personal improvement and growth. Part two is encouraging your child to pat herself on the back and feel a sense of pride and appreciation for her efforts and hard work. This is an important emotional and self-esteem skill that will serve your child well throughout all of her life.

Lessons of Winning and Losing

Competitive activities present other opportunities for your child to learn lessons about winning and losing. Some of these lessons are painful for loving parents to watch. If your thirteen-year-old daughter competes in the state band competition and her school band loses out in the first round of competition, don't make more of this momentary loss than it warrants. It is indeed a disappointment to the children who worked hard and tried their best. Your job in these moments is to listen as your child expresses her disappointment and later acknowledge that you are sorry your daughter feels disappointed, but that you were pleased to

Signs That a Child is Having Difficulty with Competitive Feelings (Overly Competitive)

1. Child becomes furious and aggressive toward others if he is losing.
2. Child has tantrums in the middle of the game (on the sports field or during a board game).
3. Child tears up the game, kicks, throws sports equipment, and so on.
4. Child threatens or attempts to beat up his opponent.
5. Child taunts other players during the game or shows consistently poor sportsmanship (whether winning or losing).
6. Child cries excessively after each losing game.

Help Your Child Accept Winning and Losing as Parts of Life

1. Listen to your child's feelings, but stop the destructive actions he is directing to others. Set a very clear limit that hitting, pushing, taunting, tearing, and kicking are not acceptable, but you are happy to sit and listen to his feelings.
2. Create opportunities at home in which you and your child will compete at board games, backyard basketball, and so on. Let young children set the rules of play part of the time, giving an advantage to your child. When your child wins, do not heap praise upon her or make this win an example of how smart, clever, or creative she is. Move on to the next activity without great fanfare over her win.

    Part of the time, you will undoubtedly win the competition. Be a gracious winner, but move on to another fun (noncompetitive) experience with your child shortly after winning.

spend the afternoon watching her play. Later, when appropriate, remind her that she is a talented musician who will have many, many other opportunities to perform and compete.

Winning with good sportsmanship and grace is something that children learn over time with consistent guidance from parents. Some kids will find it more difficult to win gracefully than others. Some kids may get so caught up in the excitement of winning that they boast to, or put down, their opponents. Other kids may criticize their own teammates who they feel played below par. Parents must discourage this unsportsmanlike behavior every time it occurs.

When Your Child Has Lost the Contest or Competition

Do

1. Listen to your child's feelings of disappointment. Don't immediately try to make it all better or erase his feelings of disappointment or sadness.

2. After hearing your child's feelings, gently take note of one or two things your child did well during the competition. Tell your child you enjoyed being at her game and watching her play.

3. Help your child begin to construct a way to rebound from the disappointment: "You and I can practice tomorrow in the backyard. I like pitching to you."

4. Say a few carefully selected words about how there will be another opportunity to try again and that the way to get better is to practice and grow.

5. Help your child remember how much she has improved since last year, or her first soccer game, and so forth. Help her chart her own personal skills progress.

Don't

1. Criticize his performance.

2. Encourage your child to give up because she's not skilled or talented.

3. Discount or minimize his feelings of disappointment by saying things like, "It was just a neighborhood game," "This game doesn't matter," and so on.

4. Compare your child (negatively) to other players or past players or siblings.

5. Yell at the coach or criticize other players or parents.

Children may also see other children and adults who are poor sports in various competitive events. This is a potential opportunity for you to editorialize quietly to your child about your beliefs, values, and reactions to this behavior.

Realistic Assessment

Competitive events also offer children the chance to appreciate the talents and values of others. Children will see over time that there are indeed better spellers, better athletes, and better musicians, artists, and actors in some of the competitive events in which they participate. If parents keep the right attitude, most kids will be able to accept this condition without too much threat to their own identities.

When Competition Goes Awry

Some parents, teachers, and coaches miss the boat on the value of competitive events and take competing against another child or team so seriously that the child's self-worth becomes very much dependent on whether he beats his opponent. This is a misguided use of competition that has potential to limit your child's experience and wound his self-esteem. He may perceive himself to be worthwhile only when he beats someone else.

Some children decide on their own that they must win every competition or prevail at every try. These kids may need some extra role modeling from their coaches and their parents. The loss of a contest or the winning of an award does not alter who he is. This is an important truth for you to live by and for your child to come to understand.

Everyday Opportunities for Competition
Infant: Birth to Twelve Months

Competition is a foreign concept to babies. Unlike other ingredients that begin in infancy or toddlerhood and develop slowly throughout all of childhood, competition usually doesn't come into play until the preschool years.

> "I wouldn't introduce a competitive game at the age of four. It's just too difficult. You can turn almost every game into a game that has no winner."
>
> —Patti Greenberg Wollman, preschool teacher for over twenty years and author of *Behind the Playdough Curtain*

All you need to know about competition at this stage is that in time it will become a part of your child's life, and you will be required to offer guidance to help your child balance competition with cooperation and compassion. For now, shower your baby with love, attention, and care. If there are older siblings in the family who may act out feelings of competition and jealousy toward the baby, keep a watchful eye to protect your baby.

Toddler: Twelve Months to Two-and-a-Half Years

Your toddler is indeed very self-centered, but this is quite different from competition. He may play alongside another child and be curious about what his "playmate" is up to, and he surely will take any toy away from his playmate and claim it to be his own, but he is not yet capable of competing with another child in a purposeful way.

Preschool Child: Two-and-a-Half to Four Years

This is the age at which many children begin to put competitive feelings into action in play with peers and siblings. Your assistance is needed to help your child find appropriate ways to express these feelings and also to set clear limits when you see inappropriate behavior.

Daily Opportunities to Learn

- Be supportive of your child's "pretend" play in which she becomes a superhero and lives out feelings of competition in fun play. (This is a positive way for your child to experiment with competitive feelings.)
- Talk with preschool teachers and care providers about how your child is getting along with others. Encourage cooperation and taking turns.
- Praise your child's good sportsmanship when you see it in action.

- Editorialize in private with your preschooler whenever you both observe a poor sport in public or encounter poor sportsmanship in a story or movie.
- Play age-appropriate board games with your child. Focus on the fun of playing together rather than winning or losing.
- Don't overpraise your child for winning a game; it will come back to haunt you later when your child loses and believes he's disappointed you.
- Manage sibling squabbles: set clear rules that hitting is not allowed. Ignore minor disagreements and separate siblings with a brief time-out when misbehavior escalates.

> "So we as parents really need to understand that sports participation can be a two-edged sword. It can have marvelous, positive potential for facilitation of the growth of the child. At the same time, it also has the potential to damage children if things are not run and supervised correctly."
>
> —Dr. Ron Smith, sports psychologist and coauthor (with Frank L. Smoll) of *Way to Go Coach*

School-Age Child: Five to Ten Years

School-age children can express their competitive feelings in academic contests (spelling bees, science fairs, and so on) as well as sports and creative contests. Help your child use these competitive feelings in a way that enriches his life and enhances his development.

Daily Opportunities to Learn

- Encourage your child to try an age-appropriate sport such as soccer. Find a good coach who embraces the philosophy of skill development and personal improvement.
- Attend your child's performances, sports events, and contests. Be a supportive spectator, not a personal critic.
- Recognize (and praise) your child's good sportsmanship, personal improvement, and skill development as they occur.
- Listen to your child as she expresses feelings of disappointment over losing or over a poor grade.
- Don't make your child's worth contingent upon his success in competitive events or the grades he receives at school.

> "In the professional model, winning is rolling up a larger score. Professional sports are an entertainment business, so are big-time college sports. I define winning in terms of striving to do the best that you can. That's when people win; when they put themselves on the line, they give maximum effort. The outcome is less important than the whole process."
>
> —Dr. Ron Smith, sports psychologist and coauthor (with Frank L. Smoll) of *Way to Go Coach*

- Editorialize quietly, in private, about unfair play that you and your child observe.
- Switch your child to another team or another sport if after careful consideration, you are convinced the coach or sport consistently has a negative impact upon your child.
- Regularly spend time with your child that is unrelated to competition or performance (so that these events do not take center stage in your important parent-child relationship).
- Manage and minimize sibling squabbles: give each child individual time alone with you, ignore minor squabbles, enforce the family rule that hitting is not allowed.

Preteens/Early Teens: Eleven to Fourteen Years

Preteen girls and boys can benefit greatly by incorporating healthy competition into their lives. Help your child stay on course, using competition for personal improvement and development rather than dominating others.

Daily Opportunities to Learn

- If your child shows interest, help her find a sport that suits her interests, talents, and personality (consider both individual sports and team sports).
- Strive to keep school performance a personal matter and not an arena for competition.
- Find a competitive activity that allows every team member to participate. No one improves by sitting on the sidelines.
- Attend as many of your child's performances, contests, and sporting events as possible.

- Don't pressure your child to win. Maintain an attitude that focuses on improvement and personal best.
- If your child is involved in sports, encourage him to take note of his progress; give him a "Progress Report Card" that details his efforts and improvements in skills, teamwork, fair play, attitude, determination, and so on.
- If your child becomes overly competitive, help her put competition (and perhaps winning) back in perspective. Although you may take pride in your child's contests, games, and schoolwork, be careful not to focus all of your approval and recognition on these talents and efforts. She may come to believe she is valued only so long as she is the best violinist, artist, athlete, or student.
- Maintain a realistic attitude about sibling rivalry; plan to manage and minimize it throughout childhood. Strive to let each child feel loved for himself or herself.

> "When children become involved in sports, they enter a miniature life situation which mimics in many ways the kinds of challenges that they're going to face all through their lives. So they have an opportunity in what should be a relatively nonthreatening environment to learn good attitudes toward striving for success, dealing with failure, toward cooperation and competition."
>
> —Dr. Ron Smith, sports psychologist and coauthor (with Frank L. Smoll) of *Way to Go Coach*

Teens: Fifteen to Nineteen Years

Teenagers have many opportunities to compete with one another: in academic competitions, sports, creative arts, and in the workplace. Older teens may focus on competition to get into college, secure scholarships, get summer jobs, and get into enrichment programs.

Daily Opportunities to Learn

- Encourage your teen to strive for her personal best and compete against herself in sports and other activities.

> "The key is to make each child feel unique and special and at the same time be responsive to all of them."
>
> —Dr. Steven Shelov, pediatrician and author of *Your Baby's First Year*

- Attend your child's competitive events and be a positive spectator.
- Clip out articles that your teen might enjoy reading about individuals (artists, musicians, scientists, athletes, and so on) who have incorporated competition, perseverance, and integrity into their lives in an admirable way.
- Find an activity that you can do with your teen: chess, golf, tennis, canoeing, sailing, and so forth. Focus on the time spent together rather than winning or losing.
- Give your teen plenty of respect and recognition for his many efforts, accomplishments, and endearing qualities rather than simply praise for his wins in competition.
- Don't pressure your child to fulfill your unfulfilled dreams in sports or other competitive pursuits.
- Help your teen manage and minimize competitive feelings toward her siblings. Continue to get to know your nearly grown child so that she will feel loved for her unique qualities.

• • • • • • • • • • •

chapter nineteen

Learning to Cope with Stress

Elizabeth was so nervous about the math exam that she tossed and turned all night and woke up feeling sluggish. At breakfast, she refused her favorite blueberry muffins and said her stomach didn't feel very well. By the fifth period at school, she was ready to fall asleep. As she realized she was so tired that she might fall asleep during seventh period in math class, her stomach really started to churn with anxiety.

All children experience some measure of stress during childhood. A small dose of situational stress can motivate your child to excel. When she is studying for a test or preparing to participate in the regional track meet, for example, stress immediately preceding the event can be beneficial to her performance. But too much stress can also overwhelm your child and stifle her development.

As a parent, you must take on a threefold responsibility with regard to stress in your child's life. First, you must oversee your child's daily life and schedule to ensure that there is not too much pressure bearing down upon him or ongoing stress and trauma in the family. When you see a situation that overstresses

> "A parent should recognize that the child is not an adult and should not be scheduled as an adult is. Allow them to pay serious attention to the things of childhood."
>
> —Bob Keeshan, TV's Captain Kangaroo and author of *Good Morning, Captain*

your child, you must shift into your problem-solving mode and find a way to reduce the stressors. Second, you must help your child work through significant changes in his life that can cause acute stress: a divorce in the family, serious illness or death in the family, a move to a new school, neighborhood, or city, and so on. And third, because your child will eventually become an adult confronted with various real-life stresses, you must gradually teach your child how to manage and cope with stress on his own, and how to enter adulthood with healthy coping mechanisms for stressful situations.

The Pace and Rhythm of a Child's Life

A child's view of the world, of time, and of priorities is distinctly different from that of adults. Children are not mini-adults; they are small, trusting, dependent beings in the process of learning about themselves and the world around them. They exist in a child-friendly time zone, where the hands of the clock stay in the present. When they're young, their days are filled with continuous moments in which they are simply playing for the sake of learning. As teenagers, their world revolves a great deal around school, friends, and social activities. All of the important ingredients that your child needs to grow occur during a gradual passage of time, with one day of play and experience spilling into the next.

Adults, by contrast, live a part of each day in a work world that rewards productivity and efficiency and part of the day in a family life that requires time management skills to get everything done. If you require your child to take on your adult pace and perspective (and live as a mini-adult), she will be hurried through childhood with stress as a likely outcome.

As a parent, you must learn to operate simultaneously in the adult world and the world of your child—shifting pace daily from one to the other. This means you shift gears at the end of your workday for small stretches of time to embrace your child's life and time frame where play's the thing or "pretend" is the thing or blocks are what matter. You may have laundry piled sky-high on the laundry-room floor, but your child needs you to share her childhood for a part of each day in which the other demands

Parents' Role in Learning to Cope with Stress

You are the "stress detective" in your child's life. You set the pace of your child's routine, you help set expectations for your child's performance in school, and you help establish the kind of family in which your child lives.

Job Description for "Stress Detective"

1. Pay attention to signs of stress: physical symptoms, behavior problems, and changes in sleep and eating habits. Begin to investigate the cause and implement solutions to reduce stress.
2. Provide a stable daily routine that is respectful of your child's pace and need to play, create, and daydream.
3. Provide your child with a safe neighborhood and school.
4. Protect your child from violence in the media.
5. Help your child learn to cope with small doses of frustration as she plays and works.
6. Encourage your child to excel, but don't pressure your child to be perfect.
7. Be available to listen to your child's troubles and concerns each day.
8. Help your child discover enjoyable ways to relax—through exercise, creative play and projects, making music, or time alone.
9. When a significant upset occurs in your child's life, remember that his essential needs for love, security, nurturing, limits, and your ongoing commitment and presence in his life are unchanged. Use this thought to guide you through difficulties.
10. Take an honest look at stress caused to your child by your family; work to improve the way your family functions.
11. Be a good role model. Manage the stress in your life in healthy ways.

are momentarily silent. It is a magical time and a space that you should try to visit every day. Some of the magic of childhood may even rub off on you while you're there as a visitor.

Protect the Innocence of Your Children

In addition to shifting gears from the adult routine to your child's world, your child needs a lifestyle that is child friendly and free from constant stressful messages. We live in a society that appears to have lost respect for the innocence and vulnerability of the growing child. We are bombarded by graphic violence on television news and the radio, in print media, and in movies. Unfortunately, your child has access to the same violent entertainment and sensationalized reporting that you see. It does not appear to be a friendly world for children to be growing up in. I suspect that in reality our country is still made up largely of good and decent people who cherish the rights and needs of children. But we can't know this for sure, since good and decent people generally do not have broadcast powers to project their values and beliefs into the black box in your living room. They are simply going about living their lives quietly.

The media advertises violence as power and glamour as surely as they advertise toothpaste. This may not be intentional, but rather a by-product of generating revenue. If the advertising of products shapes the beliefs and actions of American consumers (as every profit-making company and every politician in America clearly believes), then surely a steady diet of viewing violence on television and in movies also shapes the beliefs and actions of viewers too.

> "Bedtime is not the best time to ask children what they're afraid of, you're opening up Pandora's Box. 'What's bothering you' is a daytime question!"
>
> —Dr. Harold Koplewicz, director of the Child Study Center at New York University School of Medicine and author of *It's Nobody's Fault: New Hope and Help for Difficult Children*

It's confounding to me that the debate still goes on, unresolved, about whether watching violence on television influences a society to become more violent, and indeed whether it has any effect on children and teenagers who are trying to find their way in life.

Nothing good can come from your child being bombarded by violent images and words in the media. You cannot count on society or the government or Hollywood producers and scriptwriters to protect and preserve the sanctity of childhood. You must tackle this commitment for your own child with great determination and make choices to protect the innocence of childhood. Set limits and boundaries for TV viewing in your family and make yourself available to listen for indications of fear and stress in your children generated by violence in the media and the world at large.

> "Having some predictability and order in the home is a very comforting thing for children. It also helps them develop the skills to organize their own world."
>
> —Marti Erickson, developmental psychologist and director of the Children, Youth and Family Consortium at the University of Minnesota

Stress for the Overscheduled Child

Most kids overcommit themselves to activities at one time or another during childhood. At some age your child may decide he wants to be on the basketball team, in the school band, and in the photography club simultaneously. Because of the time commitment for each activity, on top of typical homework demands, stress and anxiety may soon replace joy and enthusiasm. Or perhaps your teenage daughter is on the debate team, sings in the school chorus and church choir, and volunteers at the children's hospital each week, leaving no quiet time to unwind or be creative. You will need to step in and reshape your child's schedule so that it allows a balance between activity and rest.

In addition to the stress load your child might create for herself by overscheduling her life, she is also significantly affected by your expectations for her. Some parents create tremendous stress for their children by living out their own lost dreams of becoming a football hero or the most gifted young musician in the city through their children's lives. Parents must take emotional inventory from time to time to keep these feelings and corresponding actions in check. Ask yourself this question: "Is my daughter pursuing my dream rather than her own?" "Is

> "I think it's important to help parents figure out what's the right balance between activities and quiet time alone as a family."
>
> —Dr. Mary Pipher, clinical psychologist, author of *Reviving Ophelia* and *The Shelter of Each Other: Rebuilding Our Families*

my son pressured to excel in my chosen sport or interest?" Because children desire to please their parents, their motivation to win your acceptance might not seem obvious to you at first glance. Look for the joy your child experiences and look, too, for the telltale signs of stress.

There is a very fine line between encouraging your child and pushing your child. You may need to have a good talk with yourself, as a parent, or with your spouse, and spend some time chatting with and observing your child in action to keep your expectations on track. Children may not use the words, "Mom, I'm just too stressed," but they will send this message to you in other ways. Stay tuned in to your child, and you will decipher important messages.

Helping Your Child Respond to Significant Upsets and Stress

Real life sometimes delivers significant upset to the lives of children. A large number of parents divorce, creating profound changes in the family. Also, at some point, most families move at least once, sometimes more often, leaving friends and familiarity behind. Some of these changes may actually be made with the needs of children in mind: ending an unhealthy marriage, pursuing jobs that create more family stability, or moving to a safer neighborhood with better schools.

> "Love and hugs are the most important things you can (give) as a parent and discipline just fits right in with that."
>
> —Dr. Charlotte Thompson, pediatrician, director of the Center for Handicapped Children and Teenagers in San Francisco, and author of *Raising a Handicapped Child* and *Single Solutions*

As with so much in your child's life, your first way of helping is by being available to listen to your child's thoughts, feelings, concerns, and fears. You must also remember that although your family circumstances may have changed—with a divorce, for example—*your child's needs are unchanged*. She still needs stability and security, she needs discipline and limits, she needs to play and learn, and she needs to have good food, medical care, and an education. Your child needs you in the same way that she has always needed you. Let this concept be your road map to recreate a new life of stability for your child. Your ability to respond to her needs may have changed owing to your own pressures. Perhaps there is now only one adult available for parenting or the finances are greatly reduced. The challenge, then, is for you to figure out, "in light of our new circumstances, how do I provide for my child's essential needs?"

Monitoring Stress in Your Child's Daily Life

Stress visits children in some of the same forms as it does adults: frustration, anxiety, worry, unresolved anger, unrealistic pressure from ourselves and others, and fatigue. The signs of childhood stress might be physical in nature—headaches and stomachaches—or perhaps behavioral—acting out through aggression— or perhaps a severe change in habits—sleeping problems, frequent nightmares, and eating problems. Some of these symptoms can also be signs of medical conditions that require treatment. Throughout your years of parenting, you must become a good detective who combines communications skills (listening and talking to your child) with intuition and knowledge about your individual child to piece together what is troubling him. Is it an illness, are there emotional problems, school problems, trouble with peers, or is your child being affected by dysfunction within the family?

When your child shows symptoms that could possibly be stress of one kind or another, your first line of defense is to listen and talk with your child about what's going on. Some problems will be easily articulated; others your child may not be able to put her finger on or may be reluctant or fearful to talk about. You must also work with your pediatrician to uncover possible medical causes for changes in your child's sleeping or eating habits, chronic stomachaches, headaches, and so forth. This detective work may also require your talking with day care workers, teachers, and others who work with your child to uncover the causes of stress and find remedies to your child's stressful situations. Because every child is a unique individual, each experiences stress in a different way. Some children are more verbal than others about their frustration or worry. Some act up or act out whenever they experience

> "We say that self-quieting skills are needed to get to sleep, they're needed to go back to sleep in the middle of the night, they're needed for playing with friends at preschool or with siblings, and they're needed for dealing with your own parents."
>
> —Dr. Edward Christophersen, clinical psychologist and author of *Beyond Discipline*

any significant, unfamiliar situation, such as a new day care center, school, or baby-sitter. Your detective work in the stress department requires you to factor in what you know about your individual child to help her find a way to minimize and manage stress.

Teach Children to Recognize and Manage Stress

Teaching your child to be a good problem solver is a great step toward stress management. Teaching older children about the necessity of balance between hard work and relaxation is an important skill for living. Adults who never develop healthy ways to cope with stress might be more inclined to dull their feelings of stress with alcohol, drugs, and artificial relaxants than adults that develop healthy ways to solve problems and deal with stress.

Preteens and teens are capable of understanding cause-and-effect relationships. They should, possibly with a little prodding from you, be able to see the connection between fatigue and poor performance on a school exam, for example, between staying awake until 2:30 A.M. at a sleepover and subpar performance in the band recital the next day. Talk with your child about what he feels like when he is overstressed and overtired. Ultimately, he will make the connection between the crankiness, short attention span, and perhaps the headaches, stomachaches, and stress.

Parents must still enforce limits, even with a teen. For example, many parents have a family rule that there can be only one sleepover per weekend, knowing that their child's sleep routine is likely to be disrupted when spending the night at a friend's house. Two nights in a row of sleeping only six hours or less is asking for trouble. This is a reasonable rule even for teenagers.

Children who are raised over the years by parents who pay attention to their own sleep needs, diet, and exercise will be more likely to see that we must all take responsibility for caring for our health and well-being. Parents should not hesitate to be honest about their own needs—telling their child after a hard day's work, perhaps: "Daddy had a busy, busy day today, and I'm a little tired and crabby, so I must rest for a few minutes. Let's read one story, then I need to take a nap to make myself feel better." Ordinary conversations like this accomplish several things. First, the child will understand that Daddy's crabby mood is not her fault. Second, she'll understand the importance of taking care of oneself. And third, she'll realize her parents are human too.

Some children will respond touchingly by trying to help their parent. Your five-year-old son might bring you a cup of cold water with a tea bag stuck inside it and say, "Now you'll feel better, Daddy. This is what Grandma drinks every time she feels crabby or tired." Amazingly, it probably will make you feel better.

Another big step in teaching your child stress management skills is to help her identify healthy, relaxing activities that she truly enjoys in the middle years or teen years of childhood. Perhaps it's time spent drawing, building models, or creating music. Perhaps it's playing a sport or exercising to burn off nervous energy. It's important to make that connection between doing what you enjoy and relaxing. This will help your child to handle stress even years later.

Everyday Opportunities to Cope with Stress

Infant: Birth to Twelve Months

Babies experience stress and fussiness when they become overtired or overstimulated. Get to know which activities overstimulate your baby and create a relatively stress-free routine.

Daily Opportunities to Learn

- Watch your baby's reaction to the stimulation around her; learn which noises and activities disrupt her calm mood.
- Provide a comfortable, safe, quiet place for your baby to sleep at nap time and bedtime.
- Be respectful of your infant's sleep routine. Plan errands around his sleep schedule.

"I always tell patients that how you sleep affects how you feel and function during the day. You cannot be as good a parent, as good an employer, employee, as good a student if you're sleep deprived."

—Dr. Martin Scharf, director of the Tri-State Sleep Disorder Center in Cincinnati, Ohio, and author of *Waking up Dry*

Toddler: Twelve Months to Two-and-a-Half Years

Toddlers by definition maintain a hectic pace of walking, exploring, and doing. This new activity is a source of excitement and frantic energy for your child. She can become overtired in the blink of an eye.

Daily Opportunities to Learn

- Maintain a firm nap and bedtime routine for your child.
- Plan errands and outings around his sleep schedule whenever possible.
- Help your child learn to tolerate small doses of frustration when playing. Don't rush in to save the falling tower of building blocks. If necessary, step in briefly to refocus her play to try it again or substitute another quiet activity (like reading) when she is overloaded with frustration.
- Remain calm when your child experiences a temper tantrum. Try to redirect his attention, if possible, but don't fuel the chaos by losing your temper too.
- Set clear limits to discourage inappropriate behavior when your child is stressed (throwing toys or books or hurting others, for example).
- Stay alert to any signs of significant stress or physical signs of trauma. Seek expert help when you are confused or concerned.
- Be a good role model: handle stress and challenge in a way you'd like your toddler to imitate. Maintain a balance of hard work and relaxation.

> "I cannot stress enough how important it is for children to be able to go to sleep easily and sleep through the night because it makes everyone happier the next day. It makes the parents better parents because they're not cranky and tired and it also makes the child better because he's getting a complete night's sleep."
>
> —Dr. Jodi Mindell, child psychologist and author of *Sleeping through the Night: How Infants, Toddlers and Their Parents Can Get a Good Night's Sleep*

Preschool Child: Two-and-a-Half to Four Years

Preschoolers are capable of learning how to modulate their behavior. They can learn to distinguish between appropriate and inappropriate behavior when they are frustrated or stressed.

Daily Opportunities to Learn

- Maintain a predictable bedtime routine for your child; continue daily naps as long as your child seems to need them.
- Help your child accept small doses of frustration in her play; teach her to take a short break when she's having difficulty with a project or in play and return to it later to try again.
- Set clear limits with consequences for inappropriate acting out when frustrated with play or playmates.
- Help your child become a problem solver with a can-do attitude when challenges occur.
- Provide your child with free, unstructured time for play and "pretend" each day; don't overschedule your child with planned lessons and activities.
- Select a day care center or baby-sitter that is responsive to your child's need for a balance between activity and quiet time.
- Encourage your child's interest in creative or quiet play—drawing and making things, listening to music, looking at books.
- Help your child learn to shift gears to a quieter pace and comforting activities an hour before bedtime.
- Be alert to signs of significant stress. Consult with your pediatrician when you need help understanding changes in behavior or sleep or eating habits.
- Be a good role model: handle stress and challenge in a way you'd like your preschooler to imitate.

> "With toddlers in the family, each day is a bit of a challenge, but there is so much growth going on at this period that it's going to be worth it. Just hang on to your hat!"
>
> —Dr. Claire B. Kopp, developmental psychologist and author of *Baby Steps: The Whys of Your Child's Behavior in the First Two Years*

School-Age Child: Five to Ten Years

School-age children are just beginning to learn to juggle their schoolwork, friendships, and family activities. They need your careful guidance to develop a healthy routine.

Daily Opportunities to Learn

- Provide time for free, unstructured play each day.
- Maintain a predictable bedtime for your child.
- Be regularly available to listen to and chat about your child's concerns and fears.
- Be respectful of your child's need to unwind at home after a full day at school.
- Encourage your child to learn to handle small doses of frustration in his play and schoolwork and know when to take a break.
- Help your child find enjoyable, relaxing activities that burn off stress and nervous energy.
- Encourage your child to adopt a can-do, problem-solving attitude when life throws her a curveball.
- If your weekdays are highly structured, encourage a free, uncluttered schedule each weekend, with time for spontaneity and family togetherness.
- Watch for signs of stress and pressure in your child's behavior and habits. Consult your pediatrician or your child's teacher or counselor when you are confused.
- Set clear limits with consequences for inappropriate outbursts triggered by frustration and stress.
- When significant upsets occur, continue to respond to your child's essential needs for love, security, stability, and setting of limits to provide a foundation for coping.
- Be a good role model: handle stress and challenge in a way you'd like your child to imitate.

Preteens/Early Teens: Eleven to Fourteen Years

The preteen years bring the potential for increased school and peer pressure and hormonal and physical changes too. This is a time when children need careful stress management guidance from parents as well as a good night's sleep, exercise, and a healthy diet.

Daily Opportunities to Learn

- Spend time alone with your child to listen to his concerns, problems, and fears.
- Be alert for significant changes in your child's behavior, eating, and sleeping habits. Consult your pediatrician or your child's teachers or counselors when you are concerned or confused.

> "During the adolescent years, it's really important to give kids a safe place where they can question values and beliefs. If they can do that comfortably and openly in a safe place, they're much more likely to end up with the values that you would want them to have. That really prepares them to go out into the world on their own and be able to find their center and hold on to their beliefs in a world that maybe doesn't line up with what they have been taught."
>
> —Marti Erickson, developmental psychologist and director of the Children, Youth and Family Consortium at the University of Minnesota

- Oversee your child's schedule, set limits for the number and frequency of extracurricular activities. Be on the lookout for signs of overcommitment.
- Encourage your child to develop organizational skills in order to manage homework and school responsibilities.
- Set limits to ensure your child gets a good night's sleep.
- Encourage your child to find enjoyable, relaxing activities: creative writing, art, music, exercise, model building, and so on.
- Help your child learn to recognize the early warning signs of stress and understand a cause-and-effect relationship.
- Talk with your child about dating and friendships and the pressures that can arise from them.
- Encourage your child to shift gears to a quiet kind of activity a half hour before bedtime—reading for pleasure, listening to music, or writing—to establish a calming routine.
- Be a good role model: handle stress and challenge in a way you'd like your child to imitate.

> "We have a very critical job in helping our children develop the skills for managing their own anger and for responding to the anger of others. It's a job that starts very early in the child's life. The skills develop over a long period of time, all the way through adolescence and into adulthood."
>
> —Dr. Rebecca Kantor, professor of early childhood education at Ohio State University College of Education

"What I've found in my research over the years is that we grow when we're dealing with the tough moments. That's how our children grow too. Teaching children how to get along rather than to fight each other is certainly a growth moment for our children."

—Ellen Galinsky, cofounder and president of the Families and Work Institute and author of *Ask the Children: The Breakthrough Study That Reveals How to Succeed at Work and Parenting*

Teens: Fifteen to Nineteen Years

The teen years can be a stressful time of childhood. Schoolwork often accelerates in anticipation of college opportunities; peer pressure is a motivating factor in your child's behavior; her pace of life is quickened because she gains more mobility by learning to drive. It's a time when your child needs your careful attention to the daily stress in her life and an extra dose of training in stress management skills.

Daily Opportunities to Learn

- Spend time alone with your child to listen to his concerns, problems, and fears.
- Be alert to significant changes in your child's behavior and eating and sleeping habits. Consult your pediatrician or your child's teachers or counselors when you are concerned or confused.
- Be on the lookout for signs of overcommitment to sports and other activities; help your child streamline his schedule.
- Praise your child's problem-solving skills; encourage a can-do attitude when faced with a challenge.
- Encourage your child to find enjoyable activities that she associates with relaxation. Help her recognize the early warning signs of stress.
- Talk with your child about dating and friendships and the pressures that can arise from them.
- Continue to set appropriate limits for your teen's safety and well-being. Unlimited freedom causes chaos and stress.
- Be a good role model: handle stress and challenge in a way you'd like your teen to imitate.

• • • • • • • • • • • •

chapter twenty

Humor

It is an altogether funny day for nine-year-old Morris. Everything seems to tickle him today, everything inspires a joke. Last night his grandpa, who is visiting from Michigan, told funny stories at the dinner table about the mischief he got into as a young boy. Everyone in the family laughed until they cried. Today, Morris has decided he likes the idea of making his family laugh too. He started the day out by putting plastic wrap over the toilet bowl in the bathroom adjacent to Grandpa's room. Next, he put a whoopee cushion on Mom's chair at breakfast. He wrote knock-knock jokes on small pieces of paper and placed them under the napkins at the lunch table. Just now he is scheming with his sister to put Vaseline on the doorknob to Grandpa's bedroom. His parents are ready to cry "Uncle!"

Humor is a wonderful bridge between parents and their children. A shared laugh, a funny story, or silliness between parent and child affirms time and time again that joy and delight are important ingredients of life.

At every stage of your child's growth, you can see her marvelous sense of humor unfolding. Your child's ability to appreciate and express silliness and humor will be shaped by her age and personality. Her style will, of course,

> "If things are not so heated, there are other ways that a power struggle can be defused or minimized. For example, humor. I know a father in a particular situation where the child was escalating about wanting dessert before dinner. The father said, 'I can't believe it! You really mean that you want dessert before dinner,' and he kind of made these funny faces and started clowning around about how totally unbelievable this request was. And the child started laughing along with the father about how daring this request was. Then, when the child was distracted, the father started directing him into doing something else that didn't have anything to do with food and the child forgot about it."
>
> —Dr. Alicia Lieberman, senior psychologist for the Infant-Parent Program at the University of California at San Francisco and author of *The Emotional Life of the Toddler*

change as she grows, but at each age you will discover a great deal about your child by enjoying and observing her sense of humor. You can see, for example, how she thinks, how keenly she notices the events and people around her, what makes her laugh, and how much she desires to delight you and others.

Why Humor

Humor helps us connect with others. It is a way that grandparents can connect with grandchildren, siblings can share a laugh instead of a squabble, and parents can celebrate the amusing side to life with their children. Humor can also help defuse a tense situation between you and your child. A shared joke or funny off-the-cuff comment can sometimes reframe the events of the day and provide a much-needed fresh start on a problem. Many parenting veterans say that parents must maintain a sense of humor in order to hold on to their sanity! Others say humor is good medicine that helps keep us healthy. And certainly humor is a common thread tying us all together. We all have experienced a funny joke or story that had the capacity to connect a large roomful of strangers for a moment of shared recognition.

Because humor is a shared experience between two or more people in a family, humor helps to identify the family and to preserve important memories and stories among its members. Parents incorporate funny, delightful stories about the foibles of each child into the family history: "When you were only two years old, you said something funny about the red hammock in our backyard that I'll never forget." "I knew you were destined to become a singer or performer. I'll always remember the time we went to the Mills Cafeteria when you were only four years old. You started singing 'You Are My Sunshine' to everyone in the restaurant. And at the end, you took a bow facing one end of the restaurant and then turned and bowed to the people in the back of the restaurant, and everyone applauded." These funny stories help define the spirit, character, and experience of the family and its individual members.

> "None of you are going to remember grades...years from now, but you will remember the quality of your relationship. So adding laughter and lightening up makes for a more enjoyable day-to-day routine."
>
> —Judy Ford, family therapist and author of *Wonderful Ways to Love a Child* and *Wonderful Ways to Love a Teen*

Then, too, there are family jokes or funny themes that keep cropping up in a family to the delight of its members. Dad's stories about his championship high school football game in which he scored the winning touchdown gets retold to the children year after year. And as the children mature, they realize that the number of fans in the stands of Dad's ancient football game keeps growing and growing each year in his retelling of the story. Suddenly this begins a series of ongoing family jokes about good ole Dad's memory and his amazing strength. This good-natured teasing helps create parameters for family fun that everyone seems to enjoy. And Dad, impressed with the wit of his now teenage children, is tickled by the jokes that surface time and again at his expense because he appreciates the gentle loving spirit in which his children poke fun. Each family has rich opportunities to express a shared sense of delight, to shape and refine a sense of humor that ties its members together.

How Children Develop Their Sense of Humor

Children are capable of sharing a laugh with you long before they can tell a joke. Your baby learns in the earliest months of life that he can make you laugh, and that you in turn know just how to get him to squeal with delight. Children learn that humor is a special way of communicating pure joy or merriment.

When your child is an infant of five months old, she has already learned what sounds and gestures she can make to cause you to laugh or smile. Your two-year-old learns that she can make the whole family

Parents' Role in Humor

Perhaps you do not think of yourself as particularly funny, or maybe you consider yourself to be a great comedian. In either case, your sense of humor will likely be enhanced by the young company you keep.

Job Description for "Accomplice in Merriment"

1. Learn to shift gears from your chores and responsibilities to an attitude of playfulness for part of each day with your child.
2. Find activities that are genuinely fun and playful for you and your child.
3. Read funny books and stories that delight your child throughout all of childhood.
4. Put your joint creativity to work: invent songs, word games, and jokes together.
5. Look for humor in the ordinary or even mundane activities of your day.
6. Laugh when your child shows a clever or funny perspective on her experience.
7. Enjoy movies and plays together that are lighthearted.
8. Encourage your child to express his amusement in drawings, stories, and poems of his own making.
9. Help your child understand what attempts at humor are actually cruel, mean-spirited teasing, put-downs, or gross.
10. Let your child see you good-naturedly laugh at yourself as an expression of your own style of humor.
11. Preserve funny stories, poems, pictures, and episodes in a family treasury book or box to share with your children again later as they grow.

laugh every time she stretches your big floppy sock onto her head and grins. Your ten-year-old daughter tells knock-knock jokes that are so silly you roar each time she repeats them. Your teenage son has developed a wry sense of humor that reframes the monotony of your household chores and always seems to lighten up your attitude. Humor is, in part, a form of communication that takes its audience's or participants' perspective and experience into account. At each age, your child's sense of humor reflects her keen sense of perception. She learns to read your facial expressions, your body language, and your reaction to her humor. She also learns from your response which things are funny and which are mean-spirited or just plain gross. These are important tools for understanding and communicating with others.

Where's the Humor?

The wonderful thing about humor is that it is portable. Its opportunities are found in many circumstances of life. You have dozens of opportunities to share a joke, a pun, or silliness with your child wherever you happen to be. For example, you might both see something hilarious as you're driving down the freeway together after a trip to the dentist. Driving up to the speaker at your local fast-food restaurant to order your food almost always offers potential for a laugh or two. The screeching microphone and speakers and confusion over what was really said can create hilarious situations that your kids will remember for some time to come. The opportunity to appreciate and express humor with your children is everywhere and in every day. The real question is not what is funny but what is funny to us today, given our ages, our experience, and our moods. As a parent, you'll experience times when your child's brand of humor might seem so juvenile (or gross) that it's hard to laugh along. Some of these jokes are told truly in innocence, others are told for the shock value by a preteen who is testing the limits of acceptability. Aside from the pure delight created for you by your children's

> "The terrible thing that sometimes happens is that people enjoy the playfulness or silliness or gleefulness of their children…and then about the time that the children start to school, they tend to say, 'Now, honey, we have to be serious.' Oh, never say that to a child!"
>
> —Steve Allen, comedian, composer, and author

> "Use stories, plays, songs; anything that exposes the child to the music of words and to the majesty of language. And of course we mustn't forget games such as Scategories, Scrabble, Scrabble for Juniors…anything that harnesses language. And every time we can hitch up language with laughter, we win and the kids win!"
>
> —Priscilla Vail, learning specialist and author of *Emotion: The On/Off Switch for Learning* and *Words Fail Me*

emerging sense of humor, you do have a responsibility to help your child learn which jokes are cruel and which are funny.

Parents' Role in Humor

Your role in encouraging your child's sense of humor begins with your own ability to appreciate and express humor. Parenting can be pretty serious business. Fulfilling all of your work and family responsibilities in the course of each twenty-four-hour period is an ongoing, stress-inducing proposition. But it doesn't have to be so every moment of the day. Some people keep humor on tap throughout each moment of their lives. These parents have a finely developed sense of humor that stays engaged at work, in rush-hour traffic, and when scrambling to make dinner in the evening. The majority of busy parents, however, may have to make a conscious effort to shift gears at the end of the workday and on the weekends to a pace that invites humor to visit their lives.

Your child's sense of humor is much like his appreciation of beauty, art, or music. It is highly individualized; dependent upon tastes, preferences, and style; and also is a reflection of his age. With this said, just as you can help encourage your child's interest in music or art by purposeful exposure to these things, you can also encourage your child's sense of humor, although you can't regulate his personal tastes and preferences or style of wit.

In addition to creating your own spontaneous fun together, make an effort to expose your child to lighthearted entertainment. Read lively and humorous books to your child. There are of course many funny stories for young children, but there are also stories you can share with your older child or preteen that hone in on her brand of humor. Select movies at theaters and your neighborhood video rental shop that are funny in the best sense and watch these movies together. Encourage your child to write poems, songs, and stories that express her humor-

> "A joke will sometimes absolutely dissipate the argument and the tense situation. Some of the time it looks as if nothing is ever going to succeed, but a well-placed joke can help everybody."
>
> —Patti Greenberg Wollman, preschool teacher for over twenty years and author of *Behind the Playdough Curtain*

ous perspective. And don't be afraid to let your children see you acting silly sometimes. Children of all ages get a charge out of parents who will agree to play a round of Simon-says, Twister, and charades.

The telling of stories is in danger of disappearing in today's families. Videos and games have taken over the "family storytelling" time slot for many families. This is a distinct loss. Find the time to tell your children stories about past family members and occurrences that are funny or in some way help connect your child to his ancestors in a vivid way. Nearly every family has some characters that are lovable, well-meaning people who have gotten into sticky or otherwise humorous situations. Tell these stories to your children in the car, at dinnertime, on vacations, or spontaneously as you are reminded by a current thought or event. Your children will be encouraged to tell their own stories too and to make observations about the current life you share together.

Children will also learn from your behavior that you sometimes poke fun at yourself, telling a story about the unbelievable thing you did today in the grocery store—"running into a display of soup cans and sending all the cans flying as our neighbor stopped her grocery cart to greet me." The ability to laugh at your own foibles is an important, humbling quality for children to see in their parents, and to emulate. Kids learn too that some of these embarrassing but funny episodes in your life are shared in a trusting way, without fear that the other family members will bring up this particular memory the night your boss and her husband are over for a family dinner. This respect and trust runs two ways. That funny story about your daughter losing her diaper on the swing set is shared in the family, but is not a story to be told to your daughter's thirteen-year-old peers at a slumber party. These subtle but important rules of family humor and trust are learned gradually by your children, with guidance from you and the good example you set.

Many parents rediscover their sense of humor, long forgotten in the process of being parents. This is just another example of the hidden surprises in store for those merely trying to be good parents for the sake of their child.

Everyday Opportunities for Humor

Infant: Birth to Twelve Months

Study your baby closely to see what delights him. You'll see his capacity to understand and appreciate your gestures and words grow right before your eyes.

Daily Opportunities to Learn

- Respond to all your baby's smiles with smiles and chatter of encouragement.
- Play peek-a-boo and other baby games to create laughter.
- Read stories and nursery rhymes to your baby that are cheerful and interesting.
- Find age-appropriate toys like a jack-in-the-box that are surprising and amusing to your child.
- Use your voice and facial expressions to show your delight in her play and clever antics designed to get your attention.

Toddler: Twelve Months to Two-and-a-Half Years

Toddlers are tickled by funny voices, silly hats and props, and facial expressions. They are beginning to perfect humorous antics designed to get your attention.

Daily Opportunities to Learn

- Allow yourself to get silly with your child on a regular basis; discover the toddler brand of humor!
- Read stories and poems that are funny and appealing to toddlers, enjoy yourself, and put drama and special effects into the story.
- Invent stories that are silly and lighthearted. Incorporate familiar animals like the family dog and include events that your child would think are funny.
- Find short videos to share with your child that are age appropriate and truly funny.

- Be a good role model: Make humor a part of your way of looking at the world.

Preschool Child: Two-and-a-Half to Four Years

Preschool children have a great understanding and command of language, so they can begin to understand and tell jokes and stories of their own.

Daily Opportunities to Learn

- Spend time reading funny stories and poems to your child that are especially appealing to preschoolers. (Ask your local librarian for suggestions.)
- Give your child a sturdy child-proof cassette recorder and a supply of tapes with fun and funny music and encourage your child to sing along.
- Invent stories and jokes with your child's interests in mind.
- Encourage creative play that incorporates humor.
- Be a good role model: live a life that includes laughter.

School-Age Child: Five to Ten Years

Children of this age are quite sophisticated in their appreciation of humor and their ability to make spontaneous jokes.

Daily Opportunities to Learn

- Spend time with your child pursuing light-hearted fun; tell jokes and stories that appeal to your child's age and interests.
- Help your child learn the difference between humor that is in good fun and humor that is hurtful or taunting: set clear limits and reactions to show the distinction.

> "One of the things about a four-year-old is that he has a wonderful sense of humor. Sometimes you can really use that to your advantage. If you get in a difficult situation with the child, you can make a joke and lots of times the child will laugh himself out of bad humor."
>
> —Patti Greenberg Wollman, preschool teacher for over twenty years and author of *Behind the Playdough Curtain*

- The next time your child asks, "What can I do?" answer with one of these suggestions: (1) you can write a funny story about [fill in the blank] to send to Grandma (or Aunt Sharon, etc.); (2) you can draw a picture of the silly thing that happened at school this year; (3) you can write a little booklet with all the knock-knock jokes you know and we can send it to [fill in the blank].
- Go to see movies and plays with truly funny wit and humor.
- Laugh at yourself in a lighthearted, generous way.

Preteens/Early Teens: Eleven to Fourteen Years

Many preteens have a sophisticated sense of humor that plays upon the subtleties of life and personalities of the characters they encounter. They sometimes, however, need to be reminded which things are funny and which are just plain gross or cruel.

Daily Opportunities to Learn

- Make a conscious effort to shift gears into a lighthearted mood after work whenever possible; spend time with your child telling about a funny thing that happened in your life.
- Help your child learn the difference between humor that is in good fun and humor that is hurtful or taunting.
- Continue to read funny articles and stories (for teens) during quiet time in the family.
- Encourage your child to incorporate humor into creative projects—artwork, writing poems, stories, and songs.
- Be a good role model: find time for humor and laugh at your own foibles and follies.

Teens: Fifteen to Nineteen Years

Teenagers sometimes seem to wander off the path of humor into pranks. Help your teen keep humor alive in a positive way that doesn't have a negative impact upon himself or others.

Daily Opportunities to Learn

- Spend time with your child each week pursuing lighthearted (nonconfrontational) activities you both enjoy.
- Encourage your child to discover comedians, writers, satirists, and others that you think she will enjoy.
- Encourage your child to incorporate humor and whimsy into his creative projects—papers, stories, poems, music, art, and so on.
- Encourage your child to share laughter with smaller children and learn what it's like to delight a much younger child.
- Share the funny movies, stories, and plays from your childhood with your teen.
- Encourage your child's humor that is genuinely playful and clever, discourage humor that is mean-spirited or spiteful.
- Be a good role model: live a day-to-day life that has humor woven through it.

caring about others

• • • • • • • • • • •

chapter twenty-one

Learning
Respect

Six-year-old Leah loved to play "school" and pretend to be the teacher. Sometimes she played school alone, with an imaginary class full of students. She always started her game in the same way—teaching the kindergarten children the rules of participating in class. "Now, class, you must always raise your hand whenever you have something to say or a question to ask. Every question is a good question in my classroom. You must never, never, never laugh when a classmate asks a question that you think might be silly, because that would be disrespectful to another child."

Respect is a concept with many different practical definitions. Respect in the South might mean saying "Yes, ma'am," and "Yes, sir," whenever you are spoken to by someone older. Respect in one family might mean that their child is forbidden to address his best friend's parents as Paul and Marilyn; instead, they must always be called Mr. Jones and Mrs. Jones. The way in which you show respect varies greatly from one family to another, and one region of the country to another.

Parents' Role in Teaching Respect

Showing respect is a fairly sophisticated communication skill, based upon a guiding belief in the importance of expressing consideration to others. The first rule is patience—your child will learn these skills slowly.

Job Description for "Solicitor of Respect"

1. Show respect to your growing child through all of your daily ups and downs together, even when setting a limit or consequence for misbehavior.

2. Begin early to teach your child about the feelings, ideas, and opinions of others; find everyday opportunities to repeat these messages as your child grows.

3. Meet respectful behavior with praise and recognition; privately express disappointment and disapproval when you see disrespect.

4. Talk with your child in advance of real-life events about how to ask questions of the teacher, how to behave during church, how to act at a play, concert, or birthday party. Help your child plan ahead to show respect in these situations.

5. Help your child learn that everyone has different likes and dislikes; go to the art museum, listen to a variety of music, taste different foods. Teach your child to show respect for individual differences and preferences.

6. Be a good role model for showing respect in your daily interactions with others.

> "Let us behave in such a way that we respect ourselves and respect our fundamental decency."
>
> —Dr. Robert Coles, child psychiatrist and Pulitzer prize–winning author of *Children of Crisis* and *The Moral Life of Children*

While we communicate respect through our behavior, respect actually starts as a powerful idea in the mind. The basic idea is this: "There are many other people besides me who also live in this world. Those people have their own ideas, thoughts, feelings, and possessions, and I must always take that into consideration." This same principle will be applied to the playground, neighborhood, dinnertime conversations, and interactions with teachers, peers, and later coworkers. This understanding of respect will certainly affect your child's relationship with parents, grandparents, siblings, and others of great significance.

How Children Learn Respect

Children learn respect in three important ways throughout all of childhood: (1) they watch the behavior and attitudes of their parents and teachers and others, (2) they grasp the idea of respect intellectually, and (3) they learn to show respect through trial and error, when praised for their respectful behavior and scolded for disrespectful behavior.

"People have various levels of tolerance to a lot of things. A parent gets to be who he is too! It's not as if you have to turn yourself inside out to be somebody that you're not....If your limit for certain kinds of things is a certain way, then that is your privilege and that is your right. Your child needs to respect you as much as you respect him."

—Dr. Jeree Pawl, clinical psychologist and director of the Infant-Parent Program, University of California San Francisco

Parents as Role Models

The process of teaching your child to behave respectfully, of course, begins with your behavior toward your child. A child who is treated with respect expects that this is how we treat one another. Like learning to talk—and expressing respect with our actions and words is in fact a form of communication—your child is learning respect throughout his childhood by listening to what you say and how you say it. How Mom disagreed with her best friend the other day or how Dad talked with the salesclerk in the shoe store when he had to return those broken shoes last week will form your child's ideas of how to show respect.

Another aspect of showing respect that might not be so readily apparent is that children must learn that they are not the center of the universe. Other people count too. Parents who overindulge their child will soon have a child who doesn't know how to respect others.

First Attempts

The process of learning respect begins during fleeting moments with your baby; for instance, saying, "No, that hurts Mommy," when she grabs your earring. The toddler years of your child's life present the first

> "I think for each child we need to find their special qualities. Every one of us has some abilities that are different from other people."
>
> —Dr. Charlotte Thompson, pediatrician, director of the Center for Handicapped Children and Teenagers in San Francisco, and author of *Raising a Handicapped Child* and *Single Solutions*

clearly teachable moments for your child regarding respect. Toddlers are on a mission of independence. Their objective is to impose their own newfound will upon their parents and peers and others around them—and they do this without any finesse whatsoever. For example, you will never hear a toddler say, "Well, I see that you have your car keys in hand and you wish to go to the grocery store now to get our weekly food supply. I understand this responsibility; however, I would like to continue playing with this fire truck for several more minutes—say, ten more minutes. Let's postpone our grocery store adventure for a while, shall we?" No, your toddler—like all toddlers everywhere— will simply pitch a fit, the likes of which you may never have witnessed before (particularly if you are a first-time parent) to express her desire in that moment. She has absolutely no concept of your need to stay on schedule with your family responsibilities, and she doesn't yet understand respect or compromise as principles that guide her behavior—but she's learning. She's willing to listen to you during short spurts of time when she's not saying, "No! Me do it." And this is how your job begins.

During the two- and three-year-old period in your child's life, he can begin to understand the concepts, "That hurts Molly!" and, "Todd is sad now." As your child gets older, you will find many teaching moments regarding respect where your child begins to "get it." He might think to himself, "Oh, yes, other people have feelings too. That hurts Elizabeth's feelings. I remember I heard that from Daddy before." Your thirteen-year-old son, quite pleased with his newfound reasoning and arguing abilities, will have different opportunities to learn about respect. His younger sister's friend may comment about "which cars are the best," which creates a heated debate at the dinner table. When your son goes from expressing his opinion, "If I had a million dollars I'd buy a Porsche," which is fair game, to "You're the biggest idiot I've ever met. Nobody with a brain would want that pitiful car," you have disrespect in action. You will need to point out the difference firmly to your child.

Respect Builds an Individual and a Civilization

Children need to learn to show respect for several critical reasons—some of these reasons are for the good of the world we live in, other reasons benefit your individual child and set the stage for her experiences in life.

Separate from being your child, whom you are responsible to love and nurture and care for to the best of your ability, your child is now a participating member of society. He will have unique talents and perceptions and contributions to make to his family, the community, and the world, and he will have an impact upon the many people he encounters over his long life. You may not know right now, for example, that he will one day become a music teacher who works with young children. You may never guess that your son will become the harbor master for a busy shipping port with thousands of ships calling each year from around the world. But your child will progress through his own life as someone important to many people: his friends, his children, his godchildren, his grandchildren, and the many professional people he encounters.

If your child learns how to put into action the idea, "These people are worthy of my consideration and respect," it will enhance the world. It will open doors of experience to your child because although she is strong in her beliefs and opinions, she is also respectful of others. She will be able to ask tough questions of her boss about ethical issues, and she will learn to express her opinions and tastes to others in a way that is respectful of their individuality. The old saying, "If you want to receive a letter from a friend, write a letter to a friend," works with respect too. If you want to be respected by others, show your respect to others.

The Teenage Years

The teenage years present a special set of challenges for most parents. Teenagers are busy establishing their own identities separate from their parents and the process rarely goes smoothly. One day your child is still your special boy or girl, the next he or she is rude, self-centered, and impatient. Many parents ask, "Should I even expect respect from my child during these turbulent teen years?" The experts unanimously answer *yes* to this question, but they do not agree on which remarks are indeed disrespectful and which we must simply ignore.

Parents need to develop their own baseline standard of "respectful talk." Perhaps you'll choose to ignore somewhat hostile looks and disinterested stares from your teen. Perhaps you'll decide it's not that important to have the former niceties exchanged when working side by side mowing and raking the yard now that your child is a teen. And perhaps the look of disgust when you ask your child to take out the garbage is best not acknowledged. But you do have the right to expect minimally respectful language even when your child is expressing his opinion. Your teen, at the same time, can expect the same behavior from you.

When your child moves outside your limits of acceptability—for example, name-calling, swearing, or other hostility directed at you—you must let your child know that you refuse to tolerate or participate in such a conversation. You should also feel entitled to grant or withhold privileges based on behaving and communicating in a responsible way. For example, if your daughter asks (or demands) to borrow the car for the evening, and the conversation deteriorates into explosive verbal attacks, you should suspend the conversation and not provide the privilege being requested until the teen is able to talk in a minimally respectful way. Of course, this presupposes that parents themselves are diligent in their efforts to behave and talk respectfully with their teens as well. When parents lose control and engage in name-calling, verbal attacks on the child's character, or threats, it's unfair and unrealistic to expect teens to behave and talk respectfully.

Everyday Opportunities to Learn Respect
<u>Infant</u>: Birth to Twelve Months

Your baby is worthy of great love and devotion. He is also worthy of your respect. He will learn subtle lessons about respect by observing your respect put into action in his life. It is true he is very dependent upon you and others to care for him. But he is trying very hard to do for himself, with a lot to learn.

Daily Opportunities to Learn

- Your greatest way to show respect for your child is by being there for your baby to care for her needs.
- Handle your baby with care and speak respectfully to him.
- Show respect for your child's need for sleep and arrange your life so that she has the time and place to get all the sleep she needs each day.
- Begin to teach simple messages about others' feelings during the end of this first year: say, "That hurts Daddy," when your baby hits you, for example.
- Your baby is watching you behave: show respect for others in your daily interactions.

> "Parents need to recognize that their baby and child is a unique individual and will be so their entire life."
>
> —Dr. Neal Kaufman, M.D., pediatrician at Cedar-Sinai Medical Center and professor of pediatrics and public health at UCLA

Toddler: Twelve Months to Two-and-a-Half Years

Respect is a foreign concept to toddlers. Be a patient teacher. Your child will pick up subtle lessons of respect by observing your respectful behavior toward her.

Daily Opportunities to Learn

- Act and speak in a way that makes your child feel like a valued member of the family.
- Arrange your schedule to accommodate his needs for sleep.
- Begin to teach your child that others (children and adults) have feelings, too: "That makes Arlene sad," for instance.
- When you see small efforts to consider other playmates' feelings, praise your child's accomplishment.
- Let your child learn that you have rights and needs, too: "Mommy is reading now, you may not turn off the light!"
- Discipline your toddler with firmness, not force.
- Be a good role model: show respect for others in everyday situations.

Preschool Child: Two-and-a-Half to Four Years

Preschoolers pay great attention to what they see around them and imitate everything you do. Your respectful behavior and talk will make an impression on them.

Daily Opportunities to Learn

- Treat your child like a valued member of the family through all the ups and downs of your lives together.
- Help your child recognize the feelings of other children and grown-ups in the family, at day care, and so on.
- Help your child learn to begin to take turns when others are expressing their ideas or feelings.
- Let your child know in everyday situations that you have needs and rights, too.
- Rehearse the rules for new social experiences in advance: "This is what will happen at the school play—we must be very quiet and whisper if we have something to say."
- Help your child learn kind ways to say no to playmates.
- Praise your child's small efforts to show respect; show your disappointment for disrespect.
- Look for simple opportunities to talk about other children having different likes and dislikes.
- Be a good role model: show respect in your everyday interactions with others.

School-Age Child: Five to Ten Years

School-age children are very aware of other children's actions and are capable of understanding the idea that everyone is entitled to rights, opinions, feelings, and likes and dislikes.

Daily Opportunities to Learn

- Show with your words and actions that you value your child's interests, ideas, thoughts, and feelings.

- Help your child understand appropriate respectful behavior in all sorts of real-life situations—in the classroom, at a sporting event, in church, or at family celebrations.
- Encourage your child to be a good, thoughtful listener when a lively discussion is under way and to take turns in expressing his opinion.
- Role-play with your child as everyday problems arise at school, with friendships, and so on. Help her develop respectful ways to speak her mind.
- Praise your child's small efforts to show respect; show your disappointment for disrespect.
- Let your child know that you have rights and needs too.
- Look for opportunities to talk about the fact that everyone has different likes and dislikes.
- Be a good role model: show respect in your everyday interactions with your family and others.

Preteens/Early Teens: Eleven to Fourteen Years

This age provides many opportunities to learn about respecting parents, teachers, and peers. The trouble is that preteens are trying to exert their will and preferences at every turn, so you may sometimes have an unwilling student—be patient and consistent.

Daily Opportunities to Learn

- Show your child with your words and actions that you value and respect her thoughts, ideas, interests, and feelings.
- Take your child to plays, concerts, art museums, and ethnic restaurants to experience diverse interests, tastes, and ideas.
- Help your child learn the difference between friendly debate and hurtful verbal attacks.

"I think the most important thing is that we shouldn't try to rush our children. Giving them the opportunity to learn through play is a gift. If we don't give it to them when they are three- and four-year-olds, they'll never have that opportunity again."

—Toni Bickart, coauthor of *Preschool for Parents* and *What Every Parent Needs to Know about 1st, 2nd and 3rd Grades*

- Talk with your child about respectful and disrespectful behavior toward authority figures.
- Be respectful of your child's need for independence.
- Learn about other cultures, traditions, and religions with your child; teach tolerance and respect for differences.
- Praise the efforts you see when your child acts respectfully to others; show disapproval and consequences for disrespect.
- Expect your child to respect your feelings and needs too.
- Be a positive role model: show respect to others even when you disagree.

Teens: Fifteen to Nineteen Years

Your teenager is still observing you in action, despite his need to act grown-up and think for himself. He does take note of how you live, relate to others, and, of course, respond to him.

Daily Opportunities to Learn

- Praise your child's efforts to behave respectfully to others.
- Let your child know, with your words and actions, that you respect his thoughts, interests, ideas, and feelings.
- Listen respectfully to her plans, hopes, and dreams.
- Help your child learn to voice his opinion and feelings respectfully in all sorts of real-life situations—in the classroom, on sports teams, and with family members and friends.
- Keep your criticism of your child under control; express your thoughts in a respectful way.
- Make clear to your child that she must respect your concerns and feelings; if she is going to be late, she must call you, and so on.
- Expose your child to experiences and events that give him a taste of other cultures and traditions and differences. Teach your child to respect individual preferences and differences.
- Be a positive role model: behave respectfully in all sorts of real-life and potentially confrontational situations.

• • • • • • • • • • • •

chapter twenty-two

Learning Kindness and Compassion

Olivia was living up north when she learned from her first-grade teacher that a terrible hurricane had struck Florida the day before. That evening she saw pictures on the television news of the many homes, schools, and other buildings that were destroyed. In one of the pictures, she noticed a broken doll lying beside the remains of a collapsed house. That night, before she got in bed, she picked out her favorite baby doll and wrapped it in a paper grocery bag. When her mom came to tuck her in, Olivia gave her mom the package and asked her to send it to the child in Florida who lost her doll in the hurricane.

The world would be a desolate place in which to live without the obvious signs of compassion and kindness nestled all around us. If you look closely, you will see it and feel it in many places—in your family, in your neighborhood, in the hospital waiting room, and in your child's school. Many people who give generously of their time, energy, and money to help others in need say that they get more from the giving than from receiving. It is actually both givers and receivers who benefit from acts of kindness and caring. Both ingredients help hold our society together.

Kindness and compassion are essential ingredients in the life of each developing child. Through his kindness, he contributes to the strength of the world. Through compassion, he contributes to the strength of his own character.

Most children seem to come by feelings of compassion and kindness naturally. But they usually need help in transforming these feelings into acts of kindness to others.

How Children Learn Kindness and Compassion

Children who are treated kindly and compassionately by their parents and caregivers start out in life with a belief, based upon personal experience, that this is how the world operates. "Big people are kind to little people. Big people take care of us little people and help us when we are hurt and hungry. Big people also speak softly and kindly to me."

Children further learn kindness and compassion in three essential ways:

1. By observing their parents and other significant adults behaving kindly and compassionately to others.

2. By discovering how to empathize with the needs and feelings of others.

3. By discovering how to act kindly and compassionately; by learning skills to communicate feelings of kindness into actions.

In the early years of childhood, from birth to three years old, children are absorbed in their own wants and needs. As time goes by, your child will begin to pay more attention to other children. During the toddler stage, for example, your child will quietly take notice of another toddler playing alongside her. She will be casually interested in the other child's activities and words, but still much more focused on her own play and needs.

> "Just as the great teachers—Aesop, Socrates, Confucius, Jesus, Moses—use stories to get their lessons across to their audiences, parents can use stories, whether they're fairy tales or folk tales, to get very important cultural and social lessons across to children. They not only educate the child's mind, but they educate the child's heart as well.
> In many fairy tales, the little kindness done to a ragged wayfarer bears fruit later on in the story in a full heart, because that kindness is returned to that character when that ragged wayfarer saves them from disaster at the end of the story."
>
> —Jim Trelease, author of *The Read-Aloud Handbook*

Parents' Role in Learning Kindness and Compassion

Parents' words and actions to their children help create children's beliefs, conclusions, and expectations about the world in which they live. When you treat your child with kindness and compassion, an important lifelong standard is set for your child.

Job Description for "Minister of Kindness and Compassion"

1. Treat your child and other family members with kindness and compassion.

2. Find kind words to convey your requests to your children and others.

3. Teach your child lessons in developing empathy for others by gently asking this question, "How would you feel...?" And then, "What can we do to help?"

4. Praise your child's daily efforts to show kindness and consideration to others.

5. Encourage your child to do good deeds for others on a regular basis.

6. Set clear limits and express firm disapproval for unkind words and unkind actions.

7. Find ways for your whole family to give to other children in need.

8. Help your child identify (or brainstorm about) what she can do to make a small difference to a friend in need.

9. Tell your child about kindness shown to you or your family by others who cared, in the past and present.

10. Be a good role model: show kindness and compassion to others in your community, neighborhood, and workplace.

During the ages of three, four, and five, your child will become more interested in other children. He will desire their presence and attention. In the process of playing, he will begin to take notice of another child's feelings. He will discover that he sometimes makes a playmate sad or mad, and also that he can show kindness to his friend and make him happy.

> "I went to McDonald's one evening, put all the french fries on my plate, and said, 'Daddy is going to share his french fries with Hunter (who is my son) and Daddy is going to share his french fries with Mommy.' Maybe three times that we ate at McDonald's, we did it that way. Then three times we put all of them on Mom's plate. Then the first time we put them on my son's plate we said, 'Hunter, you share your french fries with Daddy.' And he picked out a small, brown crinkly one and handed it to me. I said 'Thank you' and ate it on the side where I didn't have any caps, because he had the right idea. None of us instinctively shares the thing that's closest to our heart. After he had shared a couple of brown, crinkly ones, then he shared some skinny ones, and pretty soon he was sharing honest-to-goodness french fries. By the way, he is now twenty-one, and he is superb at sharing."
>
> —Dr. Edward Christophersen,
> clinical psychologist and author of
> *Beyond Discipline*

Help Your Child Feel Empathy and Act Kindly

Sensitivity to others almost always starts with asking yourself this question: "What would that feel like to me?" This question is appropriate in many real-life situations that arise for both children and adults. Empathy is a knowing feeling of the heart, the ability to imagine, not only with your mind but with your heart, the plight of a fellow human being. There is a short question formed in the mind: "How would that feel to me, to my child, or someone I love?" and then a flood of feelings translated to the heart.

This question, "How would you feel?" is good to ask children of all ages when a troublesome situation arises that they helped create, such as when they've hurt the feelings of a playmate. When five-year-old Sammy's mother says, "You hurt Tommy's feelings by telling him you're not his friend anymore. How would you feel if Sammy said that to you?" Sammy begins to compare his own feelings to those of others. He then feels the first stirrings of compassion and to understand how his words and actions affect others.

The second key question is, "What can I do to help?" This is a straightforward question that even your four-year-old can contemplate. When your child takes a favorite toy away from a playmate and the playmate runs off crying, you have an opportunity to brainstorm with your child about how to make the playmate feel better. As your child grows older, the answers to this question expand to less tangible issues, to family concerns, and eventually to the world at large.

Kind and Compassionate Words, Deeds, and Actions

Children don't know instinctively how to translate kindness and compassion into action. One way to help in this regard is to ask your preschool or school-age child (or older child) to do two good deeds each day for someone in the family. Make this an ongoing request or rule. This is a wonderful way to encourage your child to look around and see what she can do for another member of the family that might make a difference. These good deeds might be quite small, like getting the newspaper from the front lawn each day for Dad, finding her brother's missing soccer ball, or helping Grandma carry her groceries. This idea starts the ball rolling by asking each child to think for a moment about the needs of others in the family, and then figure out a way to help.

From there all sorts of other good things occur spontaneously. The giver feels good about the giving. The receiver feels valued and appreciative. There will be an unmistakable feeling of interdependence in the family, a feeling that you can count on one another. And because these good deeds are happening under your roof, you will be there to recognize your child's kindness and caring with some heartfelt praise.

When your child is a preteen or teen, you may expand these two or three good deeds to be given to others at school, in the neighborhood or community, or the family. If you approach this assignment positively, you'll be surprised to see how enthusiastically children of all temperaments take to this idea of regularly doing good deeds for others.

Another concrete way for children to develop empathy for others is through your family efforts of giving to those who are struggling. In every community across America, there are many children that could use the help of your family in

> "We're basically born sort of self-obsessed. It's I, I, me, me. The parent teaches the child to start thinking about other people. If a child comes home and says that her friend Jane's mommy is sick in the hospital, you look at your little girl and say, 'Well, what are we going to do about that?' And before you know it, you go down to the card shop with your daughter and you send the sick lady in the hospital a card. And then you bring a present to her daughter because you know her daughter is suffering to have her mother in the hospital and so terribly ill. When your little daughter Mary grows up, she'll know how to act with compassion and to take action instead of just sitting home and saying, 'Oh, dear, too bad!'"
>
> —Letitia Baldrige, author of *Letitia Baldrige's More Than Manners*

some way. There are social service agencies dedicated to helping families with financial problems, children in foster care, children who are ill or abused, children who have lost their home to fire, who need a sponsor to attend a summer camp program for a week, and so on. All of these agencies can use your financial support, your special holiday gifts selected for specific children in need, and of course your time. Select a doable way that your family can help children in your community and encourage your child to participate in the giving. If you have older children in the family—preteens and teens—they may wish to help a cause or charity of their own choosing. You will want to stay involved, and perhaps, wherever necessary, guide your child to help in ways that are both effective and safe. If your child wants to volunteer to help at the soup kitchen, homeless shelter, or any other community outreach center, for example, she must still obey the family rules about safety and nighttime travel in your community.

BOBBI CONNER:
"Dr. Lane, let's talk a bit about empathy. How do kids first begin to experience a sense of looking at another child and somehow understanding that person's feelings and needs?"

DR. VERA LANE:
"Development and the age of the child become very important because as children are growing, initially they're very self-centered. They are very concerned and interested in what they are doing themselves and it's not until they get a little older—four, five, six even—that they can really see what it's like to be in another person's shoes. When you talk about empathy, you are talking about seeing how a situation looks from another person's perspective. Young children can't do that immediately. They can only look at it from their own perspective."

—Dr. Vera Lane, associate dean of
the College of Education at San Francisco State University
and coauthor (with Dorothy Molyneaux) of
The Dynamics of Communicative Development

There are also similar social service agencies that help the elderly the year round. Something as simple as arranging for your son's school choir to sing at a home for the elderly at Christmastime can create moments of joy for people who have a lonely or difficult life now.

All of these acts of kindness require you to be involved, to help your child develop empathy and kindness skills and develop a balance of caring for himself and giving to others too.

Everyday Opportunities to Learn Kindness and Compassion

Infant: Birth to Twelve Months

Your infant is aware of what she sees and feels all around her. She senses kindness conveyed in a loving tone of voice, in the soft and caring way she is being held, and in the soothing songs you sing as you rock her in the rocking chair.

> "If you share because you are told to share, it's very different than if you share because you have an appreciation for other people's needs."
>
> —Dr. Stanley Greenspan, clinical professor of psychiatry and pediatrics at George Washington University School of Medicine and author of *The Growth of the Mind, Building Healthy Minds, Playground Politics,* and *The Challenging Child*

Daily Opportunities to Learn

- Put your kind and caring feelings into words and actions each day as you take care of your baby.
- Select a child care provider or baby-sitter who is kind and compassionate to your baby and has good coping skills to deal appropriately with crying and fussiness.
- Help the older children in your family (siblings, cousins, and so on) learn to treat your infant with gentleness and kindness.

Toddler: Twelve Months to Two-and-a-Half Years

Because toddlers are extremely curious and mobile, they sometimes get into mischief. They also have trouble containing their feelings of frustration and crankiness. You may have to work hard to maintain a mood of calmness and gentleness in the family.

> "I'm sure every parent…will remember moments in their children's lives when the parent has seen the child capable of an act of goodness or kindness or thoughtfulness or sensitivity. It's a miracle of this life that I think ranks with any miracle that we read about in history books or textbooks of religion."
>
> —Dr. Robert Coles, child psychiatrist and Pulitzer prize–winning author of *Children of Crisis* and *The Moral Life of Children*

Daily Opportunities to Learn

- Treat your child with kind and compassionate words and actions each day:
  1. Be empathetic to the busy, curious stage of his development that drives his actions (and mishaps).
  2. Get enough rest each day so that you can handle the daily challenges you face with your toddler.

> "Children are like sponges. They absorb what they see in their environment. This is in every way what they learn; how they learn to speak, how they learn all of the other activities that...they see around them. And so in learning compassion, they also need to have someone demonstrate for them what that is."
>
> —Dr. Vera Lane, associate dean of the College of Education at San Francisco State University and coauthor (with Dorothy Molyneaux) of *The Dynamics of Communicative Development*

3. Find supportive friends and family to talk to when you are overwhelmed with your toddler.

- Select baby-sitters or child care providers that you know are kind and caring to your child and capable of appropriately handling their sometimes frustrating job.

- Begin to talk gently with your toddler about how her actions affect her playmates: "No, that hurts George when you hit him," and follow up with a short time-out.

- Praise any spontaneous acts of kindness your child shows another child, adult, or family pet.

- Teach by example: show compassion and kindness to the many people you interact with in your daily routine.

Preschool Child: Two-and-a-Half to Four Years

Preschoolers are quite curious about the feelings of other children, and are capable of beginning to show kindness to others with their words and actions.

Daily Opportunities to Learn

- Treat your child with kind and compassionate words and actions each day.

> "A parent who always thinks about somebody else—I call it walking through the world with grace, being aware of other people—the child picks up on that."
>
> —Letitia Baldrige, author of *Letitia Baldrige's More Than Manners*

- Select a preschool program for your child that is staffed by kind and caring adults. Establish a close working relationship with child care providers and baby-sitters in order to stay involved in the quality of your child's care.

- Encourage your child to be sensitive to the feelings of others:

  1. Praise any spontaneous acts of kindness your child shows another child, adult, or family pet.

2. If your child behaves unkindly to a playmate, gently ask her, "How would you feel...?"

- Help your child think of ways he can show kindness to a friend or playmate.
- Find books to read to your child that incorporate compassion and kindness into the story.
- Encourage your child to do one good deed each day for someone else in the family. (Help your child brainstorm an appropriate list of good deeds that she can realistically do.)
- Teach by example: show compassion and kindness to the many people you interact with in your daily routine.

> "One of the critical things is to get children out of the feeling that their own wishes and needs are the only reference point for behavior."
>
> —Dr. William Damon, developmental psychologist and author of *The Moral Child*

School-Age Child: Five to Ten Years

School-age children are out in the mainstream of society once they enter school. They will see and hear how other children and adults talk to and behave toward one another. They must learn to find their place among children of various backgrounds and temperaments.

Daily Opportunities to Learn

- Treat your child with kindness and compassion.
- Be available to listen to and talk with your child about the unkind words and actions of other children.
- Encourage your child to be sensitive to the feelings of others:
  1. Praise any spontaneous acts of kindness your child shows another child or adult.
  2. As real-life problems arise with childhood friends, ask your child to imagine, "How would you feel if you were on the receiving end of hurt feelings?"
- Encourage your child to do two or three good deeds each day for someone else in the family.
- Encourage your child to show special kindness and care to tiny children in the neighborhood or family.

- Have conversations with your child about the good deeds and kindness of others in the world as you read or hear about them.
- Read books and watch movies together that incorporate kindness and compassion into the story.
- Be a good role model: show compassion and kindness to the many people you interact with in your daily routine.

Preteens/Early Teens: Eleven to Fourteen Years

Preteens and teens are driven in part by their desire to express their own opinions, ideas, and wishes. Encourage them to open their minds to the positions of others.

Daily Opportunities to Learn

- Develop an understanding of this stage in your child's development and empathy for the many changes that your child experiences as she strives to be more independent.
- Treat your child with kindness and compassion, but also continue to set firm limits surrounding issues of safety and the well-being of your child.
- Be available to talk with your child each day as issues regarding kindness or unkindness occur at school, in sports, on the playground, or at home.
- Help your child develop an understanding of "what that might feel like to you" as situations arise that call for empathy.
- Praise your child when you see him showing kindness and compassion to others.
- Find appropriate ways for your family to help others who are struggling and encourage your child to help.
- Let your child know that she is becoming a "big person" now, and the big people of the world have a special responsibility to care for and help the small children in the family, neighborhood, community, and world.

- Encourage your child to do two or three good deeds each day for someone else at school, in the community, or in the family.
- Teach by example: show compassion and kindness to the many people you interact with in your daily routine.

Teens: Fifteen to Nineteen Years

Teens have a great capacity to help others; they are aware of the plight of others in the world, and they have developed a high degree of competency to apply to the job of doing good deeds for others.

"If the husband of one of the neighbors has died, let's say, and the woman is left a widow, and her house needs painting, I think it would be wonderful if the children or teenagers in the community were expected to go over and help her give that house a new coat of paint. This is the kind of thing that not only is good for society, it is exactly the kind of thing that fosters good values in young people."

—Dr. William Damon, developmental psychologist and author of *The Moral Child*

Daily Opportunities to Learn

- Treat your child with compassion and kindness daily, yet continue to set rules regarding his safety and well-being.
- Engage your child in conversations about specific acts of kindness and compassion in the world. Help your child learn about the goodness of the world.
- Be available to talk with your child as problems arise between friends. Help her find kind solutions to friendship troubles.
- Praise your child's spontaneous efforts to show compassion and kindness to others.
- Help your child discover ways of helping others that are in keeping with his interests and personality.
- Your child is becoming a "big person" now. In an appropriate moment, remind your teen that she has a special responsibility to help the smaller children in the family or neighborhood.
- Encourage your child to develop a balance of taking good care of himself and helping others.

the treasures of family

• • • • • • • • • • • •

chapter twenty-three

A Family Identity

The five preschoolers were playing together by happenstance; their parents were all teachers enrolled in a half-day refresher course that offered free child care. Makenzie was a bubbly four-year-old with curly brown hair and chestnut eyes. She said to the others, "Let's play house!" Everyone jumped in with a different request—"Let me be the dad." "Well, I'm the mommy." "Can I be the baby sister?" —at which time, Makenzie pulled a toy baby bottle from her knapsack. The game was under way, with a part for each child to play. These children, like millions of others before them, were actually playing a beloved game more accurately called "family."

Kids have a profound need to belong. This is one of the driving emotions that creates a lifelong desire for interdependence with others. The question regarding children and belonging is: belong to what? The first answer is, his or her family.

It only takes two people to make a family. Divorced or widowed parents who find themselves raising their child (or children) alone should take heart— you have the essential ingredients needed to sustain a family if you have love, commitment, and a belief in yourself and in your child.

Have Fun With Your Child; Remember Your Childhood

You had favorite games you loved to play as a child. Those memories are still stored in your brain. All young children and some preteens and teens enjoy playing childhood games with their parents. (Some teens will join in willingly when told the games are for the distinct benefit of the youngest members of the family.) When you are in the mood, here are a few tried-and-true old standbys you might have forgotten. But just like riding a bicycle...

- kick the can
- jump rope
- duck-duck-goose
- red rover
- hide-and-seek
- kick ball
- red light/green light
- hot potato
- four square

- broom ball
- follow the leader
- h-o-r-s-e (basketball)
- hula hoop
- Twister
- Simon-says
- freeze tag
- croquet
- whiffle ball

And quiet-time games:

license plate game (find as many states as possible)

billboard/alphabet game (start with A, find consecutive letters)

"I'm going on a trip and I'm going to take a..." (using A to Z)

"I'm going to the store and I'm going to buy..." (using A to Z)

- Scrabble
- Monopoly
- checkers

- go fish/old maid card games
- hangman
- tic-tac-toe

Creating a Vision of Your New Family

Giving quiet thought to what kind of family you would like to have is the first step. This purposeful reflection requires you to put your values and ideals to work to create a vision of your family. If you've never

Parents' Role in Creating and Sustaining a Family

Think of yourselves (or yourself) as the glue that holds the family together. This is so because you are the adults, the parents. You set the standard that helps define your family.

Job Description for "Chief Executive Officers" of Your Family

- Create a vision of the kind of family you'd like to be a part of, turn this into a goal, then work toward that goal.
- Show by words and actions that family time together is important.
- Listen to your children's ideas and comments about the family activities (no matter how simple) that bring joy and definition to your family.

reflected upon your hopes and dreams in this concrete way, it might be a helpful exercise even if you have been a parent for many years.

Part of your vision of your family will be based upon your past experiences as a child. Some of your positive childhood memories will enhance your vision of your new family. Other childhood experiences may lead you to say, "I'll do that part of parenting differently now that I'm raising *my* children." It's wonderfully empowering to realize that you are free to sift in new parenting information and skills, new hopes, and new dreams for your own children and create a family with its own unique values, experience, personality, and pizzazz.

Next, you must translate your vision into reality by seizing the daily opportunities you have as parents living with your children.

Family Activities Define Your Family

Family life is made up of many ordinary details and routines, and it is through these that the family identity takes shape. Take food, for example. It's a given that we all have to eat.

"It's a stressful society that we're dealing with right now. It takes strong parents to be able to say, 'This is the most important thing for my family right now. I'm going to need to say no to some of these other opportunities to concentrate on what's important.'"

—Dr. John Clabby, psychologist and coauthor (with Maurice J. Elias) of *Teach Your Child Decision Making*

What Do Families Need?

Bobbi Conner: "What do families need? What do they need from the outside world, from the outside communities?"

Marguerite Kelly: "They need the same things that children need. They need respect. They need encouragement. They need to be told, 'I know you're doing the best you can; keep at it.' They need bosses who are going to give them more flex time and more shared time....They need better day care, and they need on-site day care whenever possible. Parents adore it!"

—Marguerite Kelly, syndicated columnist, author of *Mother's Almanac* and *Marguerite Kelly's Family Almanac*

This situation creates a world of daily opportunities for families. There are mealtime conversations, homemade foods to be prepared, funny attempts at recipes that flop, opportunities for kids to do something helpful for their family (set the table, bake brownies, or roast a chicken), opportunities to invite new friends to dinner, numerous spills in the kitchen that require patience and perseverance, and countless other mealtime activities and mishaps that shape a family's time together.

"The environment we create, rather than the skills that we teach, is really critical to the child's long-term success and happiness. That is what we need to focus on."

—Dr. David Elkind, professor of child development at Tufts University and author of *The Hurried Child* and *Parenting Your Teenager in the '90s*

Perhaps more important, dinnertime rolls around every day. It is a predictable occasion when every family member takes a break from their individual pursuits (a day at the office or playing with friends at the day care center) and regroups with the family. It is also a forced slowdown to the pace of an otherwise hectic day. For many busy parents, dinnertime might be the first time they sit and relax all day long. If you have very young children, you're likely thinking: "Mealtime relaxing? It's chaos!" An enjoyable family dinner, then, is a goal to work toward. Children will rise to your expectations about mealtime in the long haul.

Mealtime is a sacred part of family life that needs to be honored and preserved. With today's busy schedules, it takes a commitment on the part of parents (and later their older children) to make this happen. Some of these family dinners may be less than wonderful, others will be ecstasy. Approach them with humor and respect; be creative, slow down, relax, embellish them with entertainment, and enjoy your family in action.

> "I think the point is that we all need identity, kids more than anyone. And if traditions are strong within the family, they will have an identity larger than themselves."
>
> —Richard Eyre, coauthor (with Linda Eyre) of *Teaching Your Children Values* and *Three Steps to a Strong Family*

There are many other routine activities that present opportunities for being together as a family: reading stories together, growing fruits and vegetables in your garden, taking a walk each evening after dinner, or making chocolate chip pancakes for breakfast each Sunday morning. These and other seemingly simple activities are an investment of time that helps shape and define your family.

Family Vacations

Family vacations can be adventurous, offer a needed change of scenery, and can *sometimes* be relaxing. There's no guarantee, however. They can also be stressful or frustrating, particularly if not considered and planned carefully. Here are a few short tips to consider when planning or taking your next family vacation:

1. Give realistic consideration to the age, attention span, and interests of your children and plan accordingly.
2. Consider short weekend trips close to home that include kid-friendly activities—swimming at the hotel pool, fun restaurants, children's museum, or sporting events.
3. For long car rides, establish the rules for cooperation between siblings ahead of time, take easy/healthy snacks, take "surprise packages" to be pulled out at regular intervals that contain inexpensive activities or games for the long

> "Believe it or not, a really good predictor of later academic success is whether or not parents and children have interesting conversations together at the dinner table."
>
> —Dr. Jane Healy, learning specialist and author of *Your Child's Growing Mind*

> "Every spring, we go out to the Platte River and see the sand cranes. That's one of the things that defines our family. We are a family that loves the sand crane migration. I think as my children grow up and have children, they'll probably take their children out there."
>
> —Dr. Mary Pipher, clinical psychologist, author of *Reviving Ophelia* and *The Shelter of Each Other: Rebuilding Our Families*

drive, take cassette tapes with music and stories for each child, and stop at city parks and school playgrounds along the way to let your child play outdoors and run off energy (you can read or relax on a blanket nearby while they play).

4. Select vacation destinations with something for kids and grown-ups.

5. Save the fast-paced, sight-seeing trips for the older years of childhood.

6. Visit resorts that have "children's programs" and take a break from the children for several hours each day to relax or sightsee.

7. If you are a single parent, plan a vacation with grandparents, sisters, brothers, and their children, or join another single parent with children for a planned vacation.

Single-Parent Families

> "We really came to the conclusion that any institution—whether it's a school or a country or fraternity, and certainly a family—needs three things in order to have permanence and strength: 1) it needs to have a set of laws, a set of rules, 2) it needs to have an economy or a way to motivate, and 3) it needs some strong traditions."
>
> —Richard Eyre, coauthor (with Linda Eyre) of *Teaching Your Children Values* and *Three Steps to a Strong Family*

Families who have experienced divorce are sometimes referred to as those living in "broken homes." With divorce affecting over 50 percent of families today, this thoughtless and insensitive label discredits a majority of the families in our society. Single-parent families, like all other families, can work diligently to create a strong and stable family in which their children can grow. To achieve this goal, it's important to realize that your child's many needs remain the same, whether growing up in a single-parent or dual-parent family. He needs stability, security, a safe home, encouragement, good food and medical care, and many other essentials. It's true that your circumstances have changed, but your child's needs have not. This equation requires you to be an extra-creative thinker and problem solver, to find ways within your means and energy level to meet your child's needs.

Your creativity will help you to live well on less money, to find supportive friends and family to play a positive role in your child's life, and to find trusted friends and family to whom you can talk about the joys and challenges you face in raising your child.

> "I feel like I'm the only one in the world saying this, but I think the family is in good shape and I think it's getting better allthe time."
>
> —Marguerite Kelly, syndicated columnist and author of *Mother's Almanac* and *Marguerite Kelly's Family Almanac*

You may need to organize your life so that your work, the baby-sitter, day care, and school are all close by. (A long commute is simply a time waster.) If you have a strong relationship with your extended family, you may choose to live close by so that other family members can help with your child or your chores.

Put your intelligence, determination, and creativity to work to find good, safe solutions to your parenting challenges and create a strong and stable family.

As for the thoughtless comments about "broken homes," success is the best revenge!

Comedian Steve Allen on Preserving Memories

"Have fun with your children...and make a record of your fun. For nineteen dollars you can get [a] little tape recorder, tape your children, starting right in the crib, when they are babbling. Sometimes they will babble funny little things when they are learning to say words....Every family has its own collection of stories about funny things that the little one said at two or four or six. Make tape recordings, write down, and type up the stories."

—Steve Allen, comedian, author of *How to Be Funny*

Write the Book on Your Family, Page By Page

We're all familiar with the keepsake baby books that help us jot down baby's height and weight, when she said her first words, lost her first tooth, and so on. Now it's time to start your own version of the family keepsake book. Purchase a lovely and sturdy blank photo album or large notebook and fill it with pages that create a growing record of your family over the years. Let your children contribute mementos along the way that they think are significant (you'll be surprised what they include!). Here are some suggestions of what might go inside your family keepsake book:

1. Photos of family, photos of friends

2. Locks of hair from your child's haircut and other haircuts along the way

3. Menus from your favorite restaurants (you may move to another city some year)

4. Programs from all school performances, theater, dance, music productions your children (or you) participated in

5. Baby teeth lost, separated into small jewelry pouches with each child's name on them

6. Mementos from family outings that were fun or otherwise memorable:
   - local roller- or ice-skating rink
   - miniature golf course
   - ski slopes
   - go-cart race track
   - riverboat ride
   - movie theater
   - sports events and tournaments
   - postcards from all family vacations
   - shells/shark's teeth collected from the beach
   - leaves from autumn walks (pressed between sheets of wax paper with an iron)

continued

Write the Book on Your Family, Page By Page (continued)

- boating or fishing trips
- amusement parks
- the zoo

7. Mementos from your child's school field trips
8. Report cards over the years
9. All school photos
10. Awards given to your children
11. Recognition received by parents
12. All newspaper clippings about honor roll, awards, and so on your children received
13. Audio cassettes with your children's voices (singing, talking, and so on) as well as interviews with grandparents and others
14. Locks of hair from family pets put in small plastic bags, clearly marked

Here are some handy materials to help organize the contents of your family keepsake book:

1. Get tiny, thick plastic bags with zipper locks (like the jewelry repair shop uses) to hold locks of hair and so on.
2. Purchase clear, plastic pencil pages intended for three-ring notebooks to store miscellaneous mementos inside your family keepsake book.
3. Browse a well-stocked office or paper supply store for more containers and add-ons for your family keepsake book.

Let your imagination run wild when you write the book on your family!

Create New Family Traditions and Incorporate Old Traditions

You have the right to create and carry on those family traditions that you deem to be important and to invent new traditions of your own. Exercise this right!

"You know when you put a baby in the bathtub, you don't just have to say, 'Oh, now we're going to take a bath.' You can say, 'Rub-a-dub-dub, three men in a tub, and how do you think they got there? The butcher, the baker, the candlestick maker, they all jumped out of a rotten potato. 'Twas enough to make a man stare.' My mother used to say this to us—my brother, my cousin, and me....All of these little rhymes developed as ways in which you conversed with your child as the day went along."

—Amy Cohn, children's literature specialist

"I think most people do think of family traditions as being holidays, but there are 346 other days— ordinary days—just waiting for us to make special for our kids, our husbands, grandparents, whoever!"

—Jayne Reizner, author of *A Book of Family Traditions* and *A Book of Christmas Traditions*

Many of the old traditions in your family have their origins with grandparents, great-grandparents, aunts, and uncles who have long since passed away. Baking the traditional holiday meals that your great-grandmother made, for example, may lead to the telling of long-ago family stories that help your child feel a connection to his family history and ancestry.

For example, you might be guided by your fond memories as a little boy of making homemade "blue" ice cream with your grandmother and grandfather during blackberry season. Keep this tradition alive; make your own version of special seasonal treats with your children. Or perhaps you remember building a fire in the fireplace on the first frosty evening each winter and roasting marshmallows indoors. Your husband or wife will have special family traditions that will be blended into your new family as well, making a rich tapestry of influences from past generations of both families for you and your children to enjoy.

But don't hesitate to create a new tradition. For instance, you might create an annual "first day back to school" celebration for all the young learners in your family. Perhaps this might involve placing candles on a special back-to-school cake (homemade or store-bought—it doesn't matter) representing the grade of each child in the family returning to school. You might have eleven candles this year to signify your fifth and sixth graders in the family; next year the number grows by two candles. A tradition like this marks the transition from summertime to the new school year while it celebrates learning.

This is one example—but use your imagination to embellish family life with traditions and celebrations. These traditions don't have to coincide with a holiday; they might simply be the way you celebrate your lives together.

Create a Family That Reaches Out to Others

Your family can provide a haven where its members feel loved and appreciated. Your family can also reach out to others. There are boundless opportunities to help throughout the year and holiday times. When you are formulating your vision of your family, you may wish to include "generosity toward others outside the family" as part of your family concept.

Everyday Opportunities That Honor Your Family

Infant to Teen Years

Your family is shaped and reshaped over the long years you have together. This process is much like the waves of the ocean, sometimes strong, sometimes gentle ripples that flow repeatedly across the shore to define and redefine our beaches. The need and opportunities for family togetherness are the same whether your child is an infant, toddler, preschooler, older child, or teen.

Daily Opportunities to Learn

- Strive to create a stable, loving family in which each member feels a sense of belonging.
- Spend quality time with your family on a routine basis.
- Use words and actions that honor and respect each individual member of your core family.
- Create new family traditions and preserve old family traditions that are meaningful to you and your children.
- Treat family dinnertime as a sacred part of each day.
- Tell stories and share memories that help your children feel a connection to past generations in their family.
- Celebrate life together—both the ordinary moments and spectacular occasions.

"I grew up in a home where everything was fun and every little accomplishment or little thing that needed recognition got the attention it deserved. We always knew we were special— we still do. I'm past the forty-year-old mark, and my mother and father still make events in my life just very special."

—Jayne Reizner, author of *A Book of Family Traditions* and *A Book of Christmas Traditions*

- Preserve family memories with photos, a family journal that captures happenings along the way, audio and video cassette recordings, vacation mementos, and family recipes.

The Answer Is, The Glass Is Really Half Full

There's much to celebrate throughout each year. Family celebrations can be impromptu or well planned, silly or dignified, or inexpensive or elaborate. Here are some events worthy of celebration that you might have overlooked:

- Children's Day (you select the date year after year)
- Grandparents' Day
- First Day Back to School
- First Day of Summer Vacation
- Annual Family Spring Walk Together (first day of spring, rain or shine)
- The Family Pet's Birthday
- Friends and Family Monthly Dinner (Each family member invites one or more friends for a festive dinner or party)
- Report Card Celebration
- First Day Home from Summer Camp Celebration
- Promotion Celebration (Mom or Dad)
- Parent's Night Off from Cooking Celebration (Kids cook dinner or order and pay for pizza to be delivered)
- Winter Celebration (outdoor hike, ice skating, or bonfire)
- Passed the Driver's Test Celebration
- Got My First Part-Time Job Celebration
- Got Accepted to College Celebration
- Got Scholarship to College Celebration

continued

The Answer Is, The Glass Is Really Half Full (continued)

• Paid Off the Mortgage Celebration
• Paid Off the Car Celebration

And of course there are birthdays, Thanksgiving, Christmas, Hanukkah, Easter, Passover, other religious holidays, Fourth of July, Memorial Day, Mother's Day, Father's Day, Labor Day, Presidents' Day, and Martin Luther King Jr. Day, which deserve a hearty family celebration.

Ask each child in your family to suggest important days to celebrate, and let them help shape the celebration. Celebrate with food, stories, music, family contests, noisemakers and party favors, special desserts, the place of honor at the dinner table—make it simple or elaborate—but make it a family celebration.

• • • • • • • • • • • • •

chapter twenty-four

Hidden Benefits of a Job Well Done

It was a gloomy February day in Chicago; the purple winter sky was without one ray of sunshine. But inside this house was a spark of something like human sunshine. There were three generations busy in the kitchen: Nanna, her daughter, Sarah, and the two small grandchildren. Sarah sat at the kitchen table reading Blueberries for Sal *aloud as her two children pasted macaroni on red posterboard. Four-year-old Brian and seven-year-old Niki worked intently as the story drifted into their creative minds. Nanna stood nearby at the kitchen counter making the same snickerdoodle cookies she began making for her own children thirty years ago. The combination of the story and the smell of the cookies stirred a profound realization for Nanna; her now grown-up daughter had learned something she never specifically set out to teach her—how to become a good parent in the ordinary moments of life.*

We all know that throughout childhood, our children do get taller. Your newborn son might have been twenty-one inches long at birth. When he reached fourteen years of age, you were amazed to discover that he was taller than you. In that moment of realization, it was hard to pinpoint where and how this

> "Bringing up children is often an education for oneself. It's a great opportunity not only to teach others but to learn from them."
>
> —Dr. Robert Coles, child psychiatrist and Pulitzer prize–winning author of *Children of Crisis* and *The Moral Life of Children*

mind-boggling growth occurred. If you had been measuring your child with a tape measure every evening of his life, you would never, in one single day, have seen his growth. When did he grow? Was it late at night while you were sleeping? Was it while he was away at school? Or was his growth so gradual that it was imperceptible in any one single day?

Each day, your child is also growing intellectually, emotionally, socially, and spiritually. She is growing from the everyday opportunities in life that present themselves in the kitchen, in the rocking chair as you read to her, on the playground, and in the classroom. And just like the inches that add up to create her physical growth, you cannot measure her intellectual, emotional, social, and spiritual growth at any one moment. You must simply do your job as a parent, to the best of your ability, and have faith that she is indeed growing and learning each day.

Each day of growing has special meaning in and of itself. Playing with Play-Doh, performing in the school choir, and reading a book are worthwhile experiences in their own right. When added together, all of these simple moments create layers upon layers of learning, the foundation of a lifetime.

> "It doesn't end at eighteen as I used to think. You continue to be a parent, and you continue the struggle of both giving them a sense that there is somebody there to turn to and yet also a sense that they should develop independent lives."
>
> —Dr. Sophie Freud, professor emerita at Simmons College, Boston, and author of *My Three Mothers and Other Passions*

This book has identified many of the important ingredients that children need in their lives in order to thrive in every way. It occurs to me that something extraordinary happens in the process of parenting: these essential ingredients of parenting blend together, and new elements arise.

Your child's self-esteem, for example, develops in part because you have shown encouragement, recognition, and respect to your growing child from the time she was young. Your son's confidence develops in part because he feels a strong sense of security, he was taught to be a problem solver, he was encouraged to develop self-control (through your discipline), and indeed he was raised believing exploration and creativity lead to learning. Your child's sense of optimism spills over into her values, faith, perseverance, and development of courage.

> "The second message that I really think is important is to remember to enjoy your kids! Your child is only going to be six or twelve or eighteen this year....Those are the magic moments of parenthood."
>
> —Ellen Galinsky, president of the Families and Work Institute and author of *The Six Stages of Parenthood*

These essential ingredients for good growing are like the chemical elements on the periodic table that you studied in chemistry class in high school. You will remember that each chemical element on the chart has a distinct value and characteristic of its own. But these chemical elements can also be added together to form new and distinctly different chemicals. Oxygen, for example, is a distinctive element that has tremendous value all by itself. But when you add oxygen to hydrogen, you have created another new substance (H_2O) that is essential for human survival!

This same idea can be applied to the necessary ingredients that your child needs from you, for good growing in childhood. Think of the ingredients covered in this book in the same way that you might think about the chemical elements on the periodic table of elements you studied in chemistry class. Each of these ingredients or elements is important in its own right (creativity, for example), but when added to other ingredients, they create other essentials for good growing. Unlike the scientific chart, many of the ingredients necessary for good growing are fostered through the parent-child relationship, which incorporates deep feelings, thoughts, and commitment rather than

> "My daughter just went off to college about two weeks ago. This last year, I have been grieving in a sense, expecting that loss....In the last months, in August, just before she was going off, I spent that month putting together a photo album of her entire life. I had never really sorted through all of our family pictures. I had tons of slides. I made an album really covering almost eighteen years of her life and our lives together as a family. It was a present for her. I realized when it was all done that it was really a present for me, sort of a celebration of just how wonderful it's been. I have had the good fortune to have two wonderful kids....Parenthood is a wonderful growth experience. There are so many wonderful moments to look back on."
>
> —Jim Levine, director of the Fatherhood Project at the Families and Work Institute in New York City and author of *Who Will Raise the Children?*

chemical components. These are all miraculous ingredients of the human spirit and mind. Although these ingredients of childhood can be identified in a book, only you can put them into action, in your particular way, with your individual child. This is the powerful gift that you have to give to your child.

This book was written about the growth and development of children, but it is also about the profound growth of parents. If you are dedicated to doing your very best in raising and guiding your child, your journey will bring personal growth to you as well. No matter what the current age of your child, you have already experienced profound change (and growth) simply by becoming a parent. Your interests have changed, your capacity to love and be responsible has likely grown, you have learned to juggle new responsibilities—and a good night's sleep has somehow shifted from the "taken for granted/no big deal" category of your consciousness into the "priority" category.

As a parent, you must have faith in yourself and your child; you must believe in your ability—as well as your child's ability—to grow and learn and thrive. In truth, these are the growing years both for your child and for you.

- - - - - - - - - - - -

Recommended Reading for Parents

Health and Development

The American Academy of Pediatrics. *Caring for Your Adolescent (Ages 12–21)*.

The American Academy of Pediatrics. *Caring for Your Baby and Young Child (Birth to Five)*.

The American Academy of Pediatrics. *Caring for Your School-Age Child (Ages 5–12)*.

Eliot, Lise. *What's Going On in There?: How the Brain and Mind Develop in the First Years of Life*.

Leach, Penelope. *Your Baby and Child*.

Mayo Clinic. *Mayo Clinic Complete Book of Pregnancy and Baby's First Year*.

Nowicki, Stephen, and Marshall P. Duke. *Teaching Your Child the Language of Social Success*.

Salovey, Peter, and David J. Sluyter. *Emotional Development and Emotional Intelligence: Educational Implications*.

Shapiro, Lawrence. *How to Raise a Child with a High EQ: A Parent's Guide to Emotional Intelligence*.

Spock, Benjamin. *Dr. Spock's Baby and Child Care.*

Thompson, Michael, and Daniel J. Kindlon. *Raising Cain: Protecting the Emotional Life of Boys.*

Prenatal

Curtis, Glade. *Your Pregnancy: Every Woman's Guide.*

———. *Your Pregnancy after Thirty.*

Eisenberg, Arlene, Heidi Murkoff, and Sandee Hathaway. *What to Expect When You're Expecting.*

Jones, Maggie. *Motherhood After 35: Choices, Decisions, Options.*

Kitzinger, Sheila. *The Complete Book of Pregnancy and Childbirth.*

Snyderman, Nancy, and Margaret Blackstone. *Dr. Nancy Snyderman's Guide to Good Health for Women Over 40.*

Newborn/Infants

Ames, Louise Bates, and Carol Haber. *Your One Year Old.* (A continuing series of books for each age of development.)

Barnet, Ann B., and Richard Barnet. *The Youngest Minds: Parenting and Genes in the Development of Intellect and Emotion.*

Eisenberg, Arlene, Heidi Murkoff, and Sandee Hathaway. *What to Expect the First Year.*

Greenspan, Stanley. *Building Healthy Minds: The Six Experiences That Create Intelligence and Emotional Growth in Babies and Young Children.*

———. *Growth of the Mind.*

Greenspan, Stanley, and Nancy Greenspan. *First Feelings.*

Hirsh-Pasek, Kathy, and Roberta Michnick Golinkoff. *How Babies Talk: The Magic and Mystery of Language in the First Three Years of Life.*

Meltzoff, Andrew, and Alison Gopnik. *The Scientist in the Crib: Minds, Brains and How Children Learn.*

Pryor, Gale. *Nursing Mother, Working Mother: The Essential Guide for Breastfeeding and Staying Close to Your Baby After You Return to Work.*

Sears, William, and Martha Sears. *The Baby Book: Everything You Need to Know About Your Baby From Birth to Age Two.*

Shelov, Steven P., ed. *Your Baby's First Year.*

Todd, Linda. *You and Your Newborn Baby.*

White, Burton. *The New First Three Years of Life.*

———. *Raising a Happy, Unspoiled Child.*

Toddlers

Brazelton, T. Berry. *Toddlers and Parents.*

Dexter, Sandi. *Joyful Play with Toddlers.*

Eisenberg, Arlene, Heidi Murkoff, and Sandee Hathaway. *What to Expect: The Toddler Years.*

Kopp, Claire. *Baby Steps: The Whys of Your Child's Behavior in the First Two Years.*

Lieberman, Alicia. *The Emotional Life of the Toddler.*

Zweiback, Meg. *Keys to Toilet Training.*

Preschool Children

Bickart, Toni and Diane Trister Dodge. *Preschool for Parents: What Every Parent Needs to Know About Preschool.*

Galinsky, Ellen. *The Preschool Years.*

School-Age Children

Kelly, Marguerite. *The Mother's Almanac Goes to School: Your Child From 6–12.*

Preteens and Teens

Benson, Peter. *What Teens Need to Succeed: Proven, Practical Ways to Shape Your Own Future.*

Berardelli, Phil. *Safe Young Drivers: A Guide for Parents and Teens.*

Elkind, David. *Parenting Your Teenager.*

Lieberman, Susan. *The Real High School Handbook: How to Survive, Thrive and Prepare for What's Next.*

Pasick, Patricia. *Almost Grown: Launching Your Child from High School to College.*

Steinberg, Laurence, and Ann Levine. *You and Your Adolescent.*

Wolf, Anthony. *It's Not Fair, Jeremy Spencer's Parents Let Him Stay Up All Night.*

General Parenting Books

Bingham, Mindy, and Sandy Stryker. *Things Will Be Different for My Daughter.*

Borba, Michele. *Parents Do Make a Difference: How to Raise Kids with Solid Character, Strong Minds and Caring Hearts.*

Brazelton, T. Berry. *Touchpoints.*

Caron, Ann. *Strong Mothers, Strong Sons.*

Doherty, William. *The International Family: How to Build Family Ties in Our Modern World.*

Elkind, David. *The Hurried Child.*

Eyre, Linda, and Richard Eyre. *Three Steps to a Strong Family.*

Galinsky, Ellen. *The Six Stages of Parenthood.*

Kelly, Marguerite. *Marguerite Kelly's Family Almanac.*

———. *Mother's Almanac.*

Lansky, Vicki. *Practical Parenting Tips: Over 1,500 Helpful Hints for the First Five Years.*

Pipher, Mary. *The Shelter of Each Other.*

Stuhring, Celeste. *Kid Sitter Basics: A Handbook for Baby-sitters.*

Sleep

Ferber, Richard. *Solve Your Child's Sleep Problems.*

Jones, Sandy. *Crying Baby, Sleepless Nights.*

Mindell, Jodi. *Sleeping Through the Night: How Infants, Toddlers and Their Parents Can Get a Good Night's Sleep.*

Learning

Armstrong, Thomas. *Awakening Your Child's Natural Genius.*
———. *In Their Own Way.*
Grant, Jim. *I Hate School.*
———Hall, Susan. *Straight Talk about Reading: How Parents Can Make a Difference During the Early Years.*
Healy, Jane. *Your Child's Growing Mind.*
Jacobson, Jennifer, Richard Jacobson, and Dottie Raymer. *How is My First Grader Doing in School? What to Expect and How to Help.*
———. *How is My Second Grader Doing in School? What to Expect and How to Help.*
Oppenheim, Joanne. *The Best Toys, Books, and Videos for Kids.*
Shure, Myrna. *Raising a Thinking Child.*
Silver, Larry B. *The Misunderstood Child.*
Trelease, Jim. *The Read-Aloud Handbook.*
Uphoff, James. *Real Facts from Real Schools: School Readiness and Transition Programs.*
Vail, Priscilla. *About Dyslexia: Unraveling the Myth.*
———. *Emotion: The On/Off Switch for Learning.*
———. *Smart Kids with School Problems.*
———. *Words Fail Me.*
Youngblood, Jack, and Marsha Youngblood. *Positive Involvement.*

Creativity

Amabile, Teresa. *Growing up Creative.*
Diamond, Marian, and Janet L. Hopson. *Magic Trees of the Mind: How to Nurture Your Child's Intelligence, Creativity and Healthy Emotions from Birth through Adolescence.*

Gussin-Paley, Vivan. *The Boy Who Would Be a Helicopter.*
———. *The Girl with the Brown Crayon.*
Singer, Dorothy, and Jerome Singer. *The House of Make-Believe.*

Discipline

Gootman, Marilyn. *The Loving Parents' Guide to Discipline.*
Greenspan, Stanley. *The Challenging Child: Understanding, Raising and Enjoying the Five 'Difficult' Types of Children.*
Kurcinka, Mary Sheedy. *Rasing Your Spirited Child.*
———. *Raising Your Spirited Child Workbook.*
Kvols, Kathryn, J. *Redirecting Children's Behavior.*
Madison, Lynda. *Parenting with Purpose: Progressive Discipline from Birth to Four.*
Samalin, Nancy. *Loving Your Child Is Not Enough.*
Severe, Sal. *How to Behave So Your Children Will Too! A Collection of Entertaining Stories and Practical Ideas Gathered from Real Parents.*
Turecki, Stanley, and Leslie Tonner. *The Difficult Child.*
Windell, James. *Eight Weeks to a Well-Behaved Child.*

Siblings

Faber, Adele, and Elaine Mazlish. *Siblings without Rivalry.*
Rothbart, Betty. *Multiple Blessings: From Pregnancy through Childhood, a Guide for Parents of Twins, Triplets and More.*
Samalin, Nancy. *Loving Each One Best.*
Segal, Nancy. *Entwined Lives.*
Sneddon, Pamela Shires. *Brothers and Sisters: Born to Bicker?*

Self-Esteem

Apter, T.E. *The Confident Child: Raising Children to Believe in Themselves.*
Gussin-Paley, Vivian. *The Kindness of Children.*
Olen, Dale. *Self-Esteem for Children.*

Phillips, Debora. *How to Give Your Child a Great Self-Image*.

Youngs, Bettie. *How to Develop Self-Esteem in Your Child*.

Values in Childhood

Baldrige, Letitia. *Letitia Baldrige's More Than Manners*.

Clabby, John, and Maurice J. Elias. *Teach Your Child Decision Making*.

Coles, Robert. *The Moral Intelligence of Children*.

———. *The Moral Life of Children*.

———. *Spiritual Life of Children*.

Crary, Elizabeth. *Kids Can Cooperate: A Practical Guide to Teaching Problem Solving*.

Damon, William. *The Moral Child: Nurturing Children's Moral Growth*.

Dinkmeyer, Don. *Raising a Responsible Child*.

Eyre, Linda, and Richard Eyre. *Teaching Children Responsibility*.

———. *Teaching Your Children Values*.

Grollman, Earl. *Talking About Death*.

———. *Talking About Divorce and Separation*.

Hopson, Darlene, and Derk Hopson. *Different and Wonderful: Raising Black Children in a Race-Conscious Society*.

Juggling Work and Family

Brazelton, T. Berry. *Working and Caring*.

Cochran, Eva, and Moncrieff Cochran. *Child Care that Works*.

Deutsch, Francine M. *Having It All: How Equally Shared Parenting Works*.

Galinsky, Ellen. *Ask the Children: What America's Children Really Think about Working Parents*.

Peel, Kathy. *The Family Manager's Guide for Working Moms*.

Price, Susan Crites, and Tom Price. *The Working Parent's Help Book*.

Shellenbarger, Sue. *Work & Family: Essays from the 'Work and Family' Column of the* Wall Street Journal.

Tabak-Lombardo, Elissa. *The Caring Parent's Guide to Child Care.*

Childhood Sports

Andersonn, Chris, and Barbara Andersonn. *Will You Still Love Me If I Don't Win?: A Guide for Parents of Young Athletes.*

Smith, Ron, and Frank L. Smoll. *Sports and Your Child.*

———. *Way to Go Coach.*

Thompson, Jim. *Positive Coaching.*

Special Parenting Challenges

Ahrons, Constance. *The Good Divorce.*

Blau, Melinda. *Families Apart.*

Cantor, Joanne. *"Mommy I'm Scared": How TV and Movies Frighten Children and What We Can Do to Protect Them.*

Duke, Marshall P., and Stephen Nowicki, Jr. *Helping the Child Who Doesn't Fit In: Teaching Your Child the Language of Social Success.*

Frazier-Maiwald, Virginia, and Lenore M. Williams. *Keys to Raising a Deaf Child.*

Furstenberg, Frank, and Andrew Cherlin. *Divided Families: What Happens to Children When Parents Part.*

Greene, Ross. *The Explosive Child: A New Approach for Understanding and Parenting Easily Frustrated, 'Chronically Inflexible' Children.*

Greenspan, Stanley. *The Challenging Child.*

Greenspan, Stanley, Serena Weider, and Robin Simon. *The Child with Special Needs.*

Grotberg, Edith H. *Tapping Your Inner Strength: How to Find the Resilience to Deal with Anything.*

Neuman. M. Gary. *Helping Your Kids Cope with Divorce the Sandcastles Way.*

Noel, Brook. *The Single Parent Resource.*

Pickhardt, Carl. *Keys to Parenting the Only Child.*

Pipher, Mary. *Reviving Ophelia.*

Rapee, Ronald, Susan Spence, Vanessa Cobham, and Ann Wignall. *Helping Your Anxious Child.*

Siegler, Ava. *What Should I Tell the Kids? A Parent's Guide to Real Problems in the Real World.*

Stewart, Abigail. *Separating Together.*

Swallow, Ward. *The Shy Child: Helping Children Triumph over Shyness.*

Thompson, Charlotte. *Raising a Child with a Neuromuscular Disorder.*

———. *Raising a Handicapped Child.*

Turecki, Stanley, and Leslie Tonner. *The Difficult Child.*

Webb, James T. *Guiding the Gifted Child.*

Witkin, Georgia. *KidStress: What It Is, How It Feels, How to Help.*

Celebrating Childhood and Family

Bennett, Steve, and Ruth Bennett. *365 Outdoor Activities You Can Do with Your Child.*

Bundren, Mary Rodgers. *Travel Wise with Children: 101 Educational Travel Tips for Families.*

Cox, Meg. *The Heart of a Family: Searching America for New Traditions that Fulfill Us.*

Edelman, Marian Wright. *The Measure of Our Success.*

Elgin, Suzette Haden. *The Grandmother Principles.*

Ford, Judy. *Wonderful Ways to Love a Child.*

———. *Wonderful Ways to Love a Teen.*

Hughs, Ina. *A Prayer for Children.*

Keeshan, Bob ("Captain Kangaroo"). *Family Fun Activity Book.*

Lansky, Vicki. *101 Ways to Make Your Child Feel Special.*

———. *Trouble-Free Travel with Children.*

Nyhuis, Allen. *The Zoo Book: A Guide to America's Best.*

Portnoy, Joan, and Sanford Portnoy. *How to Take Great Trips with Your Kids.*

Stillman, Peter R. *Families Writing.*

Vannoy, Steven. *The 10 Greatest Gifts I Give to My Children.*

Fatherhood

Brott, Armin A. *The Single Father: A Dad's Guide to Parenting without a Partner.*

Condrell, Kenneth, *Be a Great Divorced Dad.*

Evans, John. *Marathon Dad: Setting a Pace that Works for Working Fathers.*

Levine, James. *Working Fathers.*

Sloan, Bob. *Dad's Own Cookbook.*

Index

H

Harvard University, 139, 200
head of family security, 32
Healy, Jane, 81, 83, 85, 289
Hepp, Christopher, 97, 100
honesty and fairness teacher, 161
honesty, 160, 162
House of Make-Believe, The, 90
How to Be Funny, 291
How to Choose a Piano Teacher, 97, 100
How to Give Your Child a Great Self-Image, 30
Hughes, Ina, 185
humor, 247-253; parents' role in, 252-253
Hurried Child, The, 3, 288

I

In Their Own Way: Encouraging Your Child's Personal Learning Style, 84, 92, 112, 221
independence, 195-201
ineffective discipline, 66
infant, xii, 3, 38, 51-52, 69, 79, 80, 83-84, 97-98, 114, 129, 140-141, 149, 171, 187, 201-202, 212, 227-228, 241, 254, 266-267, 277; development, 10
Infant-Parent Program, 25, 146, 179, 190, 148, 248, 263
instructor of discipline, 59
integrity, 159-162
intuition, 6
It's Nobody's Fault: New Hope and Help for Difficult Children and Their Parents, 131, 236
It's Not Fair, Jeremy Spencer's Parents Let Him Stay Up All Night, 5, 58, 60

J

job description of parenting, 4
Jordan, Tim, 63
Joyful Play with Toddlers, 85, 129

K

Kantor, Rebecca, 245
Kaufman, Neal, 267
Keeshan, Bob, 16, 234
Kelly, Marguerite, 210, 288, 291
Kids Can Cooperate, 123, 128, 211
kindness, 275-276
Knoxville News-Sentinel, 185
Koplewicz, Harold, 131, 236
Kopp, Claire, 191, 243

L

labeling, 23
Lane, Vera, 276, 278
language, 181; using effectively, 181; using to express feelings, 181-184
learning, 77-83; early, 79-81; through play, 81-83
Letitia Baldrige's More Than Manners, 51, 54, 56, 162, 275, 278
Levine, Ann, 197
Levine, Jim, 301
Lieberman, Alicia, 248
listening, 24
Loving Each One Best, 66
Loving Parents' Guide to Discipline, The, 71, 186, 187, 204, 209

M

magic, 10
making time, 24
Marguerite Kelly's Family Almanac, 210, 288, 291
master of observation , 21
Maynard, Fredelle, 23, 92, 126, 200
Measure of Our Success, The, 118
mentor of courage, 146
Mindell, Jodi, 242
minister of kindness and compassion, 273
misbehavior, 6, 63-65
Molyneaux, Dorothy, 276, 278
Moral Life of Children, The, 54, 108, 160, 163, 169, 262, 277, 300

About the Author

Bobbi Conner has worked since 1986 as a broadcast journalist specializing in child development and parenting topics. She is the executive producer and host of the award-winning weekly radio series *The Parent's Journal,* which is heard across the United States on public radio stations and overseas on the Armed Forces Radio and Television Service. Conner lives with her family in Charleston, South Carolina.